Prehistoric Pottery for the Archaeologist

Prehistoric Pottery for the Archaeologist

Alex Gibson and Ann Woods

Leicester University Press
(a division of Pinter Publishers Ltd)
Leicester, London and New York

First published in Great Britain in 1990 by Leicester University Press
(a division of Pinter Publishers Ltd)
© Alex Gibson and Ann Woods 1990

Typeset by CG Graphics, Aylesbury, Bucks.
Printed and bound in Great Britain by
Biddles Ltd, Guildford and Kings Lynn.

Editorial offices
Fielding Johnson Building, University of Leicester,
University Road, Leicester, LE1 7RH

Trade and other enquiries
25 Floral Street, London, WC2 9DS

British Library Cataloguing in Publication Data
A CIP cataloguing record for this book is available
from the British Library.
ISBN 0–7185–1274–X hardcovers

Contents

List of Illustrations

Tosson, Northumberland; 2, Yorkshire vase, Denton Hall, Northumberland; 3, Irish vase, Craigbirnoch, Wigtownshire; 4, tripartite vase, Haugh Head, Northumberland; 5, southern bipartite vase, Belle Toute, Sussex; 6, ridged vase, Knocken, Lanarkshire; 7, globular British bowl, Ford, Northumberland; 8, Hiberno-Scottish vase, Jesmond, Tyne and Wear; 9, waisted bowl, Portpatrick, Wigtownshire; 10, tripartite bowl, Lochinch, Wigtownshire; 11, ridged bowl, Cambuslang, Lanarkshire. 1 and 7 after Gibson 1978, 2, 4 and 8 after Hurrel 1976, 3, 6 and 9-11 after Simpson 1965, 5 after Musson. Scale = 10 cm, 156.

Introduction

This book is intended as an introduction to the styles, chronology and technology of British prehistoric pottery. It is designed to be a handbook and source of reference for further study, and it was not the intention of the writers to produce a definitive work. The inception of this book came from a frequently recurring request from undergraduates, continuing-education students and colleagues in local archaeological units as to where they could look for a concise introduction to the chronological development and technology of prehistoric ceramics. Undergraduates, in particular, looked with dismay at the weighty reading list that was produced in response to this request, and continuing-education students would probably not have the time, access to suitable library facilities or indeed the inclination to use such a reading list to its best effect. Furthermore, many discourses on both the chronological and technological facets of ceramics start with the premise that they are preaching to an educated audience, to a readership already conversant with the issues being discussed. Few discussions provide a foundation course. It was decided therefore that a concise and basic reference book was long overdue.

Pottery is such a complex and varied medium that it means something different to each person who studies it. One need look no further than the authorship of this book for evidence of this. Although both authors are archaeologists and have studied pottery at post-graduate level, each has been researching into widely different aspects of the subject. Different authorities look at pottery for different reasons and, as one would expect, draw different conclusions from their studies. Indeed, different conclusions may be drawn from the same data, as can be seen in the review of beaker studies outlined in Chapter 1 below. This, however, is to be encouraged, for it stimulates discussion and reappraisal: there is no right or wrong, simply plausible and less plausible.

For this reason, the present writers have tried to be brief and general in the text and to give some broad overviews. The glossary, however, is rather more catholic. An attempt has been made to explain the terms commonly used in the discussions of the styles, chronology and technology of pottery, even in cases in which these terms may now be antiquated and no longer in current usage and, indeed, even in cases in which the regionality of a possible local style has been seriously questioned. (See, for example, Collis (1977) for a critique of the styles and groups outlined in Cunliffe (1974).) Ceramic styles have been outlined and illustrated even though the discrimination of some of these styles is no longer considered to be valid or has been seriously questioned. This approach has been adopted because these terms and labels have been committed to the archaeological literature and, rightly or wrongly, their use has often been perpetuated by this.

For example, beakers or 'drinking cups' were found in graves by many nineteenth-century antiquarians. A second type of pottery was also found in graves of roughly the same date, but, because their thickened rims appeared to make them unsuitable as drinking vessels, they were accordingly named 'food' vessels. Today, such a functional nomenclature is unlikely to be acceptable: analytical techniques, such as residue analysis, at present in its infancy, may go some way in the future to establishing the real function of some vessels. We do not know for certain that 'food vessels' contained food: nevertheless the term is now well established in the archaeological literature and is used to describe a *type* of vessel rather than a function.

It is important to know what has been thought in the past before new hypotheses can be formed in the future. It is also worth pointing out that each researcher in the past has believed his or her theories to be correct before committing them to paper. Some conclusions are clearly more acceptable, while others have been shown to be less plausible. This is largely of little consequence for the purposes of this book, however, for the initial belief was there and beliefs will be formed and repudiated as long as archaeology is studied.

The major part of this book is the glossary. Terms used in the text which appear in the glossary will be set **in bold type** the first time they appear in each chapter. Similarly, cross-references in the glossary will be set **in bold type** the first time that they appear in each entry. Subsequent usages of the same terms will appear in normal type. Once more, the entries in the glossary are intended to be introductory, rather than definitive, and are designed as stepping-off points for further reading. To this end, the entries are cross-referenced with both other glossary entries and the bibliography.

In keeping with the general nature of the glossary entries, the currency of each ceramic type has been given in the broadest terms. Many radiocarbon dates for pottery are unreliable as a result of either laboratory error or, more commonly, of the insecure association of the dated sample (Gibson and Kinnes, forthcoming). In keeping with convention, chronologies based on radiocarbon dates are expressed as bc (uncalibrated radiocarbon years), while calendrical dates are denoted by BC or AD.

In a work such as this, the glossary entries must of necessity be brief and specialists will undoubtedly find fault with entries relating to their own field of interest. This book is not, however, intended for the specialist. Thus, the world authority on, for example, situla jars should not be searching the glossary for the situla jar entry. He will probably find only a reference to his own works. However, our situla jar expert may find himself excavating an Iron Age site with residual Towthorpe bowls and then may find the glossary, and particularly the references therein, to be more useful. Similarly, the line drawings are designed to give only an illustration of the types of vessel under discussion. A work of this kind can give only examples and cannot illustrate the whole range of vessels in any given assemblage. It is essential for the reader to remember to treat this work as a guide book rather than an atlas.

Thanks are due to Liz Birkett for Fig. 18, to Marius Cooke for assistance with photography, to Nick Cooper, Ian Freestone and Tony Gouldwell for reading various drafts and discussing some of the thornier problems with one of us (A.J.W.), and to Margaret Hunt for providing the sherds and clay samples illustrated in Figs. 119 and 120.

Chapter 1   The Study of Pottery

Pottery is one of the most important sources of information for the archaeologist. This is primarily because, once fired to a sufficient temperature and for a sufficient length of time, clay is virtually indestructible. Potsherds are one of the most common finds on archaeological sites of all periods, starting with the Neolithic, *c.* 3000 bc. Roman and medieval sites, in particular, produce many thousands of sherds as a result of the increased use of ceramics and the improvement and development of firing techniques and fabrics. Even on prehistoric sites, the numbers of ceramic small finds may be well into the thousands, particularly on sites where midden material is located and excavated as, for example, on some of the second millennium sand-dune settlements of western Scotland, such as Northton on the Isle of Harris (Simpson 1976).

Small sherds of fired clay, often in a very fragile state and with a consistency that has been likened to 'wet cardboard', are meticulously kept, cleaned, conserved and studied. This, to the uninitiated, often seems strange and futile. For example, every archaeologist has experienced an encounter similar to that of the present writer, who was directing an excavation, which was generally devoid of finds, at a settlement site on eastern Dartmoor. Elated to find a chronologically diagnostic sherd from a stratified context, his euphoria was rapidly dissipated by a visiting tourist:

Visitor: 'Have you found anything yet?'

There followed a brief site tour, explaining the site and the exposed timber house.

Visitor: 'But have you actually *found* anything? You know, bones and things?'

A.M.G.: 'Well yes, we've just found this potsherd from the house.'

Visitor (on seeing the proudly presented sherd): 'Oh, is that all?' and, after a pause, 'How long did you say you had left?'

Yet that one small sherd was sufficient to date at least one phase of the site, until radiocarbon dating of the charcoal samples could provide a fuller chronology.

It is primarily as a chronological indicator that pottery has gained so much importance. In the days before radiocarbon dating and the absolute chronologies that it enabled us to construct, many of the relative chronologies were based on ceramic types. Here, changes in styles and forms and methods of decoration and manufacture could be monitored through time, and these changes could then be matched against other, associated, artefact types. Similarly, on sites where pottery of different types is found, study of the stratigraphy of the deposits may indicate the order in which the different pottery types were deposited on the site. By comparing a sequence such as this with other sites producing one or more similar pottery types, a longer relative chronology can be constructed; this is illustrated in the much simplified Fig. 1.

In addition to dating, the changes in pottery fashion over time can be monitored to distinguish between gradual development and rapid change. Some sequences, such as the **bucket urn** tradition of the late second and first millennia, clearly show an underlying trend of continuation within the ceramic record stretching back probably as far as the third millennium. In striking contrast, however, are 'intrusive' pottery styles, such as the **beaker** of the late third and early second millennia, the **La Tène** pot styles of the second half of the first millennium and, later still, the **Gallo-Belgic wares** of the first century BC, all of which have no indigenous ancestry and clearly point to Continental influence.

Such major changes are the crudest sociological usages of ceramics. Finer study of the minutiae of decoration, style and **fabric** may reveal local regional variations within more general styles. Microscopic analysis of fabrics may reveal a common source of manufacture and, combined with distribution maps of identical styles of pots, may reveal trade or exchange networks between different regional groups. Pots may also be convenient vehicles for display, the decoration and form of the pot having a greater significance than simply enhancing the appearance of the vessel. Frequency, positioning and combination of motifs, as set against form, may, for example, communicate the status of the individual within his or her society; however, this aspect of the study of ceramics has not yet received sufficient attention and must remain one of the most exciting avenues for future research.

The study of ceramics is almost as old as the study of archaeology. Prior to the late nineteenth century, pottery and other artefacts were collected by the early antiquarians as curios. With the increasing interest in archaeological techniques and the development of the methodological or scientific approach to archaeology, so too artefacts, including pottery, increased in importance. As so much of the early antiquarians' interest was centred on barrow excavations, it was not surprising that it was the pottery of the early second millennium, the most commonly found types, such as beakers, **collared urns** and **food vessels**, that received the initial interest.

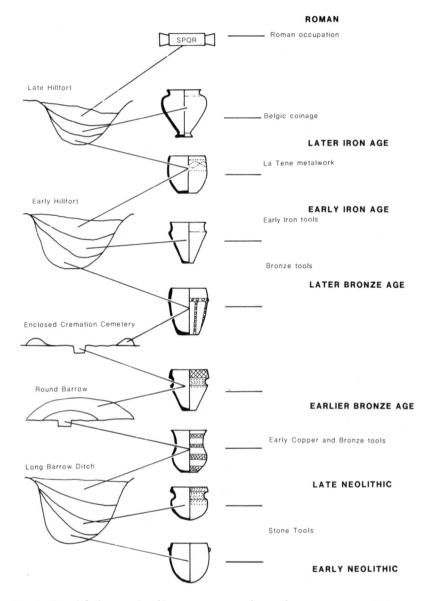

Fig. 1 Simplified example of how pottery may be used to construct a relative chronology.

In 1812, Sir Richard Colt-Hoare described the 'sepulchral urns' with which many barrow interments of Wessex were associated. Large urns containing cremated remains were named 'sepulchral or funereal urns'. These were set aside as clearly different from the more highly ornamented vessels found accompanying the inhumation burials and which, being usually empty, Colt-Hoare determined were for offerings of food or drink. These were named '**drinking cups**' and are now known as beakers. A third type of pot which Colt-Hoare encountered was described as

... perforated on the sides, and one of them on the bottom, like a colander, which circumstance induces me to think that they were filled with balsams and precious ointments and suspended over a funeral pile. I shall therefore distinguish these vases by the title of **Incense Cups**, as in the description of the numerous *tumuli* we have opened, it is absolutely necessary that these urns, so different in their nature, should be properly and distinctly discriminated. (Colt-Hoare 1812, 25, our emphasis.)

This description of the vessels that have become so typical of the early second millennium bc may seem rather quaint and certainly very inadequate by modern standards, but the discrimination by Colt-Hoare of three different types of sepulchral vessel marks the start of prehistoric pottery classifications. His term 'drinking cup' continued in use for about a century, and 'incense cup' for much longer.

In 1861, Bateman wrote his account of excavations into barrows in Derbyshire, Staffordshire and Yorkshire and recognized four main classes of sepulchral pottery:

I CINERARY OR SEPULCHRAL URNS – such as have either contained, or been inverted over, calcined human bones, and which alone are correctly styled *Urns*.
II INCENSE CUPS – so called, though their real purpose is doubtful. Diminutive vessels, only found with calcined bones, and frequently enclosed in urns of the first class.
III SMALL VASES – probably intended to contain an offering of food; usually found with unburnt bodies, but not unfrequently with burnt bones, though never containing them.
IV DRINKING CUPS – tall and highly-ornamented vessels, constricted in the middle, and no doubt named in accordance with their use, by Sir R. C. Hoare (Bateman 1861, 279).

This classification was broadly similar to that of Colt-Hoare but included one new category, category III, the small vase, later to be known as the food vessel.

As the 'drinking cup' or beaker was to become one of the most studied of the British prehistoric pottery types, it may be useful here to follow the development of the studies of this one particular type, not so much to assess the different schemes of classification but rather to consider how attitudes towards the aims of pot classifications changed over time as archaeology developed.

In 1871, Thurnham wrote an important and much-quoted essay on the burial mounds of Wessex and dealt with the pottery finds in comparative detail. Thurnham, like many of his contemporaries, was unable to comprehend the chronological depth of prehistory and thus labelled much of the pottery 'Ancient British'. He also suffered from an imprecise chronology and, noting the rareness of weapons in beaker graves, he concluded that they were Romano-British in date, the lack of weapons being a direct result of the *Pax Romana*. This error apart, Thurnham offered the first classification of Beaker pottery into (α) long-necked beakers, (β) bell or European beakers and (γ) short-necked beakers. This (α–β–γ) division was quite a revolutionary approach to the classification of ceramics and a method of discrimination that has been followed into the present time (for example, Piggott 1963; for a similar alphabetical classification of later first millennium material, follow the entries emanating from **Belgic wares** in the glossary and Thompson 1982).

In addition to this classification, Thurnham wrote about the technology of the pottery from the Wessex barrows. He noted that the pottery was hand-made without use of the potter's wheel and also that it had been bonfire-fired rather than kiln-fired, saying:

The firing of most of this pottery has been very imperfect; it was probably first partly dried by exposure to the air, and then baked rather than burnt in the ashes of a fire lighted over and around it. Cinerary Urns were perhaps sometimes baked in the ashes of the funeral pyre, while some of the finer vessels hereafter described as incense cups, food vessels and drinking cups, many of which are of a bright red colour, must have been more carefully fired, perhaps in a rude kiln of piled-up stones (Thurnham 1871, 332).

In 1877, Canon William Greenwell published an important account of material largely recovered from his excavations into many of the burial mounds of the border counties, Durham and Yorkshire. Greenwell, even by the standards of his day, was not a model excavator, but he was an avid collector and a large portion of the account of his excavations is devoted to describing the finds, albeit collectively rather than individually. Greenwell also expressed an interest in the technology of prehistoric pottery:

They [i.e. beakers, food vessels and urns] were at one time almost universally, and still occasionally, spoken of as being sun-dried. This is not the case with any of them, for they have all invariably undergone, more or less, the action of fire; though, in some instances, this has taken place to a very trifling extent. They have not been baked in a kiln, but at an open fire; and the larger vessels frequently show in their upper part a tinge of black colour, caused by the smoke of the wood with which they were burnt.

They have all been hand-made, not one showing any sign of the use of the wheel...

The clay of which they were made differs much, both in its quality, and in the preparation, by means of tempering, which it has undergone. As the vessels were probably manufactured on the spot, the clay necessarily varied with the several localities ... In the greater number of all the vessels, and in the whole of the larger ones, broken stone in various proportions is found to have been mixed with the clay. In some cases there is almost as much broken stone as clay in the composition ... The object of this mixture was to prevent the pottery from cracking in the baking, and it also had the effect of making the clay more firm before the firing, so that the shape of the vessel was better preserved ... Some of the vessels ... were formed of separate pieces [of clay] laid together, the sides being as it were gradually built up. This is apparent from the smooth and rounded edges of the pieces into which a vessel has sometimes separated ... there being a tendency for it to come asunder at those parts where the several pieces from which it was formed had originally been joined (1877, 63–4).

Not only does Greenwell notice the **ring-building** of pottery from the distinctive breaks and **join voids**, but also recognizes accurately the method of **open firing** and the role of **fillers**. He also goes on to comment on the use of **slip**:

Some of the pottery appears to be made from overlaying a coarser and ill-worked clay with a coating of finer paste; and it is not improbable that in many cases the vessel was shaped at the first out of inferior clay and partly dried, and that afterwards an additional layer of better-tempered clay was laid over the surface, upon which the ornamental patterns were executed, the whole being then fired (ibid., 64).

Returning to the classification of pottery, Greenwell retains the use of the term 'drinking cup' but constantly puts it in inverted commas and he is at pains to point out that it is most unlikely that they ever held liquid. He is clearly dissatisfied with this and other terms (such as 'incense cups' and 'food vessels') when he says:

This nomenclature is to some extent, and as regards some of them, misleading; but it has become so commonly used as to render it difficult, and perhaps unadvisable, to alter it (op. cit., 61).

Greenwell takes this point up again when he writes about drinking cups:

Like the 'food vessels', they have occasionally been found to contain a dark-coloured substance, which has all the appearance of being the remains of solid food ... No liquid could have left such a residuum and in fact the vessels are too porous in texture ever to have retained fluid for any length of time ... Retaining the name provisionally, I should class the 'drinking cups' with the 'food vessels' as having both been intended for the same purpose, that of holding food of some kind for the use of the dead (op. cit., 101–2).

In his excavations in Wessex, General Pitt-Rivers illustrated his pottery in a series of plates and included drawings of the sections of the pottery to illustrate its thickness (see, in particular, Pitt-Rivers 1898, Plate 246, and Fig. 2 here). While this reflects his interest in the advancement of the recording techniques of archaeology, with regard to the classification and understanding of pottery, Pitt-Rivers made a retrograde step. He subdivided the 'British' (i.e. pre-Roman) pottery into four classes according to the 'quality' of the **fabric**:

Fig. 2   Pitt-Rivers's illustration of pottery from the ditch of the Wor Barrow. 7, comb impressions; 8, 9, 14, incised decoration; 10, 11, 16, 17, twisted cord impressions. 10 also shows bird bone impressions and 11 also features finger nail impressions.

No. 1 Quality.—Coarse, badly-baked, containing grains of quartz, flint, chalk, or shell, sometimes one and sometimes the others; hand-made.

No. 2 Quality.—Coarse, soft, smooth without sand or large grains; ill-baked, and sometimes red on one side and black on the other, and apparently hand-made.

No. 3 Quality.—Thin, without grains, generally reddish-brown, and of fine quality; frequently ornamented with oblong punch-marks; of the quality of the Drinking Vessels of the Bronze Age; hand-made.

No. 4 Quality.—Brown colour, and mixed with sand, containing quartz and other grains. It very much resembles Romano-British, but differs from it, in having a large quantity of quartz sand in its composition. In some cases, the difficulty of distinguishing between this and the *superior* and *inferior* qualities of coarse brown Romano-British pottery is very great (Pitt-Rivers 1898, 29)

Complementing his plates, Pitt-Rivers also described each illustrated sherd, assigning it to a fabric 'quality' and indicating its stratigraphy. In his descriptions, however, he clearly shows a lack of understanding of decorative techniques which today might be considered quaint or naïve. In describing a sherd of **Mortlake ware** from the ditch of the Neolithic Wor Barrow, Pitt-Rivers writes:

Fragment of rim of No.1 quality, British; ornamented on the rim with a herring-bone pattern and on the inside by rows of oblique oval punch-marks … The peculiarity of this ornamentation consists in the transverse ribs across the bottom of the oval punch-marks, in which respect it resembles … a fragment from West Kennet Long Barrow … (op. cit., 100, Plate 261, No. 17) (Fig. 2:17 here).

The 'punch-marks' to which Pitt-Rivers refers are in fact **whipped cord** herring-bone made up from whipped cord **maggots** (hence the 'transverse ribs') on the outer rim moulding, and **twisted cord** impressions on the interior. These decorative techniques are common on **later neolithic impressed wares** and it seems strange that Pitt-Rivers did not recognize them, while many of his contemporaries clearly did (for example, Bateman 1861, 279; Greenwell 1877, 65).

Important in Greenwell's discussion of beakers is his observation of the similarity of the British material to that from the Continent and in particular the Netherlands. This was an aspect of beaker studies upon which Abercromby elaborated in 1902, when, in addition to identifying beakers as the earliest Bronze Age ceramic in Britain, he also discarded the term 'drinking cup' in favour of the now accepted 'beaker'. The reason for this change was that 'beaker' was more convenient to use and also bore similarities to northern-European words, such as *Becher* or *baeger*, used by Continental archaeologists to describe very similar pots. Abercromby continued to use Thurnham's α–β–γ classification, though modifying it and adapting it, and his introduction of the term 'beaker' took some time to become universal (see, for example, Cunnington 1926).

In 1912, however, Abercromby produced the first national corpus of prehistoric pottery, *A Study of the Bronze Age Pottery of Great Britain and Ireland and its Associated Grave Goods*. This two-volume work is a landmark in the study of pottery, bringing together a corpus of material, dividing the corpus into distinct classes, such as beakers and food vessels, and illustrating all the vessels in a series of photographs. Abercromby essentially retained Thurnham's α–β–γ classification but substituted the Latin A–B–C for the original Greek. His classification was more complex, however, with the recognition of a great many hybrid vessels—types AC, AB, BC and so on—perhaps an indication, even to Abercromby, that the typology was unsatisfactory.

Subsequent to the publication of Abercromby's corpus, an increasing amount of attention was paid to the stratigraphical sequence of pottery, its associated artefacts and its place in the increasingly more reliable relative chronologies. This led to the realization that Abercromby's A–B–C sequence, based on the degeneration of form and decoration from the elaborate to the simple, should, in fact, read B–C–A in terms of chronology (Clark 1931). In this scheme, B represents early bell beakers with close Continental parallels, C represents necked developments from type B, and A consists of elaborately decorated, long-necked beakers representing the climax of insular development. As David Clarke was to point out almost forty years later, this reversal of sequence made a 'nonsense of the alphabetical nomenclature which has unfortunately still stuck' (Clarke 1970, i).

The following decade saw similar studies which did little to advance our understanding of the beaker problem. By now, the chronological primacy of type B was accepted, and energies were devoted to both confirming this and developing, enhancing and ultimately complicating the existing typology. This was almost totally in pursuance of chronology, but also a great many words were devoted to stressing the Continental origins of the type based on both form (Crichton Mitchell 1934; Piggott 1936) and decoration (Childe 1940, 93). This brought about a major change from the attitudes of the preceding century, when pottery of the later third and earlier second millennia bc had been described as 'Ancient British'. Now, in contrast, pottery was being seen as something more cultural: contacts between British, Dutch and German ceramic must *ipso facto* mean contacts between British, Dutch and German PEOPLE. It was the beginning of the 'pots = people' doctrine, which led to theories of multiple invasions for each ceramic innovation that was difficult to parallel locally. Although it was never really stated in print, by inference it became clear that the prehistoric populations of Britain were almost regarded as a dull and unimaginative race, who were constantly behind the European fashions and who were totally unable to defend themselves as wave after wave of European invaders settled in these islands.

It may be reading too much into the political situation of the time to suggest that it had a great effect on the subsequent archaeological literature, but it may be that the constant and very real threat of invasion by the forces of the Third Reich during the second World War did much to prolong the lifespan of the invasion theories. Conversely, however, the failure of the German invasion did little to render them redundant. Pots still equalled people and therefore different pots equalled different people.

By the 1960s, it was realized that the extant typologies were rigorous in the extreme and did little to promote the study of pottery. They were based on the 'pots for pots' sake' maxim and did little to explain the people behind the artefacts. By this time, of course, the model of round-headed beaker invaders introducing the single crouched inhumation burial, the round barrow and the first metalwork was well established. The question of chronology was, however, less suited by the over-complex typologies. Piggott (1963) resolved this by reassessing the Beaker cultures, their associated burials and artefacts. He modified the typologies into a broad chronological sequence of bell beaker, short-necked beaker and long-necked beaker. This was essentially the C–B–A sequence developed before the war but used the more logical, verbal rather than alphabetical, descriptive terms to outline the scheme. It was also less rigorous and less likely to tempt classificatory hybridization along the lines of the Biαs and Biβs of the pre-war years.

In 1970, David Clarke produced a new corpus of Beaker pottery which, he was quite correctly to point out at length, increased Abercromby's corpus sixfold; all previous schemes had essentially been based on this earlier and, by now, totally inadequate corpus. Clarke's major work, published in two volumes, followed on from the classification of Dutch beakers by van der Waals and Glasbergen (1955), in which equal importance was given to form and decoration. Moreover, Clarke attempted a classification of the pottery that would not only provide a tight chronological frame for the ceramics but would also view the sociological implications, that is, what the pottery tells us about the users.

Using mathematical methodology to analyze the shape, motifs and style combinations on beakers, Clarke devised a complex system of classification which treated the intrusive European elements of the beaker corpus separately from the insular developments. By matching the motifs found on British and Continental beakers, Clarke isolated seven intrusive groups: **All Over cord (AOC)**, European (E), Wessex/Mid-Rhine (W/MR), North British/Mid-Rhine (N/MR), North British/North Rhine (N/NR), **Barbed wire (BW)**, and Primary North British/Dutch (N^1/D). From these intrusive groups developed two insular traditions, Northern and Southern (N^2–N^4 and S^1–S^4), with the northern tradition preceding the southern (Fig. 47). classification exemplified the complexity of the beaker networks both in Britain and on the Continent and was a real attempt to isolate distinct population foci by raising the question 'Who were the Beaker folk ?' Clarke's approach and results acknowledged the logical theory that Britain was tribal and far from a United Kingdom in the early years of the second millennium bc.

Clarke's fresh approach was welcomed and his schemes are still used by many archaeologists, despite the criticisms of the classification that were made shortly after its publication. These criticisms were voiced most noticeably by the Dutchmen Lanting and van der Waals. The major objection to Clarke's scheme was that his groupings lacked the foci that he had searched for. Clarke's distribution maps showed that, with the exception of the Wessex/Mid-Rhine group, each beaker group was distributed widely over the country. Lanting and van der Waals, by contrast, used Clarke's corpus and applied a regional approach to construct a seven-stage development for beakers in distinct geographical locations—Wessex, East Anglia, Yorkshire, the Borders and Northern Scotland, the last-named area being later refined by Shepherd (1986, Fig. 48). This classification allowed for obvious regional differences in the corpus, yet followed a similar path of development in each area, which was essentially the development of the neck and the diversification of the variety and complexity of the decorative motifs (Lanting and van der Waals 1972). Moreover, it was demonstrated that this ample potential for regional insular development need only have stemmed from a small-scale migration from Europe. Consequently, Clarke's complex seven-wave-invasion theory was dismissed.

In 1977, Case in turn criticized the scheme of Lanting and van der Waals in favour of early, middle and late beaker phases, on the grounds that previous scholars lacked a statistically viable absolute chronological framework, based on securely associated radiocarbon dates, against which to structure a rigid process of development. Moreover, the radiocarbon dates that were available were showing that there was increasing intra-regional, chronological overlap between the various steps, which, after all, were based on stylistic development. Case, therefore, sided with caution and saw beakers reaching Britain mainly as a result of culture contact between insular and Continental populations. It has been obvious for some time that the Wessex area played an important role in attracting beakers. The earliest examples are found in this region, perhaps because the area was in control of valuable copper supplies from Wales or even Ireland, or perhaps the developing religious importance of Wessex was already attracting foreign attention (Gibson 1982, 88).

In conclusion, the study of beaker ceramics has turned almost
From the status of 'curios', beakers were quickly classified into types in an
attempt to devise a chronological progression and, from this point, pottery
became an important chronological indicator. By the early years of this
century, pottery had reached, and still holds, an important place in the
relative chronologies, both regionally and nationally. With the extension of
the prehistoric time-span that was brought about by the discovery of
radiocarbon dating, these relative chronologies could be given absolute
frameworks, particularly in the Neolithic and the Bronze Age. In the Iron Age
or later first millennium BC, this problem was not so great. Elaborate bronze
and iron metalwork and continentally-homogeneous Celtic art could also be
used in the construction of chronologies. Metalwork, in particular, could be
related to the absolute dates of the Archaic and Classical Mediterranean
cultures and iron age pottery never achieved the importance that it had had
in the preceding periods. Conversely and ironically, prestige pottery and
artefacts of the Iron Age were initially dated by associations in graves with
securely dated Mediterranean ceramics. This is not to dismiss the importance
of, or the attention paid to, the ceramics of the first millennium, however, as
clearly they too were chronologically important. They were also well studied,
both from a regional approach, in the identifications of the developing tribal
systems well documented by the later classical texts (for example, Cunliffe
1974; Birchall 1965), and from the point of view of highlighting cross-
Channel contacts (Avery 1973).

As we have seen from the above summary of beaker studies, ceramic
typologies have been 'done to death'. The broad chronological trends have
been recognized and little altered from an early date. Some stylistic sequences
have been over-rigorous. Broad ceramic groups have been broken down with
such precision as to resemble items in a mail-order catalogue and have done
little to further our understanding of the mechanics of development and what
that development means in terms of people. The 'pots for pots' sake'
approach has outlived its usefulness and we must now direct our attentions to
the roles played by ceramics in the greater 'cultural' sphere of past
populations. Pottery must be viewed anthropologically as one facet of a past
society, and this can best be achieved by studying aspects of ceramics which
are wider and more varied than chronological, stylistic development.

Over the last thirty years, the increasingly scientific approach to
archaeology in general and the study of artefacts in particular has, naturally,
also had an effect on ceramic studies. Archaeological methodology has
always borrowed heavily from other sciences and disciplines; this is
continuing even now, as archaeological ceramists regularly use and adapt
techniques of examination and analysis that are more commonly
implemented in the physical and earth sciences.

The basic aims of most scientific artefact studies are to determine two main types of information: the composition of the material, with a view to establishing its place of origin, and the technology employed. As ceramics are potentially more likely to yield both types of information than any other class of archaeological artefact, it is perhaps a little surprising that many workers were slow to adopt the new techniques and continued to rely primarily on stylistic and typological studies.

It is also disappointing to note that, on a world-wide basis, many of the most progressive pottery studies have been made by non-archaeologists. The importance of the pioneering work of Anna Shepard in the United States on pot technology and provenance studies through the use of thin sections can never be overestimated. In Britain, some early work was done by Hodges, both on his own (1962 and 1963) and in conjunction with Cornwall, a soil scientist (Cornwall and Hodges 1964), but the real development of thin-section studies was sparked off by David Peacock, a geologist who realized that geological techniques could be applied to archaeological ceramics. In other parts of the world, another important researcher, Owen Rye, was a practising potter who later became attracted to archaeology. His work (1976, 1977, 1981; Rye and Evans 1976) involved a useful combination of knowledge acquired from modern ceramic technology, experiment and studies of contemporary potters, and he provides a personification of Shepard's statement (1980, xviii) that 'Ideally, a ceramic technologist is a specialist with multiple skills and interests'.

Although it was fashionable amongst archaeologists of the 1960s and early 1970s to sneer at ethnographic parallels, studies of contemporary traditional potters have subsequently become more scientific and more widely accepted. Rather than just being reports on methods of pottery manufacture, they have increasingly included data that may directly help solve actual archaeological problems. An excellent example of this is provided by the study by DeBoer and Lathrap (1979) of the Shipibo–Conibo people of Peru, in which, as well as noting pottery-manufacture materials and methods and vessel usage, they recorded how and where vessels broke and became incorporated into the archaeological record. Other instances of this are provided by the works of David and Hennig (1972) on the Fulani of Cameroon and of Longacre (1982) in the Philippines.

Unfortunately, many workers in Britain have felt that ethnographic parallels from other parts of the world cannot be applied to the study of British prehistoric pottery. This objection, based largely on climatic differences, is, of course, unfounded and is discussed in more detail in Chapter 2: clays suitable for utilization for hand-made and open-fired pottery have a lot in common, regardless of their geographical origin, and there is a limited number of ways in which vessels can be made and fired, regardless of the climate. The lack of contemporary traditional potters in Britain probably explains why much research has concentrated primarily on experimental studies. These, too, after a slow start, have also become more productive and applicable to the study of archaeological ceramics. With regard to firing, there has been a certain reluctance on the part of many British archaeologists to accept that prehistoric pottery was produced by **open firing**; this, despite the fact that the pottery exhibits all the tell-tale signs, such as **fire clouds**, blotchy surfaces and incompletely oxidized cross-sections and that there is a complete lack of kilns in Britain until the first century BC or even later. Most early experimental firings were of kilns, usually copies of Romano-British types (see, for example, Bryant 1970 and 1979, Mayes 1961 and 1962), and there was a general feeling that bonfires or pit firings were too easy and did not require investigation. Research at Leicester University during the last decade (Gibson 1986c, Woods 1983, 1989, and in press) has indicated that this is far from the truth and that the problems involved in open firing are more complex than had been previously thought. Little now remains to be discovered about firing temperatures, but the difficulty of recognizing sites that may have been used for the firing of prehistoric pottery needs to be investigated further; the short firing time involved in the firing of pottery in either surface bonfires or in pits has little effect on the soil underneath (Coleman-Smith 1971, 7; Gibson 1986c, 8 and 12), leaving little evidence that may be used for comparison with archaeological deposits. The solution to this problem probably lies in a combination of investigative techniques, headed by results from experimental research in conjunction with ethnographic studies.

In keeping with the increasingly scientific approach to the study of ceramics, advances have been made at the most basic levels with the development of simple tests for the macroscopic identification of inclusions in pottery fabrics. They involve **hardness tests** and the reaction of inclusions with **hydrochloric acid**, in conjunction with observation of other diagnostic properties, such as shape and texture. These tests require little in the way of equipment as they can be done with a hand lens or a low-power binocular microscope (typical magnification ×20) and have provided pottery researchers with a cheap and systematic method for the preliminary sorting of fabrics within an assemblage. (See Peacock 1977, 30-2, and Robinson 1979 for fuller descriptions of the methods involved.)

Estimation of the frequency of inclusions within fabrics may also assist in the sorting of a ceramic assemblage. **Visual percentage estimation charts** have been used for some years by pottery researchers, particularly those working with later, wheel-thrown wares. These charts have also been borrowed from the earth sciences, where they have been used to estimate the composition of sediments. Archaeologists are most familiar with the charts originally devised in Russia by Shvetsov and published in the West by Terry and Chilingar (1955). These, however, exhibit primarily angular shapes in an unspecified size range and, as such, are of limited application to archaeological ceramics. To overcome this, a more comprehensive set of charts, with a greater variety of shapes (rounded and mixed angular and rounded) and a wider frequency range, has recently been produced (Matthew and Woods, in press). This series of charts is available in a white-on-black, as well as the more usual black-on-white, format and should provide a more appropriate and accurate method for the estimation of the inclusion content of archaeological ceramics, particularly when used in conjunction with thin sections or the low-power binocular microscope.

In so far as provenance studies are concerned, it was really only during the mid-1960s that techniques such as the examination of **thin sections** of pottery with the **polarizing microscope** and element analysis techniques such as optical emission spectrometry (OES), itself in its infancy with regard to archaeological material at this time, came to be more widely utilized. Since then, the increased use of thin sections, **heavy mineral analysis** (HMA), **textural analysis** and physical methods of chemical analysis for provenance studies, along with chemical analysis of residues in pottery, has resulted in a more rigorously scientific approach to the study of ceramics, aimed at supplementing the information obtained from typological studies.

By virtue of its coarse and hand-made nature, British prehistoric pottery is especially amenable to examination in thin section. Such studies can identify the mineral and/or rock inclusions present and, if these are sufficiently distinctive, allow an area of origin to be pinpointed. In recent years, numerous thin-section studies of prehistoric pottery have been undertaken and the examination of pottery by this method is becoming commonplace. It is beyond the scope of this volume to discuss these studies in detail, but mention should be made of one well-known example of the use of the technique in establishing a provenance for pottery, viz, the case of the Hembury 'f' wares, good-quality neolithic **gabbroic wares** from the Lizard Peninsula of Cornwall. This study, published by Peacock in 1969b, looked at a wider range of material than that studied earlier by Cornwall and Hodges (1964) and, through more accurate identification of the inclusions present in the clay and comparison with clay sources, established a provenance for the pottery which was reinforced by the fact that the ceramics were found over a similar distribution area to stone axes from the same area. The use of these gabbroic clays was not confined to the Neolithic and continued throughout prehistory, through the Roman period and into medieval times (Peacock 1988, 302). Although subsequent researchers have tried to disprove Peacock's findings (see, for example, Smith 1981, Quinnell 1987), as yet no really viable alternative provenance for the wares has been suggested;

photomicrographs published later in this volume (Figs. 119 and 120) reveal the close similarity between clay and pottery from this area.

Thin-section studies can also be extremely useful in determining the methods of manufacture of prehistoric pottery. These methods are described in more detail in Chapter 2 and in the glossary, but the photomicrograph below (Fig. 3) shows a join void or junction between two straps of clay, clear evidence that the vessel was constructed by ring-building, the most common method employed for the manufacture of British prehistoric pottery. Thin sections may also reveal **particle orientation** which may be sufficiently pronounced to indicate the method of manufacture. Studies of particle orientation, however, as revealed by thin sections (Woods 1985) or **X-radiography** (Rye 1977), are still in their infancy.

Despite the many advantages of thin sections, there are also some limitations and these have led archaeological ceramists to adapt and develop other techniques of examination and analysis. Firstly, sandy wares create difficulties, because quartz sand does not exhibit any distinguishing optical properties when viewed in thin section. Much of the pottery excavated on British sites, particularly from the Roman and medieval periods, contains quartz sand as the only non-clay inclusion type. The frequency of such wares has resulted in researchers borrowing the techniques of heavy mineral analysis and textural analysis from sedimentology in an effort to obtain meaningful results from their pottery. Heavy mineral analysis is a laborious and unpleasant method to use and involves the destruction of a relatively large amount of sherd material but has yielded good results in the case of Romano-British **black-burnished** pottery and its iron age Durotrigian antecedents (Williams 1977). Textural analysis has also been used to distinguish fabrics of similar mineralogical composition. The methods used have been many and varied (see Middleton *et al.* 1985 for a summary of them) and although a certain amount of controversy still exists as to the validity of each of them, the number of grains that should be counted and/or measured and so on, successful results have been obtained, particularly in relation to quartzy fabrics. (See, for example, Betts 1982, Darvill 1979, Darvill and Timby 1982, Peacock 1971.)

Thin sections are also of little use in the examination of fine wares. They are used to identify the inclusions present in pottery fabrics and are of limited application for the examination of clay matrices, because most clay particles are too small to be identified by the use of the optical microscope and are usually destroyed in the firing process. In such instances, physical methods of chemical analysis will usually be more rewarding, yielding information on the chemical composition of pottery and, on occasions, after comparisons with clay samples, providing evidence of the origin of the pottery. A wide range of methods is available, but neutron activation analysis (NAA) is the one most

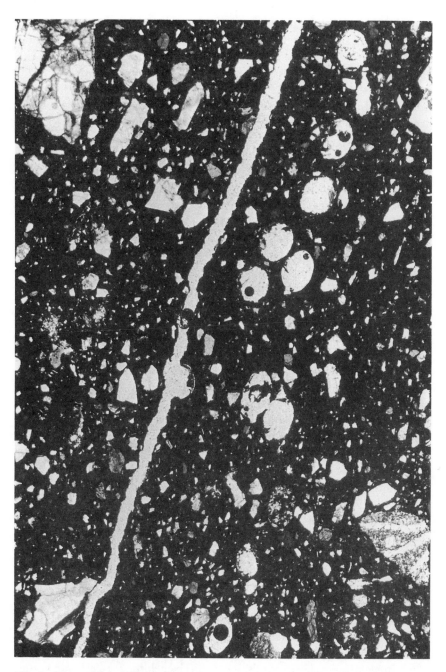

Fig. 3   Photomicrograph of a thin section of a beaker sherd from Northton, Harris. The white line is a join void between two straps of clay which were imperfectly bonded by the potter and separated as the clay dried. PPL, × 22.

commonly employed for the analysis of archaeological ceramics. It provides a complete analysis of a small sherd or sample, allowing major ($>2\%$), minor ($<2\%$) and trace (0.1-2%) elements to be detected and measured. (See Tite 1972, 273-8, for a fuller description of the technique and its applications.) It is currently the most accurate and comprehensive method of analysis. Other methods, which may be appropriate for the analysis of a particular problem, are also available; for example, X-ray fluorescence (XRF), when used non-destructively, is primarily a technique which analyses the surface of an object and as such may be useful for the analysis of **glaze** material on a pot or faience bead, enabling its composition to be detected without picking up contamination from the ceramic or frit body beneath. The use of physical methods of chemical analysis on prehistoric pottery is not, however, common; although some studies have been published (for example, Topping 1986 and Topping and MacKenzie 1988), the coarse nature of the pottery may involve sampling problems, and examination in thin section is usually a more productive method of study. Element analysis techniques generally yield better results when applied to the finer wares of the Romano-British and medieval periods.

Diatom analysis (Gibson 1986*b*) can also be used for provenance studies: although not all clays are diatomaceous, when present, the diatom assemblage extracted from the fired clay of pottery can be compared with that of clays from known sources in an attempt to find a source for the clay itself, rather than the mineral inclusions. Unfortunately, the technique is laborious and few studies have been conducted in Britain.

The continuing development in scanning electron microscopy (SEM) techniques has also been beneficial to the study of ceramics. The greater resolution power and depth of field of the electron microscope allow higher magnifications to be employed than is the case in optical microscopy, with the result that surface coatings, for example, can be examined (see, for example, Tite *et al.* 1982*a*, Middleton 1987). Other aspects of ceramic technology (such as the estimation of firing temperature from the degree of vitrification of the pottery) can also be studied (Tite and Maniatis 1975, Maniatis and Tite 1979, Tite *et al.* 1982*b*). Chemical analytical techniques, now frequently found in association with SEM, also allow provenance studies to be carried out in conjunction with these technological studies.

Many other techniques for determining the composition and technology of ceramics have also been used; of these, only X-ray diffraction (XRD) and thermal expansion measurement need mentioning here. XRD is used to determine mineral phases rather than chemical composition and, as such, is of use in identifying clay minerals. It can also be helpful in ascertaining firing temperatures, as it can reveal the mineralogical changes that occur as a result of firing. Obviously, different clays are affected by heat in different ways, but a reasonably accurate firing temperature estimation can be obtained if the clay source for the pottery is known or suspected; samples can be fired to known temperatures for defined periods of time and the results then compared with the archaeological material. Although of limited application, good results have been obtained by some workers (see, for example, Maggetti 1982, 126 ff., and Cooper and Bowman 1986). Thermal expansion measurement is another method that has been used to determine firing temperatures of ancient pottery (Tite 1969). However, as it effectively depends on shrinkage during firing, it also is of limited use in the study of prehistoric ceramics.

Finally, some mention must be made of residue analysis in pottery, as it can provide evidence of the function of pottery vessels. Few studies have so far been published, but the technique continues to develop, largely as a result of improvements in the various methods of chromatography employed, and some interesting conclusions have been drawn (see, for example, Evans 1984, Hill 1984).

This brief and superficial summary of some of the more recent developments in analytical and examination methods should provide the reader with an idea of the vast range of techniques that can be utilized for the study of archaeological ceramics. This area of ceramic studies is dynamic and challenging, but it should be stressed that no one technique will provide all the answers; the study of pottery is a multi-disciplinary one and it is through a combination of methods (such as ethnography with experiment, thin section studies with experiment or chemical analysis with thin sections), rather than by the application of a single study technique, that future progress will be made. Naturally, too, the scientific techniques cannot ever totally replace typological studies but should be used in conjunction with them.

Chapter 2   The Technology of Prehistoric Pottery

Prior to the Roman invasion, almost all native pottery in Britain was hand-made and open-fired. Despite appearances to the contrary, **open firing** in surface bonfires or in pits can be a difficult process, and the fabric of the clay vessel must be sufficiently coarse or the vessel will explode during firing. In the study of archaeological ceramics, it is worth remembering that there is a relationship between fabric, method of manufacture and type of firing: kiln-fired wares tend to be fine and wheel-thrown, whereas open-fired vessels are coarse and hand-made. This is not to say that coarse wares were never fired in kilns, but fine wares are extremely difficult to fire in open firings.

Pottery Fabrics in Prehistory

As a result of the interdependence of fabric, method of manufacture and method of firing mentioned above, prehistoric pottery was always coarse; if the clay did not naturally contain enough inclusions, potters made additions to it. Much has been written about the functions of inclusions in clay bodies, but little of the literature appears to be relevant to prehistoric pottery. Many of the explanations have been drawn directly from modern ceramic technology and writers have failed to realize that there are few similarities between the fine-bodied and high-fired wares of today and the coarse, low-fired wares of prehistory. Accordingly, many of the explanations given for the addition of non-clay materials to clay for pot manufacture are inapplicable to ancient ceramics.

The greatest problems in any type of firing occur early on, at what is known as the **water-smoking stage**, around 100°C. At this point, any water left in the clay after drying (Fig.4:3 and 4) will boil and turn to steam, expanding in volume as it does so. If the steam cannot escape through the clay, pressure builds up and it may force circular flakes of clay, known as **fire spalls**, out of the walls of the clay vessel (Fig. 5). In extreme cases, the whole vessel explodes. Such spalling produces the most commonly occurring type of waster found in archaeological contexts, regardless of the type of firing. After a vessel has been made, it is left to dry, so that the water that has been mixed with the clay to make it plastic and workable can evaporate away. However, it is not possible to remove all this water and thereby dry clay completely at

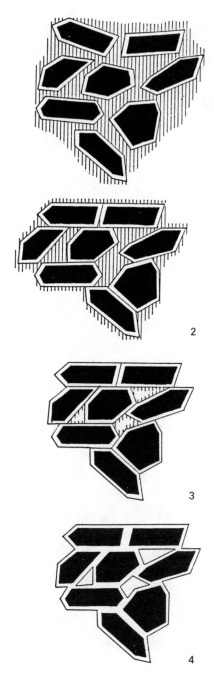

Fig. 4 Clay states with varying amounts of water between the clay particles. 4:1, plastic clay; 4:2, leather-hard clay; 4:3, air-dry clay; 4:4, clay after the water-smoking stage of firing. After Hamer and Hamer 1977, 36.

Fig. 5   Fire spalling in a pot fired in an experimental bonfire firing. Steam evolved in the early stages of the firing has been unable to escape through the fine clay and has blown large flakes out of the pot walls.

room temperature. Clay is a hygroscopic substance and will be affected by changes in the ambient atmosphere, absorbing moisture on a humid day and giving it off again in drier weather. Some moisture (3-5%) (Fig. 4:3) always remains between the clay particles of an unfired vessel, regardless of the length of time it has been drying, and this can only be driven off during the firing process itself.

In a kiln, the unfired vessels are kept separate from the fuel and from direct contact with the flames. Kiln firing is a lengthy process, as much time and fuel are used in heating the kiln structure itself. In contrast, in an open firing, the vessels and the fuel are in direct contact and the firing is rapid: the nature of fire itself ensures that the temperature will rise quickly to a maximum before cooling down at a similarly rapid rate (Fig. 6). Experimental open firings done with wood (Fig. 7) frequently take less than one hour to complete, but some other fuels can reach maximum temperature even more rapidly; sago fronds, for example, used for a firing in the Goodenough Islands, yielded a mean maximum temperature of 746°C after just four minutes, and the firing was completed after ten minutes, when the vessel was removed from the fire, the temperature of which was around 650°C (Lauer 1972, 10).

In short, open firings are quick and economical and, provided the vessels have been heated sufficiently for the clay minerals to go through the **ceramic change,** will produce fired pots that are perfectly adequate for storage, cooking and general use. Temperatures in the range 650-900°C are typical of open firings and this is quite sufficient to ensure that the clay is converted to ceramic. (The ceramic change occurs at different temperatures for all the different clay mineral types but is generally considered to occur around 550-600°C.)

Therefore, the most important reason for the coarse composition of prehistoric pottery is that it was made that way in order to ensure that it survived firing. The rapid temperature rise that is characteristic of open firing, coupled with the fact that the clay vessels are in direct contact with the fuel (and therefore with the flames once the fire has been kindled), is responsible for the problems incurred in the early stages of firing and for the risk of spalling and explosions. In a kiln, the temperature can be controlled, so that it rises slowly through the dangerous water smoking stage, but this is not possible in an open firing and alternative methods must be used to prevent spalling. The easiest way to do this is to mix plenty of **opening materials** with the clay. Almost any substance, organic or inorganic, may be used, provided that it does not become plastic when the clay is mixed with water prior to manufacture. The important factor is that there is a sufficient quantity of it. Its prime function is to open the body to allow the steam to escape in the early stages of firing, but it also performs a useful role by opening the clay during drying, allowing it to dry more quickly and evenly and with less shrinkage, thereby reducing the risk of cracking at this stage.

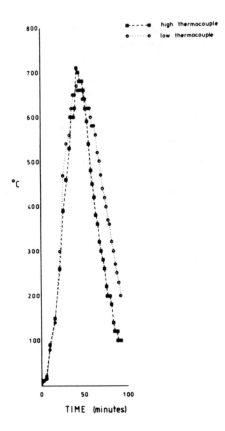

Fig. 6 Firing curve from a typical experimental open firing done with brushwood. The temperature rises rapidly to a maximum and then cools at a similar rate.

Much of the archaeological literature suggests that potters deliberately added opening materials to their clay to strengthen the fabric. However, while they do actually strengthen the vessel while it is in the clay state (they help the walls to support themselves, thus preventing collapse during the manufacturing processes), all inclusions present have a weakening effect on the fired product. This is because they interrupt and inhibit the bonding of the clay particles with one another. Rounded inclusions have the greatest weakening effect, as they do not possess any rough surfaces to which the clay particles can cling (Fig. 8).

Another popular misconception is that potters added materials to their clay to reduce firing shrinkage. However, in the early stages of firing (up to about 800°C), clay expands slightly, becoming more porous (see Grimshaw 1971, 816; Hamer 1975, 122; Woods, in press), and firing shrinkage really only

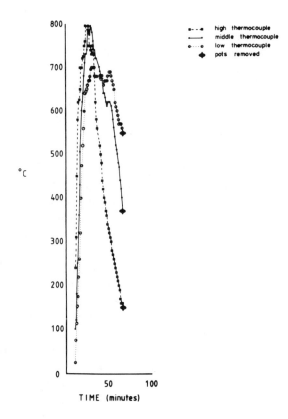

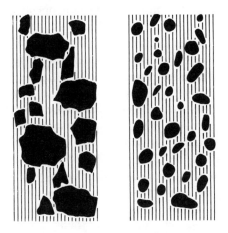

Fig. 7   Firing curve for a typical experimental open firing done with wood.

Fig. 8   The effect of inclusions on the strength of the pot body. After Hamer and Hamer 1977, 28.

occurs in ceramic bodies when they are fired to temperatures in excess of 900° or 1000°C. Such temperatures are difficult to obtain in open firing; indeed, there is evidence to suggest that many wares from the archaeological record, even those produced in kilns, were not fired at anywhere near this temperature (see, for example, Tite 1969, 139). Firing shrinkage is usually small and it is highly unlikely that potters in antiquity were actually aware of it, even when it did occur: it may have been a problem with later medieval and post-medieval pottery, but certainly not before.

It is the convention in ceramic studies to try to determine whether non-clay material in a pot body is naturally occurring or was added by the potter in order to modify the working and firing properties of the clay. In doing so, the archaeological ceramist is making an observation on past human behaviour, one of the basic aims of archaeology. Accordingly, materials which have been added to clay are frequently classified as **filler** or **temper**; the former term is now used primarily in Britain and the latter across the Atlantic. Despite the fact that both terms have largely been invented by archaeologists and are little understood by potters, they are now well established in the literature. Unfortunately, they have become open to misuse, in that they have frequently been employed to describe *any* inclusion present in the body, rather than just that which was added by the potter; for example, one writer (Maggetti 1982, 123) has recently used size as the basic distinguishing factor, employing the term 'temper' to describe anything with a greater diameter than 0.015 mm; he further compounds the problem (Maggetti, ibid.) by using the terms 'artificial' (i.e. added) and 'natural' temper. Many other terms, such as aplastics, non-plastics, grits and inclusions have also been used. However, although many of them are attempts to describe the nature of these materials, none of them actually describes their function. The term **opening materials**, although cumbersome to use and requiring clarification by the addition of *naturally occurring* or *added*, accurately describes the function of these materials, particularly in relation to prehistoric pottery, and appears to be the most appropriate general term for them.

The criteria normally employed in trying to ascertain whether opening materials are naturally occurring in or were added to the clay are the shape and nature of the rock and mineral fragments present, and their degree of sorting within the matrix. In general, angularity is often regarded as an indication that an inclusion has been added, while rounding may mean that it is naturally occurring, having become rounded as part of the transportation processes to which the clay has been subject (see **sedimentary clay**). Coupled with angularity, a polymineralic composition (i.e. when the rock fragment contains crystals of several minerals) is usually a good sign of deliberate crushing prior to addition (Figs. 212, 213), while single, separate crystals may well indicate that, even though the inclusions are angular and fresh, they are naturally occurring in the clay but have not been transported far from their place of origin or breakdown site of the rock from which they were derived. Rounding, often, as mentioned above, taken as an indicator that the inclusions are naturally occurring, can be very misleading, particularly in the case of sands, many of which can be extensively rounded by wind or water action and then added by potters, for instance, from stream or river beds.

Identification of the inclusions present in pottery is best achieved by examination of the fabric in **thin section** with the aid of the **polarizing microscope**. Bearing all the above-mentioned factors in mind, the ceramic petrologist will then examine the sorting of the inclusions in the fabric. If there are no vast differences in shape and size, although a range of sizes may be present, the fabric can be described as unimodal and the underlying assumption is that the inclusions are naturally occurring (Fig. 214). In contrast, if the fabric exhibits, for example, a number of large, rounded inclusions in a matrix containing only small, angular inclusions, then the fabric will be described as bimodal and the large, angular grains will be described as deliberate additions (Fig. 215). Similarly, any fabric can be described as bimodal if the larger opening materials occur in a different size range from the smaller ones and there is little overlap between them (Figs. 216, 217). Again, the conclusion drawn will be that the larger fragments present have been added.

Many different materials were added to clay for the manufacture of prehistoric pottery. They range from organic material, such as grass, through man-made materials, such as **grog** (crushed ceramic), to mineral and rock fragments like **calcite**, flint and granite. Choice of materials appears to have been largely determined by geographical proximity; there are few proven examples from British prehistory of potters travelling any distance to collect their raw materials.

Some substances used required an appreciable amount of preparation. The obvious example of this is flint, one of the most common opening materials used throughout antiquity but particularly in early prehistory. Flint is an extremely hard and dense rock and, owing to its cryptocrystalline structure, is most easily worked by flaking. This, however, yields sharp, highly angular fragments which are totally unsuitable for mixing with clay, as they would cause discomfort to the potter as he worked the clay and, when present in the large quantities required for a clay body that is to be open-fired, create difficulties in vessel manufacture. In addition, when heated, water combined within the molecular structure of flint is given off at around 400°C, causing cracking and disintegration of the flint, and this would have caused problems during firing. Consequently, prior to being incorporated in the clay, flint was calcined (heated) in order to drive off the chemically combined water. The resulting breakdown of the flint structure facilitated crushing and pounding

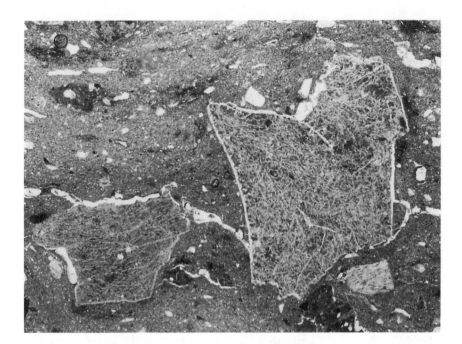

Fig. 9   Photomicrograph of calcined flint in a thin section of a neolithic sherd. The chunky nature of the fragments and the internal cracking are characteristic. PPL, × 20.

of the rock and yielded chunky, less sharp fragments which were more suitable for inclusion in the clay (Fig. 9).

It is also important to remember that not all clays used for the manufacture of pottery in antiquity needed to be modified by potters by the addition of opening materials. Indeed, many clays in Britain contain sufficiently large quantities of naturally occurring inclusions to enable them to survive open firing; the only form of modification would have been the removal of extraneous inclusions, such as pieces of organic matter and larger rock fragments. The classic example of this is provided by the gabbroic wares of south western-Britain. These originate from the Lizard Peninsula in Cornwall but spread, presumably by trade, over much of the south and are found on many Neolithic sites where stone axes from the same area are also featured (Peacock 1969*b*, 147). They were well-made, burnished wares and, although fine by prehistoric standards, are of a coarse fabric. There is some debate at present as to the validity of the provenance assigned to these wares by Peacock (see, for example, Smith 1981, Quinnell 1988), but clay samples, illustrated in the glossary of this volume, from the Helston area of Cornwall are mineralogically identical to pottery from the area (Figs. 119, 120). Origin aside, the rock fragments contained within these clays are sufficiently abundant to render the addition of other material unnecessary; these clays are, and would have been in the past, ideal for open firing.

Much is frequently made of the need for clay to be weathered, soured or generally left around for lengthy periods of time to increase its plasticity. Again, these are processes more appropriate for the preparation of clay for throwing on the wheel and it is unlikely that prehistoric potters resorted to such measures. A deficiency or excess of plasticity were probably not problems that concerned prehistoric potters; evidence for this is provided yet again by the gabbroic clays of Cornwall, many of which are fairly aplastic and difficult to work in comparison with many sedimentary clays. The vital point was that they contained the right amount of opening materials to survive firing and could still be worked into good-quality vessels. Storage and long-term weathering of clay should really only be considered when dealing with potting sites from later periods.

Until relatively recently, many British archaeologists believed that pottery was not used for cooking in prehistoric times. They considered that the vessels had been so poorly fired that they would have been incapable of withstanding the effect of fire, and accordingly suggested a number of alternative methods that might have been employed. These included the use of skins and animal stomachs as cooking receptacles and of so-called 'pot-boilers'—stones, including lumps of flint from on or near chalkland sites in particular, that were supposedly heated in the fire and then dropped into pots to boil the contents. One earlier writer (Layard 1922, 487) even included a somewhat fanciful description of a flint-knapper at work 'crooning some prehistoric chant ... and occasionally refreshing himself with a hot brew, brought to the boil by means of the pot boilers'. Some of these suggestions have been tested by experiment (see, for example, Ryder 1969, Woods 1984a) and useful information can also be obtained from ethnographic reports (for example, Cantrill and Jones 1911, 255; Layard 1922, 489; Rechnitz 1959). Although there is now some dispute over the purpose of the so-called burnt mounds and accompanying troughs found on many prehistoric, particularly Bronze Age, sites, they are widely accepted, largely as a result of the extensive experimental work conducted by O'Kelly (1954), as cooking sites. Barfield and Hodder (1987) continue to dispute this, but further work in Ireland, where the sites are particularly common, and in other areas (for example, Martin 1988) reinforces O'Kelly's conclusions. While heating stones are still used in a similar way in some less advanced societies, there is little evidence for their being employed in conjunction with ceramic vessels; instead, they are more commonly used in earth ovens, being employed for roasting, baking and steaming processes, rather than for boiling. The basic reasoning behind the early suggestions can be seen as illogical: needless to say, if a pot has survived open firing, it will not be adversely affected by contact with the heat from a cooking fire in which, typically, coals, rather than flames, are utilized, and relatively low temperatures (300-500°C) are obtained. Indeed, because of the danger of rehydration of the clay minerals (see below, p. 50, for a fuller explanation), low-fired ceramic vessels would have been more severely damaged by having water standing in them for a period of time while hot stones were dropped in.

Since the publication of Rye's important paper (1976) on thermal-shock resistance in ceramic vessels, archaeologists have become obsessed with this theory and the possible panaceas for the problem. The pages of many publications, particularly from northern America, have been crammed with research into the matter. A more technical explanation is given in the glossary but, briefly, the theory behind it all is that vessels used for cooking will crack as a result of repeated heating and cooling but that various steps may be taken to overcome the problems and thereby prolong vessel life. For example, certain shapes may accommodate more efficiently the expansions and contractions that occur as a result of heating and cooling, and some types of inclusions (those with a low coefficient of thermal expansion or one that is similar to that of fired clay) should be better for incorporating in the clay used for the manufacture of cooking vessels.

While not denying that there are some valid examples from both the archaeological and ethnographic records (Rye 1976; Arnold 1971), it appears that there is very little evidence in Britain, throughout antiquity, to indicate that potters were even aware of the problem, let alone knew how to overcome it. To take the argument about shape first, the theory is that round-based, globular vessels will be best for cooking, because their uninterrupted shape will allow the pot to expand with heating and contract with cooling: flat-based vessels, on the other hand, have a sharp, angular change of direction at the base and this is a weak spot, where stresses are created during heating and cooling which, over time, will lead to cracking and breakage. However, the change to flat-based pottery came early in Britain, earlier in fact than in many other, more advanced, parts of the ancient world, with flat-based vessels appearing at Skara Brae, for example, around 2700 bc. This change probably came about as a response to a change in living habits (such as, for example, the advent of flat work-surfaces). Whatever the reasons, round-based vessels were quickly replaced by flat-based ones, even for cooking, indicating that Neolithic man was not aware of the supposed beneficial effects of the round base.

Similarly, there is little archaeological evidence from Britain to suggest that specific inclusion types were chosen for mixing into the clay for cooking vessels. Of the materials that are supposed to be good for thermal shock resistance, grog was frequently employed, being used for all types of vessels throughout prehistory and into the Roman period; similarly, crystalline calcite and other calcareous materials, such as shell and various types of limestone, were common inclusions throughout antiquity, again for all vessel types, usually being employed in areas where these materials were abundant. In contrast, quartz, which is supposedly a disastrous opening material to have present in cooking-pot fabric because of its high coefficient of thermal expansion, is probably the most ubiquitous mineral in British clays and was in many instances, the most notable of which is the long-lasting Durotrigian and Romano-British black-burnished tradition, a deliberately added opening material (Fig. 10). The choice, therefore, of the basic raw materials for British

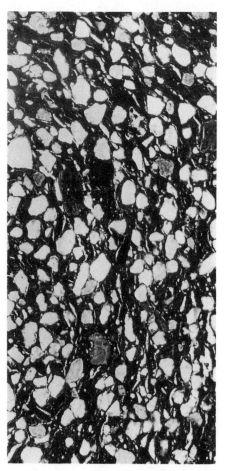

Fig. 10 Photomicrograph of a thin section of a typical sherd of black-burnished 1 pottery. Most of the grains are quartz, but some shale (dark fragments in the upper part of the photo) and limestone (grey fragment below centre) can also be seen. PPL, × 15.

prehistoric pottery appears largely to have been determined by geographical proximity and, in some instances, ease of preparation, rather than by any awareness of the properties of those raw materials effective in thermal-shock resistance.

Ceramic Technology in Prehistory

Most British prehistoric pottery was constructed of flattened rings, or straps, of clay. The basic technique was **ring-building**, a variant of coiling, in which rings of clay were applied to one another and squeezed and smoothed together. Firm bonding of the clay is essential if this method is to be successful and ring- or coil-built vessels tend to break along the junctions between the rings of clay if it is not achieved. There are various ways in which the new clay

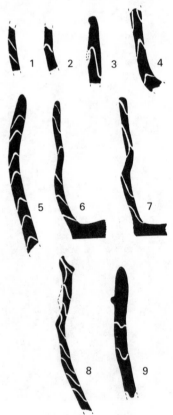

Fig. 11   Typical methods of manufacture of prehistoric pottery. The bonding methods are clearly shown in the sections. Not to scale. 1-3, after Callander 1930; 5, 6, after Stevenson 1939; 7-9, after Stevenson 1953.

may be applied: round, elongated cylinders of clay may be placed directly on top of others and then joined (Fig. 193) or the rolls may be shaped and chamferred in such a way as to provide a groove or diagonal bevel to which the next ring may be added (see Fig. 11). Basic shapes can be altered by the way in which the straps are applied: for example, a vessel can be widened by applying the rings slightly on the outside of the existing shape or narrowed by applying them internally.

The diagonal, or tongue-and-groove bonding methods should, theoretically, allow a stronger join because they provide a greater surface area of clay for bonding. They were the methods most commonly employed for the manufacture of British prehistoric pottery: many vessels and much of the sherd material from prehistoric sites show evidence, in the form of cracks running horizontally around vessels (Figs. 12, 194), **join voids** (Figs. 3, 13,

Fig. 12   This food vessel has cracked along the junctions between the rings of clay used to construct it. The cracks in the lower third of the vessel show that the straps were around 1 cm in height.

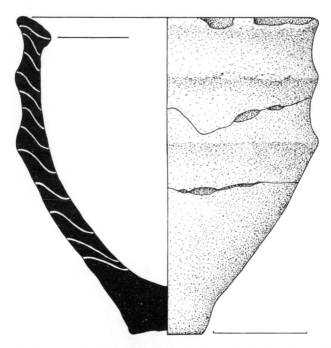

Fig. 13   The drawing of the same food vessel shows clearly the diagonal bonding technique used in its construction and the size of the straps. Scale = 5 cm.

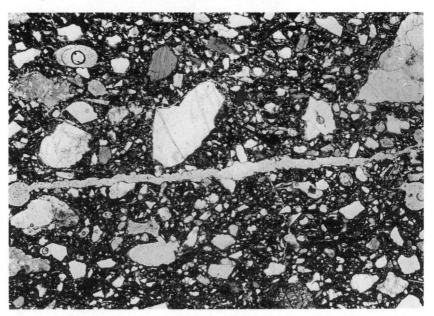

Fig. 14   Photomicrograph of a thin section of a beaker sherd from Northton, Harris, showing a join void. PPL, × 20.

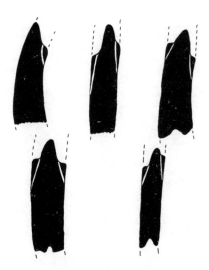

Fig. 15 'False rims' created by vessels breaking along the joins between the clay rings. Not to scale. After Callander 1937, Figure 23.

14, 194) in the vertical sections of sherds, of this method of vessel construction. Many earlier writers (for example, Childe and Paterson 1929, 269; Callander 1930, 193-5; Mears 1937, 258-9; Stevenson 1939, 233-9 and 1953, *passim*) have provided detailed descriptions and profuse illustrations of these methods of vessel construction (Fig. 11), calling the rounded facets revealed on breakage 'false rims'—for obvious reasons (Figs. 15, 105). The fact that so many vessels have cracked or broken in this way indicates that the potters were not very adept at joining the clay straps together. Although the clay has been adequately bonded and smoothed on the external and internal surfaces of vessels, the clay in the middle was not affected; it suggests that the potters may have flattened and shaped the clay straps and then allowed them to dry slightly before applying them to the vessel. (See Woods 1989, 196 ff., for a fuller discussion of this aspect.)

Although coiling and ring-building are extensively used by modern traditional potters, there is very little evidence for the use of the diagonal bevel or tongue-and-groove methods of joining the clay. These methods were used extensively throughout prehistory, not only in Britain but on the Continent as well (Figs. 16, 147), but now appear to be lost technology.

In contrast to modern practice, the construction of many prehistoric pots may have been started from the rim rather than the base. This would have been particularly advantageous in the manufacture of round-based vessels, which would have required some form of support if built from the base upwards. Join voids which show evidence of tongue-and-groove construction

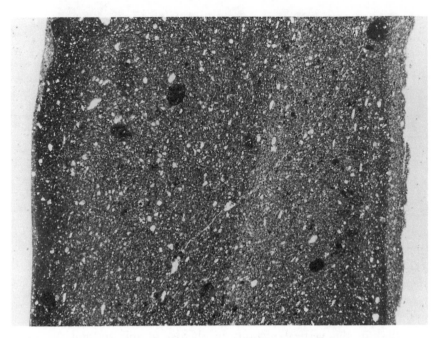

Fig. 16   Diagonal bonding revealed in a thin section of a prehistoric sherd from Herpaly, Hungary. The fabric is relatively fine and the join void between the rings appears as a thin line running from top right to bottom left. PPL, × 20.

may also be indicators of this method, in that it is easier, when building a pot with flattened straps of clay, to apply the new ring in a prepared groove rather than to push it down over a modelled, rounded, top edge (Fig. 11:5 and 9).

Some have suggested that **pinch pottery** was also made. Evidence for this method is often difficult to detect if the potter has been competent (see Rye 1981, 70, for its characteristic signs) and the claims that have been made for its use have been largely based on negative evidence. Howard, for instance, following Smith's earlier (1965) classification, suggests (1981, 23) that the smaller complement of the pottery assemblage at Windmill Hill was produced by pinching, while larger vessels were coil-built. She uses the small size of the vessels as evidence for the use of pinching, stating (ibid.) that 'the potential size of "pinch pots" (formed from a single clay lump) is limited by the hand size of the potter'. In the light of Rye's detailed work (1977; 1981, Chapter 5) on the characteristic signs of the various methods of pot manufacture, such early ceramics should perhaps be re-examined to ascertain definite evidence of their technology. There is no denying that pinching is a quick and easy way to produce small, round-based vessels, like the ones at Windmill Hill, but vessels should also be examined for evidence of alternative methods, such as moulding. It should also be remembered that pinched vessels may be made larger by placing them in some kind of support rather than turning them in the potter's hand and that pinching may be used as a preliminary technique, to be supplemented by another, such as ring-building, in order to produce larger vessels. (Such a method is utilized at present by the Gciriku potters of the Kavango region of Namibia, who produce round-based vessels by a combination of pinching, ring-building and paddling techniques (Figs. 17, 172, 193); see Woods (1984*b*) for a full description of the techniques employed.

Fig. 17   A contemporary potter from the Kavango region of Namibia using a wooden paddle to ensure efficient bonding of the clay and to expand the vessel walls. The paddle is normally used as a secondary forming technique, but this potter uses it as a primary method.

Archaeologists and ceramic technologists should be aware that combinations of techniques may have been employed and should be on the look-out for evidence of them: a single sherd that shows evidence of ring-building may not mean that the whole vessel was formed by that method, any more than a wheel-thrown rim precludes the possibility of a hand-made body below it. Similarly, large or sharply carinated vessels may have been built in halves or pieces and subsequently joined. (Evidence of this is shown by many European vessels from the La Tène period, and by early wheel-thrown ones in particular, which have broken around the mid-point of the vessel to reveal obvious bonding grooves.) The cases used above are intended as examples to stress that there are many methods and combinations thereof that may have been employed for the manufacture of British prehistoric pottery and that the twentieth-century techniques with which we are familiar are not the only possibilities.

Surface Treatments

Following the initial manufacturing and shaping processes, clay vessels would have been put aside for a short time in order to dry further, until they reached the **leather-hard** (or green-hard) stage. At this point, most of the water that had been mixed with the clay to make it plastic and workable would have evaporated off, and maximum drying shrinkage would have occurred (see Fig. 4:2). However, a small amount of the **water of plasticity** still remains at this point, allowing secondary manufacturing techniques, such as the addition of extra parts (such as handles), **burnishing** or the use of **paddle and anvil** (Fig. 17), to be executed. It was at this point, too, that decorative, as well as functional, surface treatments would have been carried out: **comb, cord, fingernail and bird bone impressions**, as well as **incised decoration**, would all have been executed at this stage.

It is, of course, possible to carry out most surface treatments before or after the leather-hard stage has been reached, but the effects are usually less satisfactory. The different effects obtained by incising clay in varying states of dryness have been clearly illustrated by Rye (1981, Figure 47) and similar results (for example, raised edges when the clay is too wet and scratching and shallow marks when the clay is too dry) would have been obtained with impressed patterns: stamps or cord used for decorating prehistoric pottery would have clogged very quickly during use if the clay were too damp and have only made shallow impressions and caused cracks if it were too dry. (See Stokes 1985, 89, for results of recent experiments.) In the case of burnish, it is essential that the clay be in exactly the right state of dryness: if it is too wet, the burnishing tool will pick up clay from the surface of the pot, and if it is too dry, it will be difficult to burnish and the effect will be patchy and uneven.

It is worth remembering that a lot of British prehistoric pottery, and the better-quality wares, such as beakers, in particular, were burnished prior to the use of another surface treatment. This was only a light burnish, intended to smooth the surface of a coarse clay and prepare it for further treatment; it was not intended to produce an obviously decorative and functional effect as it was in the case of the Romano-British black-burnished 1 wares.

Prehistoric pot-manufacturing sites are difficult to identify, largely because little equipment is needed and potting tools, if made of organic materials (Fig. 18), may not have survived. Bone combs have, however, been found at the site of Northton, Harris (Simpson 1976, 224), and were almost certainly used to impress patterns on the pottery from that site; combs have also been found in second millennium levels at a number of other sites (Fig. 19). Bone appears to have been a common material for potting tools in antiquity: even in the Roman period, it was used for pot burnishers and for handles for cheese-wires (see Woods and Hastings 1984, Figure 11). Similarly shaped implements and partly polished bone spatulae found at Northton (Simpson 1976) may have been used as pot burnishers, but there is no definite evidence for this. Heat-affected flint has been found on many sites and may, in some

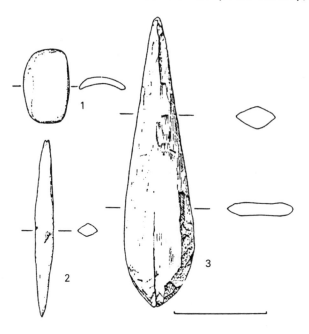

Fig. 18 Tools used by modern potters in Kavango, Namibia. 1, rib/scraper made from a fragment of gourd; 2, wooden tool with sharp end for incision and notched end for impressed decoration; 3, wooden paddle. Scale = 10 cm.

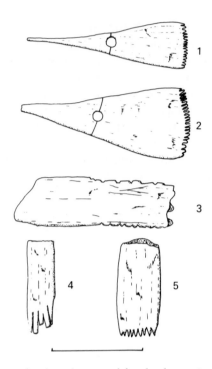

Fig. 19   Combs presumed to have been used for the decoration of pottery. 1, 2, Northton, Harris; 3, Bishops Cannings Down, Wilts; 4, Dean Bottom, Wilts; 5, Gwithian, Cornwall. 3 and 4 after Gingell 1980, 5 after Megaw 1976. Scale = 5 cm.

instances, have been prepared for use in potting. The site of Runnymede Bridge has yielded piles of calcined flint, which appears to have been graded by size for some purpose, pottery production being the most likely. In particular, excavation of Area 16 East at the site has revealed scattered heaps of calcined flint accompanied by rejected domestic pottery, burnt clay, and quernstones and pebble hammers used for crushing the flint (Needham and Sørensen, 1988, 123 and 124).

After surface treatments had been executed, the vessel would have again been set aside for a final drying period, prior to firing.

Firing

Some writers (for example, Arnold 1985, 61 ff.) have claimed that potting can really only be done effectively in dry weather; the main argument put forward to support this is the difficulty encountered in drying and firing vessels when it is cold or wet. Many recent writers have claimed that complete dryness of clay wares is essential for successful firing and, among them, Bjørn has stated (1969, 50) that vessels should be dried for at least a month before firing. Indeed, the drying of clay vessels may have been one of the bigger problems encountered in the manufacture of British prehistoric pottery, but it is highly unlikely that vessels would have been left standing around for such a lengthy period. It is impossible to dry clay completely at normal temperatures; it is a hygroscopic substance and will always be affected by the ambient atmosphere, giving off or re-adsorbing moisture from the atmosphere according to the relative humidity. Heat is required to obtain the temperatures around 100°C which are necessary to dry it completely (by driving off the **water of plasticity**) (Fig. 4:4); consequently, the weather is relatively unimportant and its effect in drying has been over-estimated by many writers who have been influenced by modern ceramics, clays and techniques. While there is no denying that it is easier to make, dry and fire pots when the weather is warm and sunny, the coarse nature of bodies required for hand-made and open-fired pottery ensures that they will dry fairly easily and evenly, both in winter and at times when the relative humidity is high.

Others have argued for seasonal pottery production on the basis of seed and **grain impressions** found in the bases or walls of vessels. Howard, for example, states (1981, 25) that 'Seed impressions on pots from all periods, including the early neolithic at Windmill Hill, suggest early autumn as the preferred potting season throughout prehistory', and she argues that clays and temper were prepared in late summer and vessels made in the autumn after harvesting and threshing. However, grain and seeds would have been fairly abundant all year round in an agricultural settlement like Windmill Hill and the presence of a few impressions in a few pots does not provide concrete evidence for seasonal pottery production. It is highly unlikely, therefore, that pottery production in prehistoric Britain was a seasonal activity and it is probable that vessels were produced as and when needed, regardless of the time of year.

British prehistoric pottery was open-fired, either in pits (Figs. 20-23) or in surface bonfires (Figs. 24-27). Archaeological evidence for this method of firing is virtually non-existent, because the short time involved rarely has any pronounced burning effect on the ground underneath the fire or on the walls of a pit and it is difficult to distinguish pot-firing sites from hearths intended for other purposes (see, for example, Gibson 1986c, 8, 12 and 14). Some claims have been staked for prehistoric firing sites, but as yet none has been definitely identified. The site of Eilean an Tighe on Harris has been described by the excavator (Scott 1951, 5 ff.) as a firing site with two kilns of 'horizontal' type and one area for open firing. Two piles of clay and a

Fig. 20   A pit firing using cow dung in Kavango, Namibia, August 1982: loading the pit.

selection of tools, supposedly for potting, were also found. However, Scott's interpretation of this part of the site, and particularly of the kilns, appears to be fanciful and his descriptions of the potting technology, as revealed by the sherds from the site, are also inaccurate; this is not to say that pottery was not made at the site but that the area described by the excavator as a pottery workshop probably had some other function. Added to this is the fact that, despite Scott's detailed descriptions of the so-called rubbish-heap on the site and his calculations of life-span for the site (1951, 13), there is actually no **waster** material in the pottery assemblage (now stored in the National Museum, Edinburgh). The site of Willington, Derbys., has been suggested as

Fig. 21 A pit firing in Kavango, Namibia: removing the fired vessels.

a possible late bronze age or iron age pot-firing site (Wheeler 1979) and areas with ashy, charcoal-rich layers and wasters have been found at several sites in Dorset and were definitely associated with the firing of Durotrigian and Romano-British black-burnished pottery (Farrar 1976).

This last example aside, however, we must rely primarily at present on negative, rather than positive, archaeological evidence and on informed inspection of the ceramics themselves. There are several tell-tale signs which immediately allow us to distinguish open-fired from kiln-fired vessels. Firstly, it is difficult to control the atmospheric conditions in an open firing and they will be constantly changing; as a result, the surfaces of open-fired vessels are

Fig. 22   An experimental pit firing at Leicester University: stacking the fuel.

Fig. 23 An experimental pit firing at Leicester University: the end of the firing.

usually blotchy and uneven in colour and frequently feature **fire clouds** (black patches caused by the deposition of carbon as a result of direct contact with the smoky flames or partially-burnt fuel) (Figs. 28, 109, 110). Secondly, the vessel walls usually exhibit a black central zone when seen in section (Figs. 29, 69). This blackness is most frequently a result of incomplete combustion of **carbonaceous material** naturally occurring in the clay and is indicative of a short firing time, as is typical of open firing; if firings last for several hours (as usually happens, for instance, in a kiln), the heat and oxidizing gases present have more time to penetrate the vessel walls and thus ensure that the clay is completely fired and oxidized.

When excavated, many prehistoric pots and sherds are in a very friable condition. This is further evidence that they have been open-fired: in short

Fig. 24   A surface bonfire firing using cow dung, Kavango, Namibia, August 1982: building the fuel stack.

firings, not all the clay minerals in the vessel walls will pass through the **ceramic change** and as a result, given several millennia of burial in wet soil, will re-adsorb moisture from the surrounding environment and become plastic again. In other words, they are reverting to their original clay state. For this reason, much prehistoric pottery is very soggy and fragile and must be handled with care while it is being excavated, cleaned and drawn.

Given the lack of archaeological evidence for pot firing in prehistory, the archaeologist must have recourse to experimental studies and the observation of contemporary traditional potters. Neither ethnography nor experiment can provide the answers on its own, but a combination of evidence from both

Fig. 25 A bonfire firing in Kavango, Namibia: removing the fired vessels.

disciplines can suggest possibilities for the way firing may have been done in the past.

Pottery was almost certainly first produced as a domestic enterprise, and Hodges (1976, 36) suggests that it may have been produced in the domestic hearth. Although some writers (for example, Howard 1981, 25) have suggested incipient specialization, the first real evidence of specialist pottery production in Britain is provided by some of the gabbroic wares of the Lizard Peninsula known as Hembury 'f' wares, better quality ceramics which were traded, either for their own value or for their contents, and which occur on numerous sites throughout southern England, spanning some 300 km

Fig. 26   An experimental bonfire firing at Leicester University.

(Peacock 1988, 302). Evidence for other pottery 'industries' within British prehistory is scarce, though there are a few examples of pots (such as the two food vessels, illustrated in Fig. 30, from Beanley and Lowick, Northumberland, some 25 km apart, clearly made, or at least decorated, by the same hand) and these may indicate a degree of specialization on the part of individuals.

Most pottery production in British prehistory should, however, be regarded as a domestic activity undertaken as and when the need arose. Experimental work (Woods 1983, 1989, and in press) has shown that vessels can be fired extremely easily and quickly in open firings, regardless of the weather, and there is therefore no need for pottery production to be confined to the warmer and drier months of the year. Even severe frost and cold need

Fig. 27   An experimental bonfire firing: the fired vessels. The rods are thermocouples used to measure temperatures in the firing.

not be a deterrent and, although they make firing more difficult (Woods 1983, 13), do not prohibit it.

It is worth remembering that prehistoric man would have had a totally different approach to fire and to fuel resources from that of modern man. We tend to consider fire as something of a novelty and, as we are largely unfamiliar with it, usually use too much fuel over too long a period of time. This is true in experimental pot firings (for example, Arnal 1988, Gabasio 1986, O'Brien 1980, P.J. Reynolds 1979, 14) and in cooking (for example, the modern barbecue). Societies that are dependent on fire for warmth, cooking and defence use their fuel resources sparingly and carefully (see, for

Fig. 28 A pot (height 18.5 cm) produced in an experimental open firing. The black area on the front of the vessel is a fire cloud.

Fig. 29 A typical sherd from a vessel that has been open-fired. The black central zone is indicative of short firing time and therefore of open firing. Other examples can be seen in *Fig. 69.*

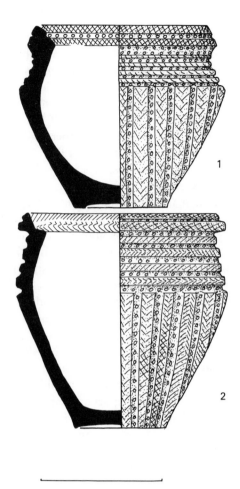

Fig. 30 Two food vessels from Beanley (1) and Lowick (2), Northumberland, which have been made and/or decorated by the same person.

example, B. Reynolds 1964), with little wastage, even in places where the climate is warm and fuel is relatively abundant. (In the Kavango region of Namibia, for example, where it is hot throughout the year and there is no shortage of firewood, pot-firings are nearly always done with cow dung; see Figs. 20, 21, 24, 25.) Similar husbanding of resources must also have been the case in prehistoric Britain, when climatic conditions were basically similar to, though perhaps a little damper than, the present day. Collection of fuel materials may well have been a daily task, in order to replace consumed supplies, and fuel would have needed to be stored in a dry place before future use.

It is highly unlikely that we shall ever discover evidence in the ground of the actual methods used in prehistory to fire pottery, and the only obtainable information is exhibited by the pots and sherds themselves. A survey of the literature dealing with ethnographic and experimental studies can provide us with a range of firing methods that *might* have been employed in prehistory. (See, for example, Arnold 1971 and 1972, Bjørn 1969, Coleman-Smith 1971, DeBoer and Lathrap 1979, Dumont 1952, Lauer 1972, Lawton 1967, Longacre 1982, Martlew 1983, Reina and Hill 1978, Woods 1983, 1984*b* and 1989.) Whatever methods were employed, it is likely that the firing would have been done as efficiently and economically as possible, with minimum wastage of human and fuel resources. In particular, the results of many experimental studies should be examined critically: the extravagant use of fuel has already been commented upon above and the complicated firing methods devised by some (for example, P.J. Reynolds 1979, 14, described and illustrated by Elsdon 1989, 54-6) also need questioning. There is, for example, absolutely no definite evidence, either archaeological or ethnographic, for the so-called 'pit clamp', a term which has been coined by British researchers but, with good reason, has not been adopted by workers anywhere else in the world. The methods used at Butser Experimental Farm, for example, yield pits in the chalk that resemble archaeological features, but almost any pyrotechnological process involving direct contact between fire and chalk, followed by cleaning of the feature, would have similar results. There is no ethnographic evidence to support burying a pile of partially fired vessels under a mound of soil or turves (Elsdon 1989, 54; Swan 1984, 30) for up to twenty hours (P.J. Reynolds 1979, 14), and the temperatures in excess of 900°C that the experimenters claim to achieve in these firings (Reynolds ibid.) are likely to yield vessels that bear no resemblance to the low-fired products of British prehistory.

With few exceptions, experimental and ethnographic studies of firing have been largely concerned with the firing methods employed and the recording of temperatures in the fires; they have paid scant attention to aspects, such as the effect of burning on the ground underneath, that may be of more use to the archaeologist. (The problem of the limited effect of burning on the soil, making it difficult to recognize firing sites, has been referred to above and there are other aspects of firing, such as **preheating** of the vessels prior to the firing proper, which do not have any characteristic requirements and leave no recognizable signs on the pots themselves.) Given the present state of knowledge, we must accept that open firing, whether in a surface bonfire or in a pit, was the method used to fire British prehistoric pottery and that, with the exception of obvious evidence, such as abundant waster material, it leaves little that allows us to distinguish it, archaeologically, from an ordinary domestic hearth or burnt rubbish pit.

Chapter 3   Chronological Sequence of British Prehistoric Pottery

Prior to the Neolithic, starting *c.* 3000 bc, Britain was aceramic. Why this should be is not fully understood, but it may perhaps have been because ceramics were too fragile and heavy to be practical for transient groups. Mesolithic hunter–gatherers must surely have had a knowledge of the hardness of fired clay as a result of the accidental burning of daubed structures, or from clay-floored hearths, but, despite this, pots were never made; clay was never deliberately fashioned into receptacles and fired. From the Neolithic, however, pottery is abundant.

The Neolithic marks the period when farming was introduced into Britain from Europe. Whether this was the result of boat-loads of farming colonists sailing over with livestock and families (Case 1969), whether it was the result of a spread of ideas (a way of life) (Bradley 1984) or whether it was the result of a combination of the two, as is perhaps most likely, is largely irrelevant here. The fact is that it arrived. Farming brought with it not only the domestic animals and cereals that are so characteristic, but also a more settled way of life, at least for some of the community. Whereas hunter–gatherers followed the seasonal migrations of animals and perhaps also seasonal fruits and plant resources (Simmons *et al.* 1981, 102-6), the introduction of farming meant that man could, to a large extent, be self-sufficient. There was doubtless still a certain reliance on wild fauna and flora, meaning that hunting parties may still have left the main settlement, even for considerable periods. However, the fragility of the crops and their vulnerability to animals, adverse weather, weeds, and hostile groups and the sheer labour investment tied up in animal husbandry and arable agriculture would mean that at least part of the community would have to stay at the main settlement. They would be needed to guard the harvest, clear forest and keep clearings open, even if only through the management of grazing herds.

The appearance of pottery is also exactly contemporary with the arrival of agriculture. The knowledge of pottery manufacture, and presumably therefore of the usefulness of ceramics, arrives as a finished product, a perfected technological process. Unlike the inception of metalwork, there appears to be no period of experimentation with ceramics in early neolithic Britain. There are no small ceramic trinkets, for example, heralding the appearance of more ambitious vessels. Instead, potting arrives with agriculture as a perfected craft.

It is clearly unlikely that the introduction of agriculture led to an overnight stability of the population (Bradley 1972), but it did lead increasingly to a less mobile life-style, allowing a new permanency of settlement, where a larger tool-kit could be developed. Pots are heavy and bulky. They are also fragile and not best suited to being transported over large tracts of country in a period when there were no roads, no wheeled transport, and when movement was by pack animal or on foot. A settled economy, however, did allow the use of heavier and more fragile artefacts, of which pottery is just such an example. such an example.

This explanation for the appearance of pottery is probably over-simplified and one needs to think about what pottery would have been used for. Storage vessels, water containers, cooking pots, and drinking and eating vessels can all be suggested and all indeed may be correct. But mesolithic hunter–gatherers would also have had to store food and carry water and have needed eating and drinking vessels just as much as neolithic farming communities. It has also been suggested above that much of the hunter–gatherer life-style would probably have continued into the Neolithic and indeed the essential population probably did not change. Lighter and more durable materials were probably already in use for each function. Storage could have been in skin bags or wicker baskets, water could have been carried in skins, cooking could have been done in troughs using 'pot-boilers' or heated stones, as experiments show (O'Kelly 1954). Cooking may also have been done simply over a fire on a spit or greenwood grill or in a pit or trough, and wooden bowls could easily be used as 'crockery'. Pottery, therefore, was not necessary. It was not essential to the farming communities and its fragility, weight and bulk would not have made it overtly utilitarian. Combined with both the time and labour involved in the manufacture and decoration, plus the 'non-functional' features of many prehistoric pottery traditions, this observation can be used to create the hypothesis that pottery might have been a high-status, display artefact used in rituals, rather than being singularly utilitarian. On present knowledge, however, purely ritual interpretations are as unsatisfactory as purely utilitarian.

In seeking reasons for the adoption of pottery in a domestic tool-kit, it may be suggested that one advantage of pottery was that it allowed direct contact with flame or embers and a good transference of heat. Water could be boiled in small quantities without the use of 'pot-boilers' and this would allow the easier cooking of stews, broths and the cereal porridges suggested by the heavy tooth attrition noticed in dental wear studies of prehistoric populations (Brothwell and Brothwell 1969; Stead, Bourke and Brothwell 1986, 99-114). Stocks and stews would also allow meat and cereal resources to be stretched farther now that settlement was less transient and man had to wait for the seasonal cycles of fruits, crops and game, rather than being able to follow them. Early excavations on Dartmoor by the Dartmoor Exploration Committee frequently found 'pot-boilers', or heat-cracked stones, in pots sunk into the floors of hut circles as, for example, at Legis Tor hut 7 (Baring Gould 1896) and analysis of the residues preserved as carbon deposits on the inside of such vessels by the same Committee proved them to be rich in fats (Baring Gould 1897). Whether or not the heated stones were actually used in the cooking process is a matter of great debate, but it is unlikely that they were ever used in pots, since the qualities of early ceramic **fabrics** would generally allow direct contact with flame (see above, pp. 33–4).

Food harvested and stored in summer and autumn had to last through winter and into spring. Seed and food corn would have to be stored and finite resources managed to allow them to last comfortably until replenishment in the following year. The bulk of the seed and food grain needed makes it unlikely that pottery vessels were used for storage of this commodity, but they could have been used for the storage of meats or foods that could be preserved by covering with fat or other dry foodstuffs.

Whatever pottery was used for, and in the majority of cases we can only guess, it was an important artefact in prehistory. Not only does it appear on domestic sites but also in what must be described as ritually structured deposits. It is found in tombs and in pits which were previously considered to be storage pits but which are likely to have served a variety of purposes (Field *et al.* 1964), and it appears with other specialized artefacts (see, for example, Clarke *et al.* 1985, 150 ff.). It is possible to consider that it was not the pot which was so important but the contents; however, it is very likely that important contents were placed in important containers. Some pots appear to have been broken before deposition, but it is often unclear whether these were broken vessels taken out of service from a domestic repertoire or whether the breakage was a deliberate act. This distinction may be largely immaterial. What is important is that some vessels achieved such a status that they were selected for ritual deposition and as accompaniments for the dead (Bradley 1984, 71-73).

3000–2500 bc

The earliest dated ceramics in Britain belong to the **Grimston Lyles Hill** series, which is also one of the longest-lived traditions. It is part of a larger western European ceramic network which reaches Britain around 3000 bc. It lasts to perhaps as late as 2000 bc, although imprecise sampling, unreliability of excavated contexts and the strictures of association have all been invoked to explain the late dates and the resulting chronological disparity with the European styles (Kinnes 1985, 22-3; Louwe Kooijmans 1976). The pots in the **Grimston-Lyles Hill** tradition are found from south-eastern England to northern Scotland and Ireland (Green 1976, 22). Nationwide, there is a conservatism of style, with simple hemispherical bowls and S-shaped vessels with a shoulder **carination** being distinctive. With rare exceptions, the pottery is undecorated. Not surprisingly in a style so widespread, there are regional variations. In Yorkshire, **Heslerton** and **Towthorpe** (Piggott 1954, 114-7) **wares** are found, though the former may not be a true style but a debased form of the norm. In Scotland, **Boghead bowls** combine classic Grimston shapes with internal, vertical finger-fluting and are closely related to Irish vessels from the type-site of Lyles Hill (Evans 1953).

In the south-west of England, there are more local styles within this western European tradition. Perhaps the best known are the **Hembury wares** from the south-western peninsula (Peacock 1969b; Mercer 1981). These also comprise remarkably uniform open and carinated bowls which, with the equal uniformity of the fabrics, suggests a common source. Like the Cornish greenstone axes, these vessels are distributed widely over south-western England and provide evidence for a third millennium 'trade' in ceramics and/or their contents. Distinctive of this style are the **trumpet lugs** applied to the exterior of the vessels.

In Wessex, a tradition of baggy pots, sometimes with rather slack, S-shaped profiles, is termed **Windmill Hill ware,** after the causewayed enclosure near Avebury where it was first recognized. The simplicity of its form and its early associations led Piggott (1954) to give this designation to the early Neolithic of southern England generally, but it has now been relegated to a regional style (Smith 1974, 107).

Towards the middle of the first half of the second millennium bc, there is an increase in pottery decoration. The surface is ornamented with **incised** and **stabbed decoration,** using a variety of points. **Stab and drag** decoration effectively combines the two aforementioned techniques, and later **twisted** and **whipped cord impressions** also appear. This decoration is found in the later phases at Windmill Hill (Smith 1965) and marks the emergence of a **southern decorated bowl tradition** (Whittle 1977, 85), once more with regional variations. The decoration is rarely ambitious either in motif or technique, yet it is often well-considered and frequently highlights features of shape, such as rims and shoulders.

Southern, south-eastern and south-western styles are discernible. Pots of the south-western style, named **Abingdon ware** (Piggott 1954, 72-3; Case 1955) after the causewayed enclosure at Abingdon in the Thames Valley, are characterized mainly by dot decoration accentuating the rim and shoulder of the pot. The south-eastern variation is known as **Mildenhall ware** after the early neolithic settlement at Mildenhall Fen (Clark *et al.* 1960) in Suffolk. Here, slightly more elaborate and profuse decoration is found, expanding over the rim and into the interior of the pot. The southern variation is known as **Whitehawk ware**, once again after a causewayed enclosure, this time at Whitehawk near Brighton (Piggott 1954, 74; Curwen 1934). This is also quite elaborately decorated with a variety of incisions, stabs and impressions. Particularly important is the appearance of **whipped cord** decoration, which becomes so common in the later half of the second millennium. In all these styles, the decoration rarely extends below the shoulder of the pot. In all cases, both simple and S-shaped profiles are found and there is also a gradual thickening of the rim, perhaps heralding the often impractically exaggerated rims of the later period.

This period, then, heralds the arrival of pottery in Britain. The reasons for its adoption are unclear, but it seems unequivocally connected with the arrival of a greater permanency of settlement resulting from the introduction of farming. This pattern of the acceptance of pottery as part of the agriculturalists' package is similarly associated with the earlier spread of agriculture across the different regions of Europe. At first simple and undecorated, though nevertheless well-made, pottery soon became a medium for art. Decorated pottery appears early in the Neolithic, at first simple in its design but becoming increasingly elaborate and heralding the display ceramics of the second half of the third millennium bc.

2500-1500 bc

The later third and earlier second millennia bc are traditionally the late Neolithic and earlier Bronze Age. They also provide, however, a continuum of development in the spheres of ritual, settlement and economy (Clarke 1970, 275; Burgess 1980) and during the period metal is adopted. Around 2500 bc, there is an hiatus in the archaeological record, when monument types are abandoned and more diverse funerary practices and a formalized, henge monument tradition develop. Clearly this change happened over a considerable period and was not as dramatic a cessation as the date suggests, but 2500 bc is used as a convenience marker for the following millennium of continuous development.

The major characteristic of the pottery from this period is increased decoration. The predecessors of this can be seen in the earlier decorated styles already outlined above (Smith 1974). This is particularly true of the **later neolithic impressed wares**, which carry profuse decoration in a variety of techniques. These impressed wares were originally called **Peterborough ware** by R.A. Smith (in Wyman-Abbot 1910) when the known distribution of the pots was dramatically south-eastern. Since then, however, our corpus has grown and the distribution has widened to Scotland and Ireland. Like Windmill Hill ware in the earlier Neolithic, Peterborough ware can now be relegated to a regional variant within the impressed ware tradition.

The development of Peterborough wares has been discussed earlier. The traditional **Ebbsfleet–Mortlake–Fengate** progression can now be seen to be relevant only to the south-east of England and to have limited chronological significance: it is a purely stylistic development. The Ebbsfleet style can be seen to be a direct development from the southern decorated styles of the first half of the second millennium bc. The carinated profile and the simple decoration are still present. The rim form, however, is often expanded, though not over-heavy, and the decoration rarely extends below the shoulder of the vessel. Internal decoration is rather more common. The decoration of Mortlake ware is more profuse, incorporating a greater variety of decorative techniques, among which are **whipped cord, twisted cord, bird bone, fingertip** and **fingernail impressions**. The abundance of bird bone impressions has led to the suggestion that wild fowling probably played a substantial role in the economy of the makers of the pot. In this style, decoration may extend over the whole of the outer surface as well as the internal surface of the rim and neck, though usually the bottom quarter of the vessel is left undecorated. The rim expands dramatically to form a broad platform, presumably designed to carry decoration, because it is too accentuated to be overtly functional. This development continues into the Fengate style, in which the rim is larger still and has tilted to the extent that it forms a collar. With this rim development comes a constriction of the neck. The sinuous profile of preceding traditions becomes more angular and in the Mortlake and Fengate styles the neck is a deep but narrow **cavetto zone**. The Fengate style will be discussed again below.

As has been already stated, local styles within this impressed ware tradition are becoming increasingly more common as our corpus grows. In Yorkshire, the **Rudston style** is recognized by its T-sectioned rim and the flowerpot-shaped body (Manby 1975). In the Borders, heavy, rounded T-sectioned rims with cord decoration and deep neck cavettos constitute the **Ford style** (Longworth 1969; Gibson 1986a), while rims with external **rim mouldings**, internal **bevels** and with deep necks characterize the **Meldon Bridge style** (Burgess 1976a). There is still more variation within the impressed tradition in Scotland and more detailed study in this area would doubtless be productive. Vessels with heavy rims and sparse but all-over decoration were found at Glenluce in south-western Scotland (McInnes 1964); vessels with impressions and **cordons** have been recovered from excavations at Brackmont Mill in Fife (Longworth et al. 1966).

In the islands and on the western coast of Scotland, there was a rich variety of local styles of pottery during the late third millennium bc. In the area of the Firth of Clyde, **Rothesay** and **Beacharra** pots are associated mainly with chambered tombs and recognized respectively by their baggy profiles and carinated forms, with sharply constricted rims which are much narrower in diameter than the shoulders of the vessels (Scott 1964, McInnes 1969). Decorated with incisions above and, to a lesser extent, below the carination, these vessels have close parallels, as one might expect, in the north of Ireland. Further north, in the Outer Hebrides, multi-carinated bowls with incised decoration constitute the **Hebridean bowl** tradition (McInnes 1969; Simpson 1976). Rim forms are rarely elaborate, though often heavy, and interrupted herring-bone is the most common motif. In the far north and west of Scotland, round-based bowls with heavy collars are called **Unstan bowls**, after the chambered tomb of that name where they were first recognized. Incised decoration covers the collar of these vessels, while the belly is invariably left plain (Henshall 1963).

So far, we have mainly been considering round-based pots. Pottery of the earlier third millennium is invariably round-based and in the main continues in this form until the end of the second millennium, but with notable exceptions that will be described below. Within the impressed ware tradition, flat bases are only found in the Rudston and Fengate styles. Meldon Bridge pottery may also be flat-based, but this is inferred from the body angles for, as yet, no base sherds have been recognized (Burgess 1976a, 173). The flat bases of Fengate and Rudston pots are not, however, terribly practical. The bases are both uneven and, in the case of Fengate ware especially, too small in relation to the maximum rim diameters of the pot to give the vessels stability. Round-based pots, on the other hand, are rather more practical and more utilitarian in a society without level surfaces. A flat-based pot, no matter how well proportioned, does not stand well on an uneven surface: how often do cups or tumblers tip over on a picnic? A round-based pot, in contrast, could easily fit into a small depression in the ground and be perfectly stable. Similarly, if used for cooking, a round-based pot would sit in a depression in the glowing embers of a fire or would be supported on stones over the flames and would be much more practical than a flat-based vessel. This could also explain why so few impressed wares have decoration extending much below the shoulder and very rarely over the base: namely that the lower, undecorated portion, when sitting in a ground depression, would be hidden from view.

It is also possible that round-based pots were intended not to stand but to be suspended. The S-shaped profiles, and later the overhanging rims, of the pots would all serve to keep string or cord in place if suspension of the vessel was intended. So, too, would perforated (or even unperforated) **lugs** and **strap handles**. However, this may not have been too practical if pots were used for cooking over an open fire. As has been suggested above, the absence of decoration on the lower third of the body does suggest that this area was generally unseen and that the vessels, therefore, stood. The S-shaped profiles and developed rims would allow the lifting of hot vessels, using sticks as tongs or even the hands, just as easily as they would suspension (Woods 1984*a*, 27-9). Even on flat surfaces, a round-based pot would stand quite securely if placed in a frame, such as a ceramic ring or rope quoit.

Nevertheless, from the end of the third millennium, bases are invariably flat, even if impractically small or uneven, as discussed above. A case has already been made for the practicality of round rather than flat-based vessels and, although a number of reasons can be suggested for the adoption of the flat base, none of them is necessarily the whole answer or even partly correct. One reason may be a result of external influence. At about this time, **beaker** pottery and flat-based wares were in use on the Continent, reaching Britain in subsequent centuries, and **grooved ware** had been developing in the north of Britain parallel to the impressed and incised wares (Clarke 1976, 1983). Both beakers and grooved wares are flat-based and played important roles in the archaeology of the later third and earlier second millennia. In the use of some pots, the base was unimportant. **Collared urns** of the subsequent centuries were commonly used for burial and in such cases are invariably found *inverted* over cremated remains. There may also have been, quite simply, an increase in the number of flat surfaces. This is probably an over-simplified hypothesis that can never be proved, for we know nothing of the development of furniture in prehistory until very much later. Work in the Somerset Levels does at least further our knowledge of the extent of carpentry at this period (Coles and Coles 1986, 85-113) and wooden furniture or floorboards in sill-beam houses would all have been within the scope of contemporary wood-working technology and would have created flat surfaces for flat-based pottery. Such carpentry would do away with the need for pot supports, scoops or quoits, as indeed would simple, flat stones set within earth floors. None of these suggestions is entirely satisfactory and the reasons for the adoption of the flat base remain a mystery. The flat base itself presupposes level surfaces or the dictates of tradition and is otherwise difficult to explain.

The adoption of the flat base in Scotland seems to have taken place earlier than in England. In the Orkney Islands, grooved ware was developing at about 2700 bc at Skara Brae (Clarke 1976). In the grooved ware tradition, bases are invariably flat. This is easier to understand in Orkney, where the Caithness flagstone is easy to split into flat slabs and was used not only for house-building but also for the construction of 'built-in' furniture, such as beds or dressers. The flat slabs produced abundant level surfaces, for which flat-based pots would be well suited. By 2000 bc, grooved ware was well established in Wessex, being found particularly at ritual and prestige sites, such as the large henge monument at Durrington Walls (Wainwright and Longworth 1971).

We have seen that the pottery of the second millennium, particularly in England, can be described as a general progression of development from Grimston through to impressed wares. Grooved ware, however, is more difficult to explain in terms of origins. The early dates for grooved ware in Scotland suggest northern origins with a southward diffusion, but this hypothesis is hampered by a paucity of dates for grooved ware in lowland Scotland and the north of England. On the basis of current chronologies and sequences, English grooved ware seems to simply 'appear' in the archaeological record as a fully developed style recognized by **barrel**-, **bucket**- and flowerpot-shaped pots with both incised and **plastic decoration** arranged in broadly geometric motifs (Wainwright and Longworth 1971).

The emergence of the flat-based traditions in southern Britain roughly coincides with the appearance of beaker pottery and early metal artefacts, which reach these shores from mainland Europe (Clarke 1970). Beakers arrive in Britain as a fully developed ceramic tradition with direct parallels on the Continent, particularly in the Low Countries and the Rhineland, where the cord-decorated variants of the northern plains merge with pottery with the **comb impressions** of Atlantic Europe (Lanting and van der Waals 1976). The earliest beakers appear in the ritual networks of Wessex, the richness and power of which probably attracted these prestige objects (Gibson 1982, 81), but, once they reach Britain, beakers quickly develop an insularity which clearly differentiates them from the European developments (Lanting and van der Waals 1972; Shepherd 1986). At first found only in graves or in ritual contexts, beakers gradually also become incorporated in the domestic repertoire and are found in association with 'native' wares (Gibson 1982).

The clear and dramatic archaeological horizon afforded by beakers and the first metal artefacts has, not surprisingly, tended to blanket the continuation of the local indigenous development. In addition, the importance of pottery also changes slightly for the archaeologist: whereas previously pottery was used as the main artefact in the construction of relative chronologies, now metal artefacts are added and are themselves chronological indicators.

Beneath the 'beaker veneer', however, the indigenous ceramic traditions continue unaltered and relatively unaffected. Once more under apparent northern influences, the impressed-ware bowls, transformed by the adoption of the flat base, develop into the **food vessels** of the earlier second millennium (Gibson 1984, 80-1). The most obvious indicator of this is the Meldon Bridge style referred to above and dated to the late third millennium (Burgess 1976a). In this style the angular rim and rim bevel of the food vessels are already present. Food vessel decoration uses the same techniques as the impressed wares with some external influencing from beakers and grooved wares—comb and plastic decoration respectively. Both bowl and vase forms of food vessel are found, but both have the same decorative repertoire (Burgess 1974, 182-4; 1980; Gibson, 1986a 35-40).

Collared urns also develop from the impressed wares (Longworth 1984). These vessels have the heavy out-turned collared rim of the Fengate style and later phases of the impressed tradition. Once more, beaker and grooved ware influence is detectable in the decorative schemes, but development is essentially an internal one with little external influence. The often-quoted beaker-derived geometric arrangements (Clarke 1970, 271; Longworth 1984, 21-2) can also be parallelled in the impressed traditions, at least in their simpler forms.

The impressed and grooved ware traditions marry more convincingly in the **food vessel urns** and **cordoned urns** of the second millennium (Cowie 1978). These are once more mainly northern or, more correctly, upland phenomena, as they extend into Wales (Savory 1980). As the name suggests, food vessel urns combine the food vessel shape with the urn function: they are **enlarged food vessels** designed to hold cremations. In a variant of these, sometimes called **encrusted urns**, plastic zig-zag decoration is used to fill the neck, and roundels of clay may be added to the resulting open triangles. **Applied** and **raised** horizontal cordons are found on the cordoned urns. Normally only one or two cordons are present, the first in the upper third of the vessel and the second a short way below this. At times, the upper cordon may have the appearance of being a residual collar, and the lower cordon the shoulder of a collared urn. Confusion of the grooved and the impressed traditions, albeit deliberate, can clearly be seen here.

During the early second millennium, a range of miniature vessels may also accompany food vessels and urns in graves as **accessory vessels** (Longworth 1984). These are **Aldbourne cups, pygmy cups, perforated wall cups** and **grape cups** of the traditional early Bronze Age. They also appear to have roots in impressed wares and, though some have been found in domestic contexts, they appear to be chiefly funerary.

Within the contemporary domestic package, however, are found not only the finer wares chosen for deposition with the dead, but also coarser wares which rarely attain a sepulchral status. These are particularly evident in a series of fingernail- and fingertip-decorated wares in southern Britain and in a range of distinctive vessel forms in the north (Gibson 1982). In Scotland, yet again, there is a regionality and assemblage richness unparalleled in the south. In the Inner Hebrides, **shouldered jars**, both plain and richly decorated, are associated with beakers and food vessels at Kilellan Farm on Islay (Burgess 1976b). Large carinated bowls with obvious food vessel connections are found in the Outer Hebrides at Dalmore and Ensay (Simpson, pers. comm.), and in the Shetlands, S-profiled, flat-based pots with incised and combed decoration appear to be strongly beaker-influenced (Henshall, in Calder 1956). The term **Shetland neolithic house ware** may be attributed to these pots as an indication of their contexts.

Complementary to the flourishing urn traditions of upland Britain, in Wessex, **Wessex biconical urns** represent a local variant (ApSimon 1972; Calkin 1962). **Horseshoe handles** perhaps represent a local variation in a degenerate form of the plastic zig-zags of the food vessel urns. Continental parallels can be found for the Wessex biconical urns in the form of the Hilversum and Drakenstein urns of the Netherlands (for example, Glasbergen 1963) and the horseshoe-handled urns of northern France (Blanchet 1984, 102-3). In both cases, these Continental wares appear to be derived from the British prototypes.

In the south-western peninsula, there is a variety of local ceramic forms similar in their degree of insularity to those of Scotland. **Cornish urn** types are recognized by distinctive handles around a carination in the upper third of the vessel but are clearly related to the collared and cordoned urns of the rest of the highland zone (Patchett 1944; 1952). These pots also have impressed decoration derived from earlier periods.

1500-700 bc

From the middle of the second millennium, the ceramic record of southern Britain is generally dominated by the **Deverel–Rimbury** series of **globular, bucket-** and **barrel-shaped urns** (Barrett 1976). The last two forms are clearly related to the large vessels of the grooved ware tradition, as they carry fingernail, fingertip and applied cordon decoration. They are found in both domestic and ritual contexts. The globular urns within the Deverel-Rimbury series, however, have constricted necks and bulbous bodies decorated in the neck constriction with lightly incised or scored chevron decoration, often considered to be beaker-derived. These globular urns are rather more difficult to attribute to earlier traditions and seem to owe more in design and fabric to degenerate beaker than to any other ceramic tradition.

Regional variations do exist within this overall tradition, however, and can be distinguished principally by differences in decorative styling and variations within assemblages. These can be broken roughly into the Dorset Group, the Cranbourne Chase group (Hampshire and Wiltshire), the Ardleigh group of Essex and Suffolk in the east, and finally the South Downs group of Sussex (Calkin 1962; Erith and Longworth 1960). These distinctive types do not seem to retain much identity after the beginning of the first millennium, when a general slackening of ceramic styles appears to take place. Barrel and bucket forms decorated with fingertip impressions still persist; also common at this time are large, angular bowls with sharp carinations and widely everted rims, copying in ceramics the bronze *situlae* of the early first millennium (Hawkes 1935).

The Deverel–Rimbury complex, confined entirely to southern England, is represented elsewhere by an abundance of regional bucket and barrel forms with, of course, smaller vessels in keeping with a domestic repertoire. These regional forms are generally undecorated or else carry simple incised and impressed designs, often haphazardly executed and frequently on the upper third of the vessel. As with Deverel–Rimbury urns, fingernail and fingertip decoration is common.

In the Midlands and northern England, cordoned urns persist in unelaborate forms (Vine 1982; Jobey 1978; 1983). Twisted-cord decoration may occasionally be found, but in the main the decoration is by incision or fingertip impressions. Undecorated bucket and barrel vessels make up the majority of the pottery, which is usually coarse, fragmentary and poor in relation to the well-made and elaborate forms of the first half of the millennium.

In northern Britain, pottery seems to lose much of its prestige at the end of the second millennium. The dynamism of previous centuries has disappeared, giving way to conservatism and decline. Bucket and barrel shapes predominate. Decoration typically consists of slight raised cordons, with or without incised decoration, or horizontal finger-dragging which results in single or multiple broad but shallow grooves (Jobey 1978; 1983). It is not known for how long this type of pottery continues in use, but it is almost certain that these bucket urn types are ancestral to later Romano-British, 'native' forms.

In the south-west of England, the middle of the second millennium sees the beginning of the **Trevisker** tradition. This assemblage consists of tub- or flowerpot-shaped vessels, which are most likely to be utilitarian, being commonly found in domestic contexts (Patchett 1951; ApSimon and Greenfield 1972). In addition to twisted cord and incised decoration on these vessels, **plaited cord impressions** are also quite common, yet they are rare in other parts of the country. The end of Trevisker is not documented and it appears from the scant archaeological evidence that, as in northern Britain, ceramic was allowed to die out as an art-bearing medium, becoming a poorly made and degenerate artefact. A lack of detailed excavation on sites of the first millennium has resulted in a lack of knowledge of contemporary ceramics. Many sites may have been almost aceramic, as was Ireland in later prehistory, and certainly pottery finds from many of the Dartmoor hut circles are rare or very poor in quality (Gibson, in preparation). Coarse straight-sided, bucket forms, as in the north, have been found, as have sinuous vessels with sparse fingertip decoration (Fox 1954), which are degenerations of earlier forms.

700 BC to AD 400

In this time bracket, covering what are conventionally known as the Iron Age and Romano-British periods, pottery loses some of its importance as a datable artefact. This is principally because other artefacts, in particular bronze weapons and ornaments, are more susceptible to chronological change and have European parallels which can often be given absolute dates by correlation with painted Greek and Etruscan artefacts which were imported into 'Barbarian Europe'. In the Romano-British period, Roman imports and/or ceramics can be securely dated with the historical record. Generally, ceramics will be labelled Iron Age A, B or C, according to the accepted chronological scheme. More recently, the terms 'Early, Middle, Late and Very Late Iron Age pottery' have been advocated (Elsdon 1989). In later prehistory, the period dates the pottery rather than the pottery being used to date the period, as in the third and earlier second millennia, though clearly the process is, to a large extent, two-way. This is not to say that iron age ceramics have been poorly studied; rather, a great deal of work has been done on the styles and fabrics of later prehistoric pottery. Some regional styles have been identified and are outlined below and in the glossary, though some of these regional styles have been seriously questioned (for example, see Collis 1977 for a critique of Cunliffe 1974).

In the later prehistoric period in the northern and western isles of Scotland, barrel forms are common, as are rather bulbous jars with everted rims, incised decoration, **plastic cordons** and **fingertip impressions**. These wares, known as **Vaul, Clettraval** and **Clickhimin** styles, are associated with stone-built fortifications peculiar to Scotland (McKie 1974) and, though it has been suggested that the jars may be influenced by southern British types (McKie 1971), a local development is now generally accepted (Megaw and Simpson, 1979, 473).

In northern England and southern Scotland, first millennium pottery has been poorly studied against an absolute chronology; in fact, until the introduction of Roman types, pottery has been insufficiently studied to provide a good dating medium. Much Romano-British 'native' pottery of poorly made, bucket-shaped vessels in a very coarse fabric can now be seen to have started well back in the pre-Roman Iron Age (Jobey 1977). These vessels are undecorated and closely resemble the earlier forms but are even poorer in quality. This coarse first millennium pottery is labelled **flat rimmed ware,** but this is a chronologically meaningless term, as flat rims are also common in the third millennium. Flat rimmed ware is also inaccurate as a descriptive term, as often the rims are very irregular and by no means flat in the accepted sense. Barrel forms with internally hooked rims are also common from a number of later prehistoric contexts in the north but as yet have no secure, chronological bracketing (Gibson, forthcoming; Jobey and Jobey 1987).

Pottery from Staple Howe in Yorkshire (Brewster 1963) consists not only of barrel-shaped vessels with fingertip-impressed cordons at the shoulder, but also of similarly decorated, more angular forms. Sharply bipartite jars with the shoulder high up on the profile and accentuated with fingertip impressions are present in the assemblage, as are **situla jars** with sharp shoulders and strongly everted rims, reminiscent of metal prototypes. Both shoulder and rim may be decorated with fingernail impressions, sometimes referred to as **cable cordons** (Harding 1974).

Vessels of a similar form (that is, angular profiled jars with finger-decorated shoulders and/or cordons) have been found at West Harling in Norfolk in association with barrel-shaped forms (Clark and Fell 1953). Harding (1974, 139-40) has made out a case for some of these angular forms being directly derived from metal *situla* prototypes, suggesting that the fingernail decoration is representative of the metal rivets which hold together the sheet bronze plates of the metal originals. The shouldered forms without everted rims might also imitate Hallstatt D types. Harding does, however, stress that by no means all angular, shouldered jars are necessarily derived from metal types, and the shouldered jars from early second millennium contexts at Kilellan Farm on Islay have already been mentioned.

Within these metal-influenced jar assemblages are also shallower bipartite bowls with relatively sharp shoulder carinations; they are usually undecorated. Rim forms are simple or slightly beaded and they resemble the situla jars in all but height. Large round-based bowls are also present, particularly in the upper Thames area (Harding 1972); they have broadly hemispherical bodies and sharply everted and internally bevelled rims, which are decorated externally with fingertip impressions. Harding likens these to class B Atlantic cauldrons of the seventh century BC.

In southern Britain, there is a clearer distinction between fine and coarse wares in the first millennium, and this continues and becomes more obvious through time. The coarse wares exhibit a great variety of form and minor features that might be expected from a basically localized industry. Bowl and jar forms are both common. They are either plain or decorated with fingertip or fingernail impressions (Cunliffe 1983, 136-7). Some vessels with characteristic multiple scratches are known as **wiped wares**. Straight-sided and slightly globular bucket-shaped vessels are also found in these assemblages and exhibit similar surface treatment.

Hallstatt influence is also apparent in some of the fine wares from southern

England. From Eastbourne (Hodson 1962), a pit group of three bulbous-bodied **pedestalled urns** can be directly related to western Continental types, as can the appearance of painted decoration. This was found on one of the Eastbourne urns in the form of a band of painted concentric lozenges on the maximum diameter of the pot.

Also based on western Continental prototypes are the bulbous, round-bodied bowls with upright or flaring necks. These are decorated around their maximum girth with a variety of incised or stabbed geometric techniques. They may sometimes be **haematite-slipped** and have a rich red surface colouration. Occasionally the decoration was highlighted in white **inlay**.

Haematite-burnishing is a technique common on many bowl forms of this period in Wessex, where powdered haematite was burnished into the surface of the pot to give a rich 'polished' copper-red colour. This technique in Wessex is particularly noteworthy in that haematite is rare in that region (Oakley 1943). Areas of Britain rich in iron ores are not, however, major centres of haematite-coated bowls, which have a wide Continental distribution and thus it is suggested that perhaps this ceramic tradition is a direct import from Continental Hallstatt groups. Haematite coatings are added to both bowl and jar forms but are best known on a range of bipartite **furrowed bowls** with upright or slightly concave necks and with multiple furrows in the lower half of the neck. They may also have an **omphalos base**, possibly a feature derived ultimately from European metalwork, and the neck tends to increase in length in the later examples.

Haematite-coated jars are found in addition to the bowls. They are usually rather bulbous vessels with rounded sinuous profiles, everted rims and with incised, geometric designs consisting chiefly of incised infilled triangles and chevrons, which were often picked out from the body of the vessel by a white inlay. These vessels are invariably in a fine fabric and certainly warrant the term 'fine ware', a term too often used to describe highly decorated pottery irrespective of the quality of the fabric. These, too, are chiefly found in Wessex, with only a few known outliers. In the later phases of iron age Wessex, these haematite bowls are decorated with cordons and labelled, not surprisingly, cordoned haematite bowls. These, too, are in fine fabrics, and tend to have bulbous bodies but with upright or slightly flaring necks, frequently giving the whole pot a shape rather like a squat thistle head. Closed bowl forms are also present. The cordons are slight in comparison with those found on the grooved ware and cordoned urns of the third and second millennia but form slight, yet distinctive, ridges, usually on the body and in the neck angle of the pot. The cordons are normally evenly spaced and the resulting cordon-bordered zones may be decorated with simple geometric incised designs. Many of these bowls also have distinctive **foot-ring bases**, seen almost as a continuation of the body cordons on to the base.

In the later first millennium, the appearance in southern Britain of sharply angular bowls in a fine, black and burnished fabric has been seen as direct evidence for European contact, particularly with the Marne area of northern France (Savory 1937). They are decorated with fairly simple geometric motifs (oblique incisions or chevrons, for example) and also exhibit a feature that was to become more common in the archaeological record, the pedestal base. **Pedestalled cups and jars** which exhibit this feature clearly recall European prototypes but in Britain rarely achieve the elaborate dimensions of the Continental forms. As with the haematite-coated wares, these types are also found in jar form, as at Long Wittenham, only more sparsely decorated with incisions or fingertip impressions. The exceptionally fine pottery of this type from Chinnor (Richardson and Young 1951) and the presence on these sherds of distinctive filled-semicircle decoration, which has a limited distribution, has led Harding (1974, 160) to suggest that they may be the work of a professional and very skilled potter or group of potters. This type of pottery and method of decoration have become known as the **Chinnor style**.

Barrel-shaped coarse wares are common in the second half of the first millennium, sometimes with slightly everted rims, as at Hanborough (Case *et al*. 1964). Decoration on these jars is almost totally absent, except for rare examples of incision. The fabrics are quite thick and heavy in contrast to the finer wares already mentioned. This form is so simple, and presumably functional, that it is almost a basic, pan-British type in the late first millennium, and we have already seen this form in northern Britain in the pre-Roman Iron Age and in the 'native' wares of the Romano-British period. Heavily **scored** or 'wiped' surfaces constitute a Midlands variant first recognized at Breedon-on-the-Hill (Kenyon 1950) and subsequently at other sites, for example, Geddington, Northants. (Jackson 1979).

From the third century BC in southern Britain, a distinctive straight-sided, tub-shaped pot makes an appearance in the archaeological record and has been given the rather misleading name of **saucepan pot**. These pots are very simple in shape, having either straight upright sides or slightly barrel-shaped profiles with simple beaded or slightly everted rims. The base angle of the pot may be accentuated by a protruding foot, but the bases are otherwise completely flat. Decoration on these vessels is invariably incised or stabbed, varying from oblique, bordered incisions (Wheeler 1943) to elaborate, curvilinear designs of double infilled incisions. These have a distribution exclusively in the extreme south of Britain.

North of the Thames, the decorated wares of this period are distinguished by globular bowls also with incised and infilled curvilinear decoration. These are simple bowl forms with the maximum diameter occurring half-way up the vessel and with a narrower rim. This rim may also be slightly upright or everted but is otherwise simple. The decoration on these forms is particularly rich, with flowing curvilinear designs and dot **rosettes** arranged in horizontal bordered bands, for example, in the case of the **Hunsbury bowls** of the southern Midlands (Fell 1936). A complementary style in the upper Thames region, the **Frilford bowl**, is recognized by similar, but less flowing decoration, for example, dot-filled double incised semicircles, and it tends to lack the horizontal borders of the Hunsbury style (Bradford and Goodchild 1939). These bowls lasted into the second half of the first century BC.

In the first century BC, Belgic influence in south-eastern Britain introduced literally a revolution in the British ceramic record. This was the arrival of **wheel-thrown** wares, recognized principally in the pottery of the **Aylesford–Swarling** complex of the south-east. In this complex, pedestalled jars are most distinctive, and tall, wide-mouthed jars with slender bases and decorated with parallel, encircling incisions are also found. There are both bulbous and straight-sided variants (Birchall 1965). Also within the Aylesford–Swarling complex are cordoned pedestalled jars and cups, and **corrugated urns** with multiple horizontal ridges running up the sides of the vessel and generally with convex bases. Sharply carinated cups with everted necks and tall pedestalled bases, known as *tazze* (singular *tazza*), are elegant vessels found in the Welwyn graves. Ceramic innovations of the final phases of the Aylesford–Swarling complex include the **butt beaker** which has an everted rim on a barrel-shaped body, giving it a distinctive S-shaped profile, with combed or incised decoration in panels on the body.

This Continental influence is widespread over southern England and the so-called 'Belgic pottery' has been reassessed and reclassified by Thompson (1982). In addition to the Belgic wares, however, there are other Continental types, such as the imported pottery and Continental copies from Hengistbury Head and the so-called **cordoned ware** from the south west of the country, originating in Brittany and northern France. Cunliffe (1974) has identified some regional assemblages amongst this late iron age pottery and based on the iron age tribal groupings such as **Atrebatic wares**, though these have not received universal acceptance (Collis 1977).

With the Roman invasion came the **potter's wheel** and **kilns** for firing pottery. These two technological aids are closely linked, for, as is explained in Chapter 2, **wheel-thrown** pottery is fine-bodied and can only be fired with safety in a kiln. Despite the fact that better quality wares can be produced in a kiln than by open firing, the local native methods of hand manufacture and

The best-known example of this is provided by the **black-burnished 1** several areas, the Romans actually adopted the native wares, perhaps employing local craftsmen, continuing to produce their less sophisticated pottery.

The best-known example of this is provided by the **black-burnished 1** **(BB1) wares** of Dorset, produced under Roman influence right through until the fourth century. These were hand-made in a coarse, sandy fabric and then burnished, frequently on the wheel. Heavy mineral analysis (Williams 1977) has indicated that the most likely source for the sand employed in the manufacture of these vessels is the Wareham–Poole Harbour area of Dorset. The shortage of kilns in this region and the presence of ashy layers, frequently containing reddened and distorted wasters (Farrar 1976, 49), has prompted the suggestion that the vessels were open-fired: the coarseness of the fabric is consistent with this. Most of the vessels appear to have been cooking pots, and the coarse fabric would again have been appropriate for this. Typologically, the wares produced during the Romano-British period are derived from those produced by the local iron age tribe, the Durotriges, and Williams's (1977) work has revealed that, throughout the existence of the wares, the quartz sand inclusions added to the clay were derived from the same source.

Other examples of the Romans adopting local ceramic traditions are provided by various types of calcareous pottery known to Romanists as **calcite-gritted wares** and including **Dales** and **Knapton wares** and **Huntcliff** types. Dales ware vessels were primarily cooking pots, characterized by a high, outspringing rim with a well-developed internal ledge or lid seat. Gillam (1951) was the first to define this ware and establish its distribution. It is found throughout northern Britain, on both military and civil sites, and was used between AD 230 and 370. The bodies of the vessels were hand-made, but shoulders and rims were produced or finished on the wheel. A shelly fabric was employed, with fossil shell being added by the potters, and the vessels were open-fired. 'Dales ware types' were also produced but, although typologically similar, they were made in a very different, sandy fabric. The most detailed study of the ware has been carried out by Loughlin (1977), who claims (ibid., 102) a northern Lincolnshire origin for Dales ware proper and sees (ibid., 89) it as a development of the local iron age shell-tempered pottery found at sites such as Dragonby and Old Winteringham. Large numbers of vessels were produced and the uniformity within the assemblage has led Loughlin (1977, 86) to suggest that this gives 'an impression of commercial potting under a degree of central control, rather than of innumerable "cottage" industries producing their own idiosyncratic variants for strictly local consumption'.

Knapton was one of the three main pottery producing sites in East Yorkshire during the third and fourth centuries. Several hundredweight of sherds, mostly derived from hand-made vessels, the fabric of which contains large amounts of calcite opening material, were excavated from the site. Vessels made in this fabric, known as **Knapton ware**, were, like Dales ware, also primarily used for cooking. They were widely distributed throughout northern England, and Yorkshire in particular, and continued to be produced at Knapton throughout the third and fourth centuries.

Other calcite-opened fabrics were also produced in Yorkshire, for example, at Crambeck and Norton (Hayes and Whitley 1950, 30) and have been found at many sites along Hadrian's Wall, as well as at the signal stations on the coast. The most common of these are the so-called Huntcliff-type vessels, characterized by a pronounced shoulder, S-profile neck and rim, with an internal groove (possibly a lid seat); manufacture of these appears to have commenced in AD 370. These vessels were largely wheel-thrown, though some may have been hand-made with a wheel-thrown or finished neck and rim. The fabric is coarse, featuring, once again, large amounts of crushed crystalline calcite. They can be seen as the logical development from the Knapton tradition, which, in its turn, had its roots in the local iron age tradition. Hull (1932, 243-4) described the Huntcliff cooking pots as being 'in a fabric essentially native, that is, of clay well intermixed with large calcite grit, as we actually see in the Early Iron Age pottery from the Scarborough site itself'.

These few examples serve to illustrate that, although they had more advanced technology in their possession, the Romans were happy to adapt the less sophisticated, 'native' potting traditions to their own uses. It is likely that these potting industries featured local craftsmen, working under Roman control and organization. Obviously, the vessels produced adequately fulfilled their intended function (primarily cooking) or they would not have continued to be produced for such lengthy periods of time; neither would they have achieved such wide distribution throughout Britain, particularly in the case of BB1 pottery, as this was largely a result of the wares being used by the army.

Glossary

Abingdon ware (Fig. 31)
A style of decorated early and middle neolithic pottery in the **southern, decorated-bowl tradition** (Whittle 1977, 77 ff.) and named after the sherds found at the causewayed enclosure at Abingdon in Oxfordshire (Piggott 1954, 72; Leeds 1928; Case 1956). The style is typified by round-based bowls, either simple or bipartite, with shoulder **carinations**. Rims may be simple, T-sectioned, everted or thickened. Deep, baggy-profiled pots are also present and these, too, are round-based. Shoulders, if present, may be accentuated by handles or **lugs** (Fig. 31:2), which may be solid or either horizontally or vertically perforated; these may or may not have been functional. Decoration is usually simple or sparse, consisting of circular **stabs**, diagonal **incised decoration** or, occasionally, **twisted-cord impressions**. It is generally restricted to the upper half of the vessel, where it is used to accentuate the rim and/or shoulder. The **fabric** is usually rich in **inclusions**, and the **fillers** used include fossil shell and calcined flint, both of which materials were finely crushed (Avery 1982, 26-30). The surfaces of the sherds are smooth and occasionally **burnished**; sometimes the fossil shell has dissolved out to leave pits in the surfaces (cf. Fig. 89). Radiocarbon dates from the pottery-producing layers of the type site range from 3110 ± 130 to 2500 ± 145 bc.

Accessory vessels (Figs. 32, 126, 179, 181)
Also known as **pygmy cups** (Fig. 181). This term is used to describe small vessels of the early second millennium which accompany **cinerary urn** or **food vessel** cremations. They are **grape cups** (Fig. 126), **perforated wall cups** (Fig. 179), **Aldbourne cups** (Fig. 32) or **incense cups**. Occasionally a food vessel may act as an accessory to another food vessel or urn but hardly ever will an urn fulfil a similar role. Where an accessory vessel accompanies an urned cremation, it is often found inside the urn and amongst the cremated bone.

See also Annable and Simpson 1964; Burgess 1974 and 1980; Longworth 1983 and 1984.

Aldbourne cups (Fig. 32)
Typically found in Wessex, these are small, bipartite cups with upright lower halves and often markedly splayed upper portions. They are one of a number of **accessory vessel** or **pygmy cup** types usually accompanying urned cremations of the early second millennium. They are richly decorated internally and externally with geometric, **incised** or **impressed** motifs and may or may not be perforated.

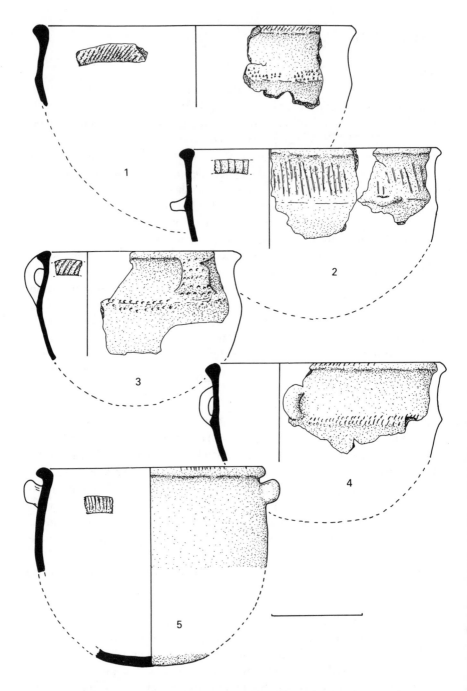

Fig. 31   Abingdon ware from the causewayed enclosure at Abingdon. 1, after Case 1955; 2-5, after Avery 1982. Scale = 10 cm.

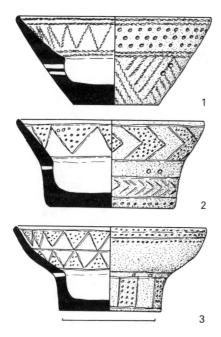

Fig. 32 Aldbourne cups. 1, Winterbourne Stoke G16(*a*); 2, Durrington G65; 3, Wimbourne St Giles G8. All after Annable and Simpson 1964. Scale = 5 cm.

See also Annable and Simpson 1964; Burgess 1974 and 1980; Longworth 1983 and 1984.

α–β inversion

The change that occurs in quartz at 573°C and which is often thought to be a problem in pot firing (see, for example, Hodges 1976, 39) and in the subsequent use of the vessel for cooking (Rye 1976). At this temperature, quartz changes during heating from the low temperature α form to the high temperature β form, and reverts back during cooling. The coefficient of thermal expansion of quartz is high in comparison with that of most other minerals but is particularly pronounced at this temperature, jumping from 3.76% volume expansion at 570° to 4.55% at 580°C (Skinner 1969, 91) and, of course, undergoing a corresponding decrease in size during cooling. Changes in the size of quartz inclusions during the cooling stage after firing are the main cause of **dunting**.

All Cannings Cross early style (Fig. 33)

A regional style of pottery identified by Cunliffe (1974, 31) as peculiar to the Wessex chalklands and datable to the eighth and seventh centuries BC. Large bulbous jars with everted rims, ornamented with filled, geometric motifs,

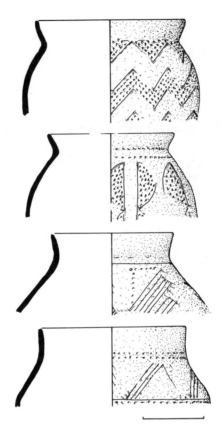

Fig. 33 Jars of Cunliffe's Early All Cannings Cross group. All from the type site, after Cunliffe 1974. Scale = 10 cm.

either **incised** or **stamped**, are common. Bipartite, **bead-rimmed** bowls with acute shoulder **carinations** and with similarly executed decoration on the upper portion of the vessel are also found in the assemblages; sometimes these vessels may be **burnished** or **haematite-coated**. **Situla jars** are also found, though they usually occur in a coarser **fabric**.

All Cannings Cross–Meon Hill group (Fig. 34)
A southern regional group of pottery, identified by Cunliffe (1974, 37-8), possibly from a single centre of manufacture and dating from the fifth to third centuries BC. **Haematite-coated** bowls are common in the assemblage (Fig. 34:1, 2) and have high shoulders and widely flaring rims. Decoration consists of grooving or **furrowing** on the shoulders, but diagonal strokes and filled

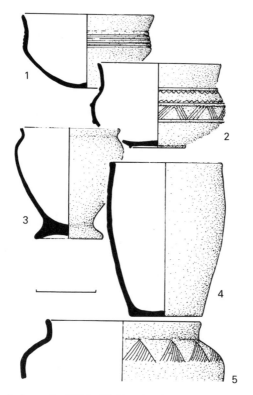

Fig. 34   Vessels from Cunliffe's All Cannings Cross–Meon Hill group. 1, 2, All Cannings Cross, Wilts; 3, Shallowcliffe, Wilts; 4, 5, Boscombe Down, Wilts. All after Cunliffe 1974. Scale = 10 cm.

chevrons are also found. Common also in this group are angular haematite-coated bowls with pronounced **foot-ring bases** and **cordons** (Fig. 34:2, 3), which accentuate the body angles and between which geometric decoration is **incised** and possibly then filled with white **inlay**. Plain **bucket urns** (Fig. 34:4) and **shouldered jars** (Fig. 34:3), some with vertically perforated handles, constitute the coarse ware. This group is found in the Wessex area, with Dorset and Somerset outliers, and may be copied from Continental, **La Tène**, pottery styles, to which they are closely related.

All Over Comb (Fig. 35)
A term used to refer to a type of **beaker** of the early second millennium, so called because of its decoration of multiple encircling lines of **comb impressions** covering the whole of the vessel. Frequently abbreviated to AOComb.

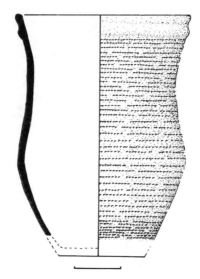

Fig. 35   All Over Combed beaker from Kilcoy, Ross and Cromarty. Individual comb lengths are clearly visible. After Clarke 1970. Scale = 5 cm.

All Over Cord (Fig. 36)
Similar to **All Over Comb** but the decorative technique used is **twisted cord**. Frequently abbreviated to AOC.

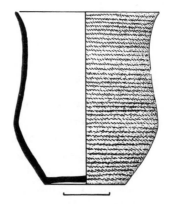

Fig. 36   All Over Cord beaker. 1, Grassington, Yorks. After Clarke 1970. Scale = 5 cm.

Ancaster bowls (Fig. 37)
This is not a generally used term but is used here to describe **La Tène**, decorated pottery of the third century BC from Lincolnshire (Elsdon 1975).

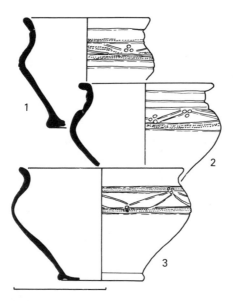

Fig. 37   Ancaster Bowls. 1, 2, Ancaster Gap, Lincs; 3, Old Sleaford, Lincs. After May 1976. Scale = 10 cm.

The assemblages comprise round-shouldered bowls with concave necks and slightly everted rims. They are usually decorated on the upper portion of the body with a band of **incised decoration** and/or **rouletting** in simple, geometric motifs. They belong to the eastern style of La Tène, stamp- and roulette-decorated pottery.

Anglesey neck (Fig. 78:2)
Regional type of **collared urn** found in Anglesey and North Wales and identified by its somewhat upright neck and its rim diameter, which is usually less than the shoulder diameter (Lynch 1970, 142). The urns often also have deep, internal, decorated, rim mouldings.

Anvil
A tool used primarily in secondary methods of manufacture and pressed against the inside surface of the wall of a vessel to support it while the exterior is worked with a **beater** or **paddle**. Ethnographic evidence indicates that various materials, including stone, ceramic and even the potter's hand, can be used (Fig. 17). Indentations left by the anvil can frequently be felt in the vessel wall and may be detected by **X-radiography** (Rye 1977).

AOC
See **All Over Cord.**

AOComb
See **All Over Comb.**

Applied decoration (Fig. 38)
A **surface treatment** involving the addition of clay, in various forms, to the surface of the vessel. **Cordons**, which may be applied in any direction or combination of directions, are a typical example, as are **rosettes** or pellets of clay. On some vessels from the Romano-British period, for example hunt cups, applied parts were frequently produced in a mould prior to being stuck on to the surface of the vessel with **slip**, and further plastic modelling was added by slip-trailing Such surface treatments often break away from the body of the vessel, leaving a distinctive scar; conversely, they may be very well bonded and be undetectable as applied, except in **thin section**, when **join voids** or differing **particle orientation** may indicate that they have been added (Fig. 38).

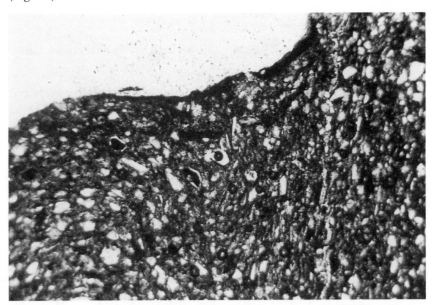

Fig. 38 Photomicrograph of a thin section of a vessel with applied decoration. Although the applied piece occupying most of the photo can be seen to be of the same clay as the pot body underneath, it can be distinguished by the different particle orientation and the presence of a thin line demarcating the original vessel surface. PPL, × 35.

Ardleigh urns (Fig. 39)
Barrel or **bucket urns** which are characterized by their profuse **fingernail** and **fingertip decoration** and which, being concentrated mainly in Essex and

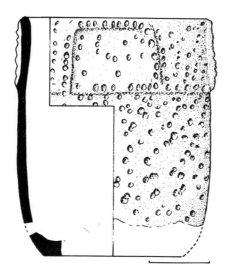

Fig. 39 Ardleigh urn from the type site. After Erith and Longworth 1960. Scale = 10 cm.

immediate surroundings, form the eastern component of the **Deverel–Rimbury assemblage** (Erith and Longworth 1960). The vessels may carry horizontal and vertical **cordons** and also roughly horseshoe-shaped cordons on the upper third of the pot.

Arras group (Fig. 40)
The name given by Cunliffe (1974, 40-1), on typological grounds, to the large, everted-rim and **shouldered jars** of the Yorkshire wolds and dating approximately from the fifth to the third centuries BC.

Fig. 40 Shouldered jar of the Arras culture from Burton Fleming, Yorks. After Stead 1979. Scale = 5 cm.

Atrebatic wares (Fig. 41)

A ceramic style identified by Cunliffe (1974, 89-92) and found mainly in the areas of Hampshire and Essex occupied by the Iron Age tribe of the Atrebates. The validity of the group has been questioned by Collis (1977). The pottery is

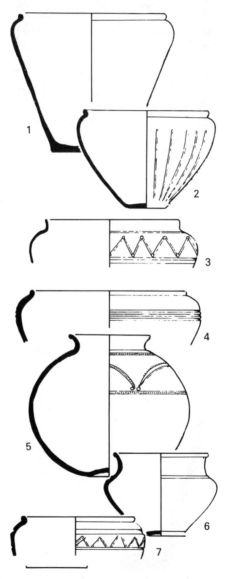

Fig. 41   Atrebatic wares, as defined by Cunliffe. 1, 2, Horndean, Hants; 3, Charleston Brow, Sussex; 4, Oare, Wilts; 5, Saltdean, Sussex; 6, Worthy Down, Hants; 7, Boscombe Down West, Wilts. After Cunliffe 1974. Scale = 10 cm.

one of the first **wheel-thrown** types in Britain and is **Belgic**-influenced. Cunliffe divides this style into three sub-regional zones:

Eastern, extending along the Sussex coast as far as the River Arun and recognized by **globular jars** with everted rims and with either simple flat or **foot-ring bases**. Other jars may have high, rounded shoulders with a short, upright or everted neck and rim. The pots may be ornamented with **incised decoration, rouletting, stamps** or painting; **cordons**, which may be **applied** or **raised**, may be used to divide the body of the pot into zones of either rectilinear or curvilinear decoration. This type of pottery was developed under Belgic influence, in the mid first century BC, from the **saucepan pots**.

South-western, occurring mainly in West Sussex and Hampshire and characterized by rounded jars with high shoulders and wide, open mouths or with upright rims. There may also be bipartite jars with everted rims and with a cordon accentuating the junction between the neck and the body.

North-western, occupying the area centring on Salisbury Plain, bearing a strong resemblance to the previous style but often featuring a groove on the **beaded rim**.

Aylesford–Swarling (Fig. 42)

A tradition of **wheel-thrown** pottery, distributed around Kent, Essex, Hertfordshire and Bedfordshire, and named after two cemeteries in Kent dating to the first century BC. The complex dates from *c*. 60 BC and has Continental parallels in Normandy, Picardy and Champagne, extending also into Belgium. The tradition reached Britain with the so-called Belgic invasion of the first century BC and may also be loosely termed **Belgic ware**, though this is an unacceptably broad label. Nine distinctive ceramic types have been identified from grave groups by Birchall (1965) as constituting the assemblage. They are as follows:

1 **Pedestalled urns** with pear-shaped bodies and everted rims (Fig. 42:1*a*, 1*b*)
2 **Corrugated urns** with wide mouths and everted rims (Fig. 42:2)
3 Large, S-profiled bowls with everted mouths, rounded shoulders, **cordons** and often with a zone of decoration (Fig. 42:3)
4 Small, S-profiled bowls with everted rims, cordons or corrugated shoulders and **foot-ring bases** or small bowls with single shoulder **carinations** (Fig. 42:4*a*, 4*b*)
5 Biconical jars with rolled rims, corrugated or cordoned shoulders and short necks (Fig. 42:5*a*, 5*b*)
6 **Butt beakers** with heavy rims and with decorated zones on the bodies (Fig. 42:6)
7 Plates or shallow dishes (Fig. 42:7)
8 Neckless bowls with rippled shoulders (Fig. 42:8*a*) and rims internally grooved to hold lids (Fig. 42:8*b*)

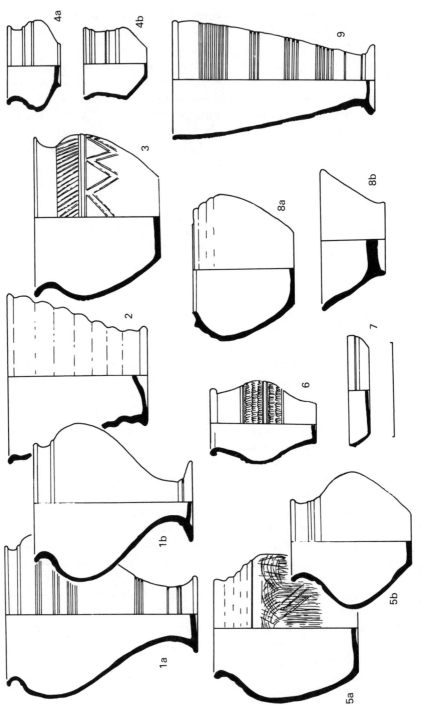

Fig. 42   Pottery from the Aylesford–Swarling complex from the type sites. After Birchall 1965. Scale = 10 cm.

9 Tall, conical urns with foot rings or pedestalled bases and body grooves or cordons (Fig. 42:9).

Birchall also identified a tenth ceramic component, the **tazza,** which was common in graves in Hertfordshire but rare elsewhere. This exclusive distribution was also found in the case of the corrugated urns, which have been found only in Kent.

Balevullin style (Fig. 43)

Late iron age pottery from the north-western Atlantic province of Scotland and particularly the Hebridean islands. Typical vessels are **barrel**-shaped pots with **fingertip impressions** on the **cordons** decorating their maximum diameter. They may have **incised decoration** above this cordon. MacKie (1963) divided Balevullin-style pottery into three classes as follows:

Class A consists of small thin-walled vessels in a well-fired and well-made **fabric** with vertical **wipe marks** on the surface. A1 vessels are roughly barrel-shaped with everted rims and protruding foot bases. They are decorated with a cordon which is either fingertip-impressed or incised and the vessel may be either incised or stabbed above this feature (Fig. 43:1). A2 vessels are undecorated but otherwise similar (Fig. 43:2).

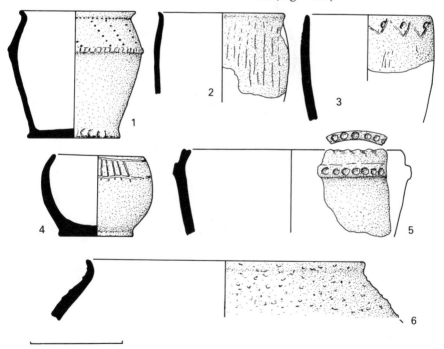

Fig. 43 Balevullin pottery from the type site. After MacKie 1963. Scale = 10 cm.

Class B vessels are rather more coarse than class A. They are usually undecorated or decorated with simple fingertip impressions on the rim and crude, incised decoration on the upper third of the vessel (Fig. 43:3, 4).

Class C (Fig. 43:5, 6) covers a variety of large coarse vessels. These are divided into three sub-types: C1 – with deep fingertip-impressed cordons, C2 – larger, undecorated pots in a coarse fabric, and C3 – large vessels in a hard, smooth fabric though still containing abundant **inclusions**.

Barbed wire impressions (Fig. 44)

A rather anachronistic term used to describe a decorative technique similar to **whipped cord** impressions (for a full discussion, see Bakker 1979, 178). In the case of barbed wire decoration, the cord was loosely wrapped around a sharp core (possibly a flint blade), so that lengths of the core showed through between the coils of the cord. This was then impressed into the clay, resulting is a straight line crossed at right angles by numerous short impressions. The technique is especially common on **Beaker** pottery.

See also Clarke 1970.

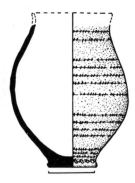

Fig. 44   Barbed wire beaker from Erriswell, Suffolk. After Clarke 1970. Scale = 5 cm.

Barbotine

An alternative name for slip-trailing, used primarily in descriptions of Romano-British fine wares.

Barrel-shaped

See **barrel urn** and **closed vessel**.

Barrel urn (Fig. 45)

A generic term for a flat-based urn with a smooth, curving profile. They are **closed vessels**, with the maximum diameter occurring in the upper half of the vessel. Rim forms vary but are rarely, if ever, everted. The term is not

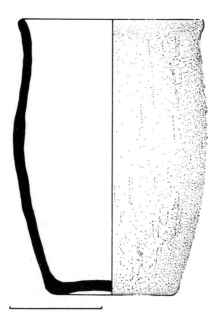

Fig. 45 Barrel urn from Rose Ash, Devon. The urn was found with a cremation and dated to 1030±70 bc (HAR 2992). After Wainwright 1980. Scale = 10 cm.

indicative of date, but barrel urns appear with the **Deverel–Rimbury** complex in the south and contemporary equivalents elsewhere (Calkin 1962; Barrett 1976), and then continue throughout prehistory. They are found in both domestic and sepulchral contexts.

Beacharra bowls (Fig. 46)
Bipartite round-based bowls found mainly in the coastal region of southern and central western Scotland and associated with the chambered tombs of the Clyde estuary (Scott 1964; McInnes 1969). The bowls are sharply bipartite, **closed vessels** with the maximum diameter occurring at the shoulder. The rim may be accentuated by being slightly upturned but otherwise simple forms

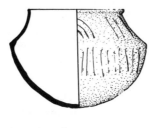

Fig. 46 Beacharra bowl from the type site. After Scott 1964. Scale = 5 cm.

prevail. Ornamentation is mainly by **incised decoration** and occurs almost invariably above the **carination**. Motifs may be either straight lines or single or concentric semicircles. They have close parallels in the north of Ireland.

Bead (or beaded) rims

Form of rim commonly found on later iron age and Roman pottery, where the rim is externally rounded as if a round-sectioned ring of clay had been **applied** to the top of the vessel. In reality, however, the bead effect is a result of carefully working the rim.

Beaker (1)

A generic term used to describe a drinking vessel of any date. When used in an early second millennium context, however, it refers to the **Bell Beaker** (see **Beaker (2)**) derived from European types and developed independently in Britain throughout the first half of the millennium. The term 'beaker' is derived from the German word *Becher*, but the early antiquaries frequently referred to this type of pot as a '**drinking cup**'. The arrival of Bell Beakers in Britain is traditionally regarded as the beginning of the early Bronze Age. In later contexts, the term is usually applied to drinking vessels of the first century BC, such as the **butt beaker** (Fig. 42:6) and **girth beaker** (Fig. 121:4) of Gaulish or Roman influence.

Beaker (2) (Figs. 35, 36, 44, 47, 48)

Highly decorated, fine ware reaching Britain from Europe at the beginning of the second millennium bc as either a result of invasion or of trading contacts. Opinion is divided as to which but is generally tending towards acceptance of the latter hypothesis with perhaps some small-scale movement of individuals from the present Netherlands. Formerly called '**drinking cups**' by the early antiquaries, 'Bell Beaker' is a term used on the Continent to distinguish this later pottery from earlier and similar forms, such as the funnel-neck beaker (*Trichterbecker* or TRB) and the protruding-foot beaker (PFB or occasionally SVB (for *Standvoetbecker*)). These forms have not as yet been found in Britain and so generally in the British literature the 'bell' component is dropped, as the distinction is unnecessary.

The distinctive features of beakers are the fine **fabric** and the distinctive decoration. Two main types are found: all-over-decorated and comb-zoned. The all-over-decorated style takes either an all-over-cord (Fig. 36) or an all-over-combed (Fig. 35) form, in which the decoration consists of encircling lines of **twisted-cord** or toothed-**comb impressions**, usually covering the whole of the exterior of the vessel, and occurring sometimes inside the rim. The comb-zoned vessels carry bands of comb-impressed, geometric motifs interrupted by undecorated bands (Figs. 47, 48).

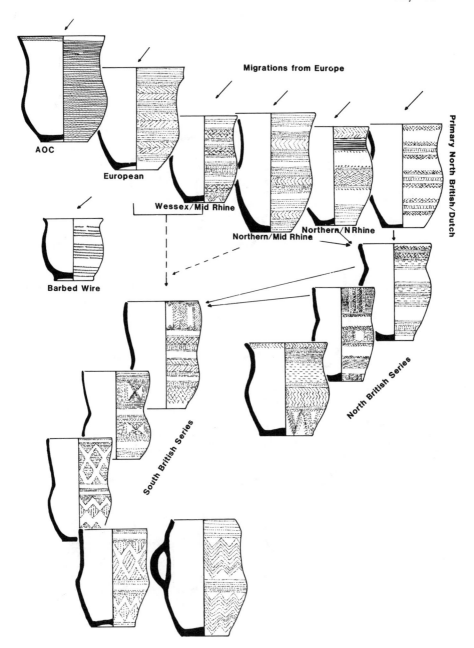

Fig. 47 Clarke's scheme of beaker invasion and development. Intrusive groups AOC, European, Wessex/Mid-Rhine, North/Mid-Rhine, North/North Rhine, Primary North British/Dutch and Barbed Wire giving rise to the North British and South British Series, the last itself developing under North British influence. All beakers after Clarke 1970. Not to scale.

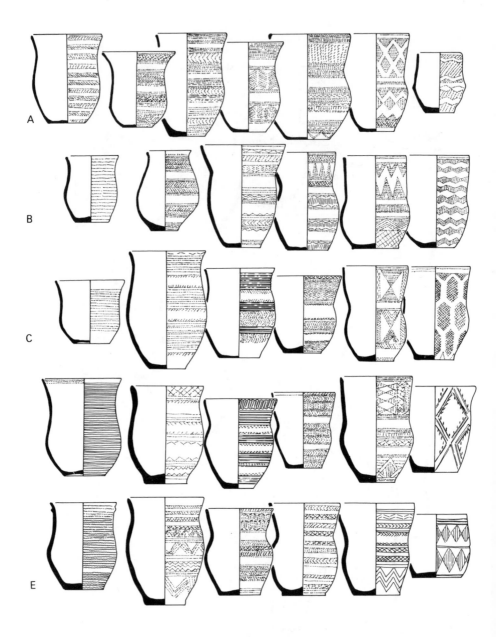

Fig. 48 Lanting and van der Waals' step scheme for British beakers for A, Wessex, B, East Anglia, C, Yorkshire, D, Borders, E, North-east Scotland (after Shepherd). Beakers after Clarke 1970 and Shepherd 1986. Not to scale.

In 1963, Piggott arranged beakers into three chronologically and stylistically consecutive types (bell, short necked and long necked), seeing the earliest beakers as being like those of the Continent with a sinuous, S-shaped profile and with the elongation of the neck being indicative of chronological development. In 1970, Clarke produced a corpus of Beaker pottery and introduced a complex classification, in which he saw a sevenfold-invasion theory with a North British and South British tradition developing out of the immigrant pots (Fig. 47).

Clarke's intrusive groups were based on vessels with Continental similarities and these were challenged by Lanting and van der Waals in 1972 for two reasons: firstly, the Continental groups had no cohesion; secondly, Clarke's distribution maps lacked the nuclei of consolidation expected of an invading group prior to their expansion. Instead, Lanting and van der Waals offered a seven-step development theory (Fig. 48) based essentially on neck elaboration and decoration complexity in four focus areas: Wessex, Kent and East Anglia, Yorkshire, and northern England and the Borders. Their scheme did not work in northern Scotland, though a similar development has recently been advocated by Shepherd (1986) (Fig. 48e). Lanting and van der Waals' scheme has not gained universal acceptance, however, as it is perhaps over-rigorous and pays little attention to the domestic material.

Until such time as a statistically meaningful sample of radiocarbon dates will allow a typology to be constructed alongside an absolute chronology, Case (1977) considered that we should stay clear of over-detailed classifications and offered a broad, three-zone scheme of early, middle and late, based on the available radiocarbon data and associations. This bears a striking resemblance to the typology proposed by Piggott.

Beakers are studied mainly from burial sites associated with individual burials in pits or cists beneath barrows, or in flat graves and with a variety of other grave goods. Beakers are also found on domestic sites, however, where the fabrics and decoration range more widely than those of the sepulchral counterparts (Gibson 1982). Fine ware is found on the settlements but also plain, coarse ware or pots decorated with random or ordered **fingernail** (Figs. 93, 107, 108) or **fingertip impressions** (Figs. 43:5, 98:5, 6). Vessels decorated with this type of **rustication** also tend to be larger than the fine wares and are more common in southern Britain, having close parallels with Continental forms sometimes called *potbekers* (see **potbeaker**).

Beater (Fig. 49)

Used in conjunction with an **anvil**, usually as a secondary forming method. The technique is frequently used to expand and compact the walls, particularly of water vessels, and to alter the shape and close the bases of

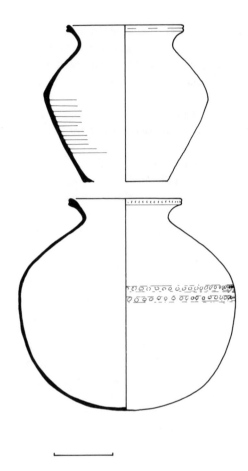

Fig. 49   One example of the effect of the use of the beater (paddle) and anvil. The walls have been expanded and thinned and the base of the original wheel-thrown vessel has been sealed and made round. After Dumont 1952.

wheel-thrown vessels. The term is usually synonymous with **paddle** but Raven Hart (1962) used it to describe a thicker type of implement than is normally called a paddle.

Belgic bowls (Fig. 50)
See also **Belgic wares** and **Aylesford-Swarling**. These are **grog**-filled bowls subdivided by Thompson (1982) as follows:
D1 Bowls with distinct necks and occasionally emphasising **cordons**
D2 **Cordoned bowls** or bowls with rippled shoulders

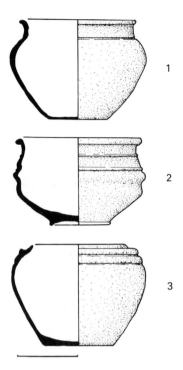

Fig. 50 Belgic bowls, as classified by Thompson. 1, D1, bowl, Welwyn; 2, D2, bowl, Wendens Ambo; 3, D3, bowl, Swarling. After Thompson 1982. Scale = 10 cm.

D3 **Globular** bowls with or without rim grooves for lids, and **corrugated** conical bowls.
Further subdivisions exist within each group.

Belgic Coarse Ware jars (Fig. 51)
See also **Belgic wares** and **Aylesford–Swarling**. Jars containing **grog inclusions,** subdivided by Thompson (1982) as follows:
C1 **Bead-rim** jars
C2 Plain, everted-rim jars
C3 Plain jars with thickened rims
C4 Round-**shouldered jars,** frequently with decoration on the shoulder
C5 Jars with rims moulded to provide a seating for a lid
C6 Large storage jars
C7 Rilled jars with multiple, horizontal grooves

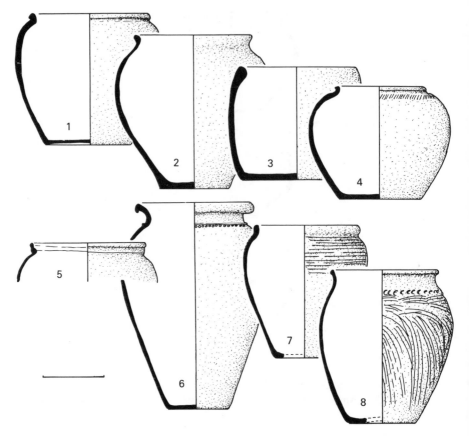

Fig. 51   Belgic Coarse Ware jars, as classified by Thompson. 1, C1 type from Colchester; 2, C2 type from Danbury; 3, C3 type from Colchester; 4, D4 type from Colchester; 5, C5 type from Puddlehill; 6, C6 type from Colchester; 7, C7 type from Nazeingbury; 8, C8 type from Wheathampstead. After Thompson 1982. Scale = 10 cm.

C8   Small, shouldered and everted-rim jars with stabbing on the shoulder and combing, rilling or scraping below this.

Further subdivisions exist within each of Thompson's groups.

Belgic cups (Fig. 52)

See also **Belgic wares** and **Aylesford–Swarling**. Small vessels with **carinations** subdivided by Thompson (1982) into three main types:

E1   Simple, carinated cups with or without one or more **cordons**

E2   Squat, carinated cups related to E1, with wide mouths and, occasionally, **omphalos bases**

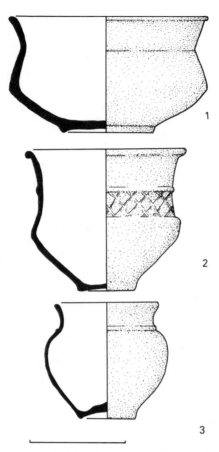

Fig. 52 Belgic cups, as classified by Thompson. 1, E1 type from Canewdon; 2, E2 type from Colchester; 3, E3 type from Radwell. After Thompson 1982. Scale = 10 cm.

E3 Plain, everted-rim cups often with tall extended necks.

Further subdivisions exist within each of Thompson's groups.

Belgic Fine Ware jars (Fig. 53)

See also **Belgic wares** and **Aylesford–Swarling**. These jars are class B in Thompson's classification of Belgic, **grog**-filled pottery and have been subdivided by her (1982) as follows:

B1 Plain jars with everted rims

B2 Rippled or **corrugated** jars

B3 Shoulder-cordoned jars with a convex bulge between two **cordons**

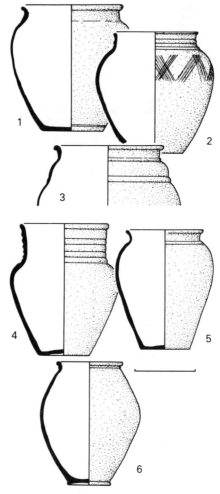

Fig. 53   Belgic Fine Ware jars as classified by Thompson. 1, B1 type from Prae Wood; 2, B2 type from Deal; 3, B3 type from Broughing; 4, B4.1 type from Berkhampstead; 5, B4.2 type from Holborough; 6, B5 type from Colchester. After Thompson 1982. Scale = 10 cm.

B4 Jars with exaggerated, cordoned necks
B5 Tall **barrel-shaped** jars.

Belgic lids (Fig. 54)
See also **Belgic wares** and **Aylesford–Swarling**. Lids are quite rare and often poorly finished, though some finer forms are present. Thompson (1982) has subdivided these forms into ten types as follows:
L1 Bell-shaped lids with out-turned rim

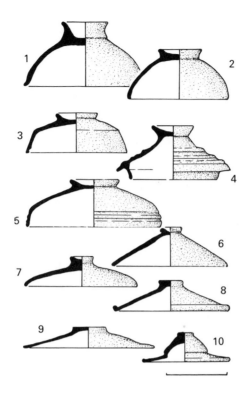

Fig. 54 Belgic lids as classified by Thompson. 1, L1 type from Colchester; 2, L2 type from Colchester; 3, L3 type from Clifton Reynes; 4, L4 type from Braintree; 5, L5 type from Heybridge; 6, L6 type from Colchester; 7, L7 type from Colchester; 8, L8 type from Colchester; 9, L9 type from Colchester; 10, L10 type from Ipswich. After Thompson 1982. Scale = 10 cm.

L2   Bell-shaped lids without out-turned rims
L3   High lids with **carinations**
L4   Elaborate lids with hollow knobs and flanged rim
L5   Lids with grooved and cordoned, vertical rims
L6   Plain conical lids with no differentiated rim
L7   Conical lids with an in-turned or vertical rim
L8   Conical rims with out-turned rims
L9   Shallow out-turned, conical rims
L10 Domed and flanged rims
Some of these rim forms survive into the Roman period.

Belgic wares (Figs. 42, 50, 51, 52, 53, 54)
A general term to describe the **cordoned jars, pedestalled cups and jars, butt beakers** and, for the first time, **wheel-thrown** pottery, which entered Britain in

the middle of the first century BC. See **Aylesford–Swarling** (Fig. 42). Thompson (1982) suggests that this pottery is predominantly **grog**-filled and, having questioned the validity of Birchall's (1965) Aylesford–Swarling series, breaks the series down into nine basic types, all with internal variation:

A Pedestalled urns
B Jars in finer fabrics
C Jars in coarser fabrics
D Bowls
E Cups
F Pedestalled bowls, cups, etc.
G Copies of Gallo-Belgic, Samian and Roman forms
L Lids
S Special miscellaneous forms.

These forms are all described separately under **pedestalled urns** (A above), **Belgic Fine Ware jars** (B above), **Belgic Coarse Ware jars** (C above), **Belgic bowls** (D above), **Belgic cups** (E above), **pedestalled cups** (F above), **Gallo-Belgic imitations** (G above), and **Belgic lids** (L above), **strainers, tripod vessels** and **strainer-spouted bowls** (S above).

See also Cunliffe 1975; Harding 1974; Hawkes 1968; Wheeler 1936.

Bell Beaker
See **Beaker** (2).

Bevel (Fig. 55)
A flat, sloping area inside the rim of a vessel frequently, though not universally, used as a platform for decoration. It does not appear to have been functional. Bevels enter the ceramic repertoire with the developed rims of the later third millennium **impressed wares** and are common on **food vessels, collared urns, food vessel urns, cordoned urns, accessory vessels** and pots of the **Deverel–Rimbury complex** and their regional equivalents. Bevels are generally not as common after the end of the second millennium.

Fig. 55   Examples of different rim forms, each with a rim bevel treated in different ways. Not to scale.

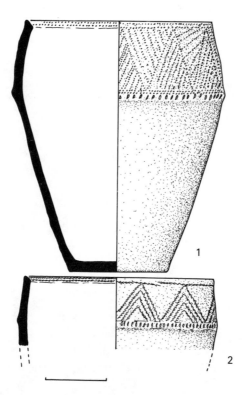

Fig. 56 Biconical urns. 1, Cherhill G1, Wilts; 2, Collingbourne Ducis G8(*a*), Wilts. After Annable and Simpson 1964. Scale = 10 cm.

Biconical urns (Fig. 56)
Generic name given to a variety of urns of the first half of the second millennium. It refers basically to an urn with two components: a body with straight but splayed sides leading to a shoulder and an inwardly angled neck ending in a closed rim (ApSimon 1972). A variety of types is found within this class, for example pottery in the **Trevisker** Series, **Cornish urns**, **handled urns** and **Wessex biconical urns**; many **cordoned urns** and food vessel urns may also fall into this category.

Bird bone impressions (Fig. 57)
Decorative impressions made in soft clay by the end of a small bone. These have been identified as being from birds, but the term may be used as a blanket to include impressions made by small mammal bones. Insufficient work has been done on this subject, but the variety of impressions that can be made in this technique, using different bones and degrees and angles of

Fig. 57   Experimental bird bone impressions, as featured in Liddell's (1929) paper. Photo reproduced by courtesy of *Antiquity*.

impression has been admirably demonstrated by Liddell (1929) after the discovery, during the excavations at Windmill Hill, of a bird bone associated with sherds of **Peterborough ware.**

Black-burnished wares (Figs. 10, 58)
Pottery of the Romano-British period directly descended in raw materials and technology from the iron age **Durotrigian** pottery of south-western England. Two main categories, black-burnished 1 (BB1) and 2 (BB2) were

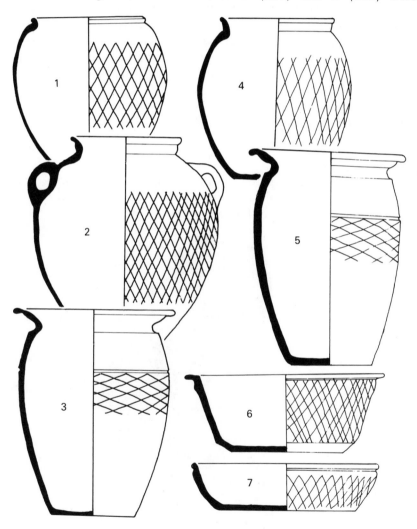

Fig. 58   Black-burnished ware, category 1. 1-3, after Gillam 1957, 4-7, after Williams 1977. Not to scale.

distinguished by Gillam (1960), and these categories have been supported by **heavy mineral analysis** studies carried out by Williams (1977). BB1 wares were hand-made and extensively burnished (some were probably done on the wheel) prior to firing. They were open-fired and the shiny black colour is most likely to be the result of the deposition of carbon on and immediately below the surface in a post-firing, **smudging** technique.

Black coring

The dark zone sometimes found in the middle of sherds. It is caused by localized **reduction** during firing and really only occurs in kiln-fired vessels. Care must be taken to distinguish between real black coring, which is caused by the reduction of **iron oxides** within the pot walls, and the black zone that can be found in many **open-fired** pots and which is the result of incomplete oxidation of the **carbonaceous matter** present in the clay (Figs. 29, 69) (see **oxidizing conditions**); the latter is an indicator of a short firing (as there has been insufficient time to burn out this material) and therefore, frequently, of **open firing**.

Bloating (Fig. 59)

Distortion of the body caused by the evolution of gases during firing, particularly when the firing has been too rapid and **sintering** has occurred before organic matter has been completely burned out.

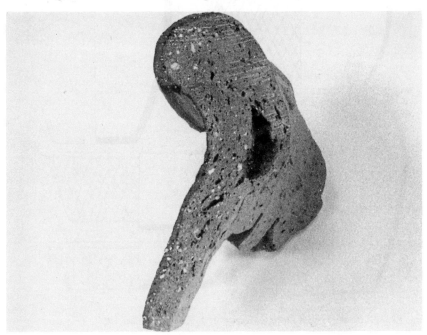

Fig. 59   A sherd which has bloated as a result of gases being unable to escape during firing. Sherd height 6 cm.

Boghead bowls (Fig. 60)

Round-based bowls with **carinations** in the **western neolithic** tradition occurring in northern Scotland and being a regional relative of the **Grimston–Lyles Hill** tradition (Henshall, in Burl 1984). The **fabric** is often fine, dark and **burnished,** and the pots carry the characteristic decoration of vertical **fluting** or rippling on the exterior and interior of the neck, as well as on the top of the rims (Henshall 1983). This fluting may be shallow and light or quite pronounced and appears to have been executed with either a rounded spatula or by the potter's fingers in the still-damp clay. Similar sherds are found at the traditional type site of Lyles Hill (Evans 1953). Radiocarbon dates from Boghead centre around 3000-2900 bc.

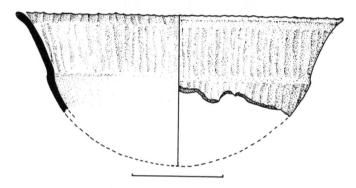

Fig. 60 Boghead bowl from Easterton of Roseisle. After Henshall 1983. Scale = 10 cm.

Body

The term used to describe clay and any **inclusions** present in it, particularly prior to firing, though it may also be used to describe the finished product. Synonymous with **fabric** and paste.

Breedon–Ancaster group (Fig. 61)

Term used by Cunliffe (1974, 328) to refer to **Trent Valley A ware.**

Briston Channel B pottery (Fig. 92:4)

The term suggested by Kenyon (1954) to refer to the linear-decorated and **duck-stamped** pottery of the Severn region.

Bucket-shaped vessels (Fig. 62)

Simple, straight-sided vessels, the rim diameter of which is usually the maximum diameter. See **bucket urn.**

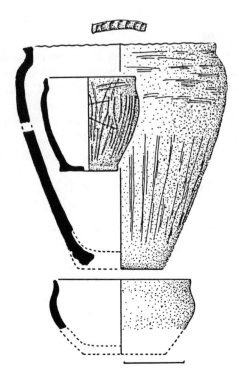

Fig. 61   Cunliffe's Breedon-Ancaster group or Trent Valley A ware. From Breedon-on-the-Hill, Leics. After Cunliffe 1974. Scale = 10 cm.

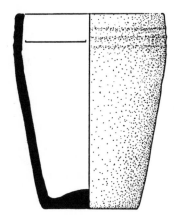

Fig. 62   Bucket urn from Eggleston, Co. Durham. Scale = 10 cm.

Bucket urn (Fig. 62)
The term used to describe a large, flat-based and straight-sided vessel, the maximum diameter of which occurs at the rim. The term is not indicative of date but is generally used in connection with urns of the **Deverel–Rimbury** complex (Calkin 1962), their regional equivalents (Gibson 1986a, 50-3), and later prehistoric pottery, particularly in northern Britain. Bucket-shaped **food vessels** and **food vessel urns** are also found in the second millennium and called such because of their simple shape.

Burnish (Figs. 63, 64, 132)
The smooth, sometimes facetted effect on the surface of a vessel produced by rubbing **leather-hard** clay with a rounded tool. It can be done with a circular motion but more commonly was done with short, linear strokes; some Romano-British vessels were burnished on the wheel, producing long facets running all the way round the pot (Fig. 63). The process compacts the surface, slightly reducing permeability, and often imparts a high shine; it is thus both functional and decorative. On occasions, mineral particles (for example, graphite or **haematite**) were applied to the surfaces of leather-hard vessels and burnished in (Fig. 132), the burnishing providing the most effective method of keeping the pigment in position. It is sometimes called polish (U.S.), but this term is more correctly used to describe a post-firing treatment of glazed wares. Water-worn pebbles are common burnishing tools used by modern

Fig. 63 A sherd of Romano-British black-burnished 1 ware. The burnishing facets can be seen running horizontally along the sherd and are quite long, indicating that the vessel was burnished on the wheel.

Fig. 64   The interior of a platter that has been burnished in two directions. Scale in centimetres.

traditional potters (for example, Reina and Hill 1978, Plate 204) but other materials, such as bone, may also have been used, for example, at Rushden, Northants. (Woods and Hastings 1984, 110-1). (The lattice pattern common on **black-burnished 1** vessels is not deep enough to be called incision and is a type of burnish probably executed with the aid of a tool similar to the rounded bone points illustrated by Woods and Hastings.) See **haematite-coated wares**.

Butt beakers (Fig. 42:6)
A style of drinking vessel, common in the pre-Roman Iron Age and surviving well into the Roman period, which takes its name from its distinctive, barrel shape with the maximum diameter occurring about midway up the vessel and narrowing to a rim which has a similar diameter to the base.

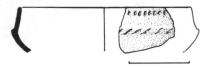

Fig. 65   Bowl with cable cordon from Staple Howe, Yorks. After Harding 1974. Scale = 10 cm.

Cable Cordons (Figs. 65, 76:8)

Style of **cordon** frequently found on early-first-millennium pottery, particularly from northern Britain, decorated with S-shaped, **fingernail impressions** formed by swivelling the fingernail as it is impressed into the clay. The result is a cordon resembling the twist of a rope.

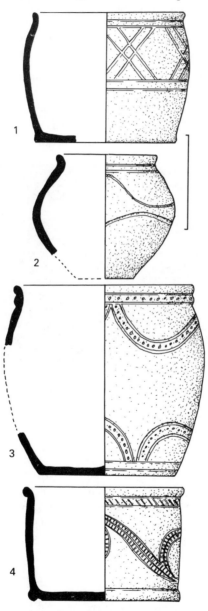

Fig. 66 Caburn-Cissbury style, as identified by Cunliffe. 1, 2, Cissbury, Sussex; 3, Park Brow, Sussex; 4, The Caburn, Sussex. After Cunliffe 1974. Scale = 10 cm.

Caburn-Cissbury style (Fig. 66)
One of a number of styles of iron age pottery defined by Cunliffe (1974, 42), in this case named after two hillforts in Sussex. The pottery is decorated with simple **incised** curvilinear or geometric designs. **Saucepan pots** with thickened rims are common, as are more bulbous bowls. Cunliffe's style zones have, however, been seriously questioned by Collis (1977).

Calcareous inclusions (Figs. 67, 68, 72, 73, 74, 89, 95)
Inclusions composed of calcium carbonate (for example, **calcite** (Figs. 67, 68, 72, 74), limestone (Fig. 73) or shell (Fig.95)). Such materials frequently occur naturally in sedimentary clays but were also often added by potters. Problems are incurred in the firing of these inclusions at temperatures between 650° and 900°C because of **lime blowing**. Rye (1976) has suggested that calcareous inclusions may be good for **thermal shock resistance.**

Fig. 67   Calcite crystals showing characteristic rhombohedral shape. Scale in centimetres.

Calcination (Fig. 9)
Strong heating of a substance. Some materials (for example, flint and shell) can be crushed more easily after they have been heated. In the case of flint, heating it to around 400°C drives off water that is found within the crystal lattice, resulting in macro and micro-cracks within a nodule. These make the flint easier to crush and yield chunky pieces (Fig. 9) rather than the sharp, angular flakes that are obtained by breaking unheated flint.

Calcite (Figs. 67, 68, 72, 73, 74)
Crystalline calcium carbonate, readily recognized by its rhombic **cleavage**

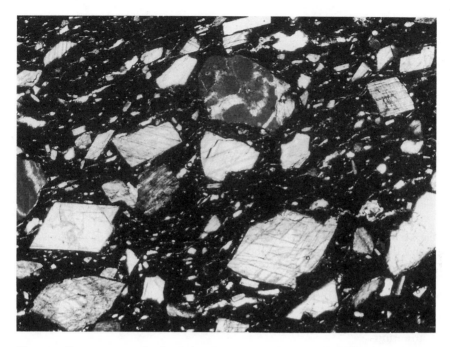

Fig. 68 Photomicrograph of a sherd of Huntcliff ware with abundant calcite and limestone opening material. The characteristic shape and internal cleavage of many of the calcite fragments should be noted. XPL, × 18.

and form. It can be scratched easily by metal (hardness 3 on **Mohs' Scale**) and reacts with **hydrochloric acid**. An **opening material** used throughout antiquity, it was particularly utilized for the so-called **calcite-gritted wares** (Fig. 68) of northern England during the early centuries AD.

Calcite-gritted ware (Figs. 68, 89)
See **calcite**, **Knapton ware** and **Huntcliff ware**.

Carbonaceous matter (Fig. 69)
Finely divided organic matter present in nearly all clays and, in particular, in those of **sedimentary** origin, when it is frequently responsible for grey colouring. During firing, it is burned out at temperatures above 250°C, although most effective combustion is achieved between 700° and 800°C. If not removed during firing, it may result in the black centres exhibited by sherds of open-fired vessels (Fig. 69) (see **open firing**). If **sintering** occurs, particularly in kiln-fired wares, before it has been completely removed, **black coring** and **bloating** may result.

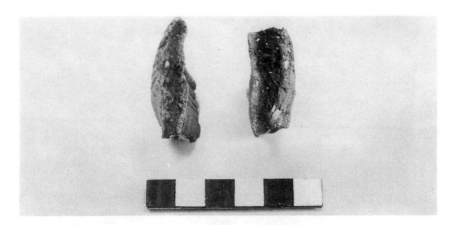

Fig. 69 Black-centred sherds produced in open firings. The sherd on the left is from a food vessel and the one on the right is from an experimental firing. In both cases, the firing time has been too short to allow for total burning of the carbonaceous matter in the clay and it has only been charred, resulting in the characteristic black centre. Scale in centimetres.

Carination
A sharp change in direction or ridge in the profile of a pot, often forming a shoulder. In hand-made vessels, such sharp changes of direction are often the result of the method of manufacture, in particular, at the junction between two rings of clay. As such, they provide weak spots in the vessel wall which are likely positions for breakage to occur. Carinations are a distinctive feature of pots in the **Grimston–Lyles Hill** Series (Fig. 127) and **later neolithic, impressed wares** and persist into pottery of the **food-vessel** (Fig. 114) tradition, some of which vessels may be multi-carinated. A carination is a distinctive visual feature but is not indicative of date, occurring, as it does, on many of the angular-profiled fine wares of the Iron Age (see, for example, the **Darmsden–Linton** style (Fig. 97:1-3).

Cauldron pots (Fig. 70)
Large round-based pots from the upper Thames area, dating to the seventh and sixth centuries BC and thought to be derived from sheet-bronze prototypes (Harding 1972; 1974, 139-40). The rim is usually everted and has an internal **bevel** and it is also usually just less than the maximum diameter of the vessel. The vessels are usually undecorated save for **fingertip impressions** on the rim.

Cavetto zone (Fig. 115:2, 3)
Sharp concavity encircling the body of a vessel. The term is also used to

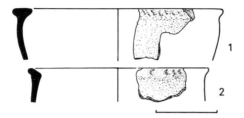

Fig. 70   Cauldron pots. 1, Dorchester on Thames, Oxon; 2, Blewburton Hill, Berks. After Harding 1974. Scale = 10 cm.

describe a deep but narrow neck, especially on later **Peterborough wares** (Fig. 180). Cavetto zones are frequently found between multiple **carinations,** particularly on **food vessels** (Fig. 114), **collared urns** (Fig. 79) and related pottery. The term is descriptive and is not indicative of date, though it is most commonly used when describing pottery of the third and second millennia (Gibson 1986*a*, 9).

Ceramic change
The point at which clay becomes ceramic. It is brought about by the removal of the hydroxyl groups from the chemically combined water in the clay molecules. The point at which this occurs varies according to the type of clay mineral involved but is generally considered to take place at 550°-600°C; afterwards, the clay is fired and will not regain **plasticity** when in contact with water.

Chinnor style (Fig. 71)
Fine-ware bowls with **carinations** and everted rims. They are plain or decorated with simple **fingertip impressions** or **incised** filled triangles or arcs. Harding (1974) has suggested that they may be the work of a single, highly skilled potter or pottery centre. See **Chinnor–Wandlebury group.**

Chinnor–Wandlebury group (Fig. 71)
Style of pottery of the fifth to third centuries BC, identified by Cunliffe (1974, 39) and occurring from the Chilterns to the edge of the Fens and southwards to the Berkshire Downs and the Thames Valley.

  Shouldered bowls with flaring rims (often the maximum diameter of the vessel) and simple, geometric, **incised** decoration characterize the style; occasionally **rosette** stamps were also used. Some bowls were in a black, **burnished** fabric with pronounced **foot rings** and with scratched zig-zag patterns made after the vessel was fired. Coarse wares also have shouldered forms but are decorated on the rim with **fingertip impressions.**

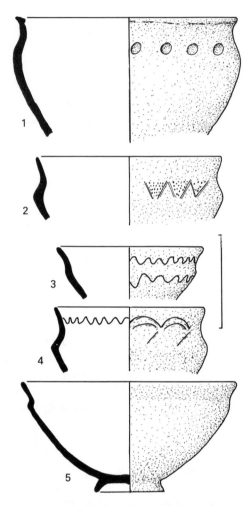

Fig. 71   Chinnor-Wandlebury group, as identified by Cunliffe. 1, 2, 4, Chinnor, Oxon.; 3, Great Wymondley, Herts.; 5, Wandlebury, Cambs. After Cunliffe 1974. Scale = 10 cm.

Cinerary urn

A large vessel used to hold a cremation burial. The term is not indicative of date but is generally used to describe sepulchral vessels of the second millennium, such as **collared urns**, **biconical urns**, **food vessel urns**, or urns of the **Deverel–Rimbury** complex and related regional styles. The term is now rather antiquated and is generally abandoned in favour of the more specific vessel names, such as those listed above.

Clacton style
Sub-style of **grooved ware** (Fig. 131).

Clamp
A structure used for firing bricks, in which the raw bricks are stacked on the ground surface, often with fuel in between them. The pile of bricks may be enclosed within an outer wall or covered with a thin coating of clay. (See Peacock 1982, 15-7, for fuller descriptions and illustrations of contemporary brick clamps.) The term should *not* be used to refer to pot firing techniques, as it is not strictly synonymous with **open firing**. Unfortunately, it is a term widely used in Britain and has become established in the literature (for example, Swan 1984, Elsdon 1989).

Clay
The American Ceramic Society has defined clay as 'a fine-grained rock which, when suitably crushed and pulverized, becomes plastic when wet, leather-hard when dried and on firing is converted to a permanent rock-like mass'.

In general, clay is considered to be hydrated aluminium silicate and can be represented by the general formula $Al_2O_3 2SiO_2 2H_2O$. (This is the formula for kaolinite, one of the purest clay minerals; others, which contain more impurities, have more complicated formulae.)

Clays are formed by the breakdown of feldspathic rocks, particularly granites, diorites and basalts. Two principal processes are concerned. When hypogenic or pneumatolytic action is involved, the feldspars are subjected to chemical processes from within the earth and decompose to form kaolinite (Cardew 1977, 14 ff.; Grimshaw 1971, 39-43). With epigenic action, the breakdown is primarily a physical, rather than chemical, process, involving the action of agencies such as air, water, wind and glaciers, and occurs on the earth's surface.

Two main clay types are generally recognized, **residual** (also called primary) and **sedimentary** (also called secondary). These terms are the geological classifications and are more accurate for archaeological purposes than the potter's terminology of earthenware, stoneware and terracotta.

Clay minerals
There are seven main families of clay minerals, but of these only the kaolinites, smectites and illites are of importance to archaeologists. Many clay minerals are hexagonal plates. They are extremely small, frequently measuring only Angström units in size, and usually cannot be identified using an optical microscope. Their size and platey nature allow the adsorption of water between the particles to create **plasticity**.

Cleavage (Figs. 67, 72, 73, 74, 75)

Cleavage is the ability of a mineral to break along certain planes and is determined by its lattice structure and crystal form. Macroscopically, it may allow a mineral to be identified: crystalline calcite (Fig. 67), for example, as found in **Knapton-** and **Huntcliff-type** wares of the Romano-British period, cleaves readily into small, angular rhombs which can frequently be recognized in sherds (Fig. 72). In **thin section**, cleavage may be a diagnostic optical property allowing the identification of minerals. For example, cross-sections of crystals of calcite reveal the same rhombohedral cleavage, albeit on a microscopic scale (Figs. 73, 74), as do hand specimens, and minerals of the amphibole family show cleavage traces that intersect at angles of 124° and 56° (Fig. 75); this cleavage habit is not exhibited by any other mineral family.

Fig. 72   This experimental bowl contains abundant calcite opening material crushed and added by the maker. Many of the fragments visible are rhombohedra. The outside surface of the vessel has exfoliated as a result of lime blowing.

Fig. 73 The characteristic cleavage of calcite can also be seen in thin section. The thin lines criss-crossing the crystals are the cleavage traces; many of them intersect, so that they form rhombs similar to those revealed macroscopically in Figs. 67 and 72. PPL, × 45.

Fig. 74 Typical rhombs of calcite in a thin section of an experimental pot. The shape and internal cleavage traces should be noted. XPL, × 35.

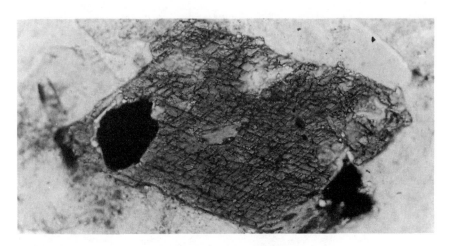

Fig. 75   Cleavage traces in an amphibole, intersecting at angles of 124° and 56°. The shape of the crystal is also characteristic. PPL, × 150.

Clettraval ware (Fig. 76)
Late pre-Roman iron age pottery from the north-west of Scotland, characterized by **globular jars** with everted rims with **fingertip impressions** on horizontal **cordons** which are situated on the point of maximum diameter.

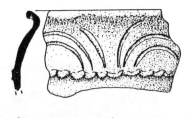

Fig. 76   Clettraval ware from the type site. After MacKie 1971. Scale = 10 cm.

Above this device, the vessels may have **incised decoration** in the form of concentric semi-circles. McKie (1971; 1974) considered this pottery to be derived from Wessex imports, but this has been contested by Ralston (Simpson and Megaw 1979, 472-3).

Clickhimin (Fig. 77)
The site at Clickhimin could best give its name to the sequence of Shetland pottery from the eighth century BC until the eighth century AD (Hamilton 1968).

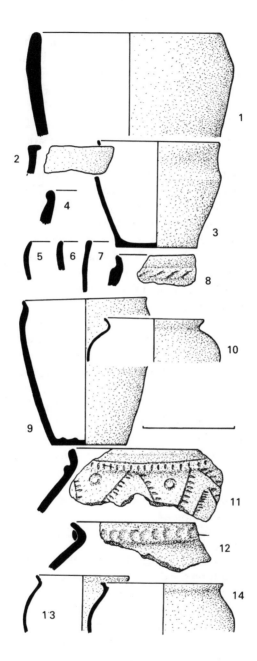

Fig. 77   The Clickhimin sequence from the type site. 1, Late Bronze Age; 2-7, Early Iron Age; 8-10, Iron Age; 11-12, Broch period; 13-14, Wheelhouse period. After Hamilton 1968. Scale = 10 cm. Nos. 9, 13 and 14 at half printed scale.

Phase I, 700-500 BC, consists of coarse **barrel urns** whose **fabric** is filled with abundant steatite fragments, many of which break through vessel surfaces. The rim forms are rounded or slightly pointed (Fig. 77:1).

Phase II, 500-400 BC, is represented by two classes of vessel. Class I consists of **bucket urn** and barrel urn shapes (Fig. 77:2 & 3) with abundant steatite **inclusions**. Class II consists of finer vessels with sharp **carinations** and everted rims (Fig. 77:4). Fine, bucket-shaped vessels are also present (Fig. 77:5-7).

Phase III, 400 to 1st C. BC, is represented by Hallstatt-influenced jars with high and sharp **carinations** and with everted rims (Fig. 77:9). More **globular** forms are also present (Fig. 43:10), as may be simply decorated vessels with plain or decorated **cordons** in the neck (Fig. 77:8).

Phase IV, 1st C. BC to 2nd C. AD, is associated with the building of a broch at the site. This pottery consists of **closed vessels** with distinct cordons and high shoulders in a hard well-fired fabric. They belong to the same tradition as the Phase II pottery but are more highly decorated (Fig. 77:11 & 12) with slashed cordons, **incised decoration**, often taking the form of herring-bone, and fringed, pendant triangles similar to **Vaul ware**. Neck cordons may be slashed, wavy or carry **fingertip impressions**. Internally, rims may have **fluting** or incision.

Phase V, 2nd C. AD to AD 800, pots are in a fine, hard and well-fired fabric with a range of forms similar to the preceding period but with a tendency towards more globular forms with less flaring rims (Fig. 77:13 & 14). Fluted rims are still present and decorated pots are also more common. Curvilinear and triangular, grooved designs are found as well as circular impressions and filled chevrons. The use of steatite fragments as **fillers** continues.

Closed vessel
A vessel in which parts of the body are of greater diameter than the rim. Amphorae are typical examples.

Coiling or coil-building
Method of pot manufacture utilizing long ropes of clay. The potter winds the ropes of clay round to form the desired vessel shape or part thereof and then joins them together by smoothing the internal and external surfaces. This basic shape is then usually further refined by thinning and expansion of the walls. Excellent illustrations of this technique are provided by Litto (1976, 158-9). It is generally almost impossible to distinguish it from **ring-building** but evidence from sherds suggests that most European prehistoric pottery was constructed by the latter method. See also **join void**.

Collared urns (Figs. 78, 79)
Bipartite or tripartite vessels of the earlier second millennium, generally used

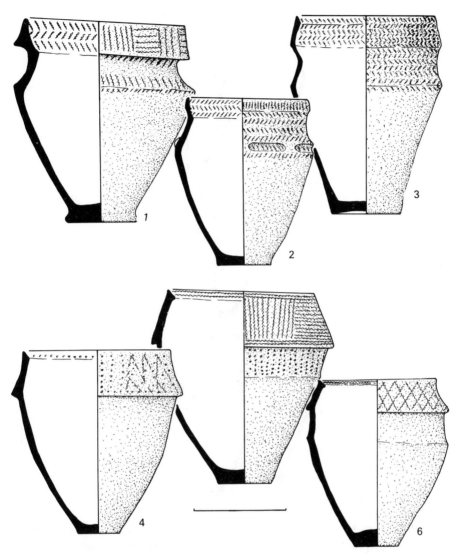

Fig. 78 Collared urns. 1-3. from Longworth's Primary Series; 4-6, from the Secondary Series; 1, Thixendale, North Yorks; 2, Pentraeth, Gwynedd; 3, Sutton, Suffolk; 4, Guisborough, Cleveland; 5, Cold Kirby, North Yorks; 6, Milngavie, Strathclyde. After Longworth 1984. Scale = 20 cm.

as containers for cremation burials and also known as **Overhanging Rim Urns**, though this term is rather old-fashioned. Collared urns are distributed over the whole of Britain and into Ireland, though there is a thinning out of the distribution in northern Scotland. They are directly evolved from **Peterborough ware** and particularly from the **Fengate style**, which has a heavy collared rim on top of a body with straight but splayed sides. **Beaker**

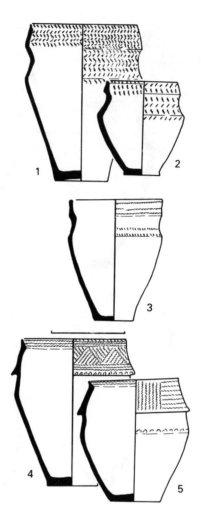

Fig. 79   Collared urns. Early (1, 2), Middle (3) and Late (4, 5) styles, as identified by Burgess. 1, Sutton, Suffolk; 2, Northants; 3, Hengistbury Head, Dorset; 4, Stockbridge, Hants; 5, Winterslow, Wilts. After Longworth 1984. Scale = 20 cm.

influence can also be seen, particularly in the use of **comb impressions** and geometric motifs, but this has been overstated by some writers. The most distinctive feature of a collared urn is a heavy rim or collar, which may be vertical or slightly inverted. This may carry **incised** or **impressed decoration**, particularly **herring-bone**, encircling lines, **hurdling** or chevron decoration. In the case of bipartite urns, this collar sits on top of a straight-sided or slightly bowed body narrowing to a small, flat base. Decoration may extend for a short way below the collar, but this is rare. In the case of tripartite urns, the collar sits on a concave neck or **cavetto zone**, which may or may not be decorated, and this in turn leads down to a straight-sided but narrowing body, as described above. Once again, decoration may extend below this cavetto zone, but this is rare. Collared urns vary in size from around 10 cm to over 50 cm high and are generally taller than they are broad, though wide-mouthed variants do occur.

Longworth (1984) has recently divided collared urns into a primary (Fig. 78:1-3) and a Secondary (Fig. 78:4-6) Series by isolating a number of traits. In simplified form, these traits are as follows:

PRIMARY SERIES
Internal rim moulding
Decoration on or below the shoulder
Straight or externally convex collar
Use of whipped-cord decoration

SECONDARY SERIES
Repetitive decorative motifs
Simple rim
Internal decoration

An urn in the Primary Series will show two or more of these traits, while an urn of the Secondary Series will exhibit one or none. In addition, the use of **whipped cord** and herring-bone decoration declines in the Secondary Series while filled triangles, cross-hatching and hurdling motifs are favoured. Internal decoration and external decoration below the collar are also abandoned in the Secondary Series. The Secondary Series can also be subdivided into the north-western and south-eastern styles, the former marked by an angled collar with an equally deep neck, the shoulder frequently being represented by a **raised cordon**. Incision is also common on vessels of this style. The south-eastern style consists of comb-decorated vessels, often with twisted cord crescents on the shoulder, as well as bipartite vessels as described above.

This is a condensed summary of Longworth's scheme. It has recently been challenged by Burgess (1986) who, using Longworth's corpus, isolates early and late traits as follows:

EARLY LATE
Internal decoration below rim
Repetitive, short, line motifs on
   collar and neck
Decoration below the shoulder
Whipped-cord decoration
Shoulder grooves
External moulding
Narrow collar

LATE
Bold decoration
No decoration below collar
Cord crescents on the shoulder
Deep collar
Pinched-out collar base
Angular profile
Smooth, continuous, internal profile
Bipartite form
Narrow base (<30% of max. diameter)
Maximum diameter equal or greater than
   vessel height

On this basis, Burgess isolates early (Fig. 79:1 & 2), middle (Fig. 79:3) and late (Fig. 79:4 & 5) vessel types. There is still, however, a great degree of expected overlap between early and late urns, and a number of vessels display both early and late traits. See also **Anglesey neck** (Fig. 78:2) and **Pennine urn.**

Comb impressions (Figs. 80, 81, 82)
Comb or combed decoration is formed by impressing a toothed implement into soft or, more usually, **leather-hard** clay, resulting in a short line of small impressions (Figs. 80, 81). These short lengths can then be joined together by re-application of the comb to make longer and/or encircling lines (Fig. 82).

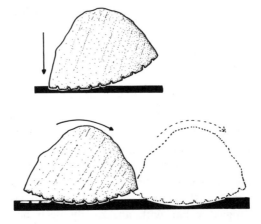

Fig. 80 Comb impressions, both short and elongated, made by the same comb pressed into the clay at different angles. After Ward 1902. Not to scale.

Fig. 81 Comb impressions on a beaker from Callis Wold, Humberside. The individual comb lengths are clearly visible. Sherd width 5 cm.

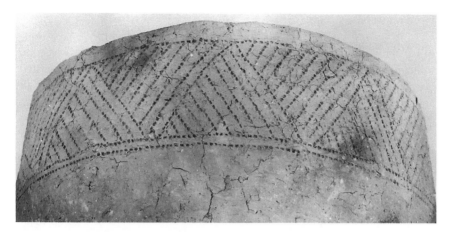

Fig. 82 Comb impressions on the experimental vessel also shown in Fig. 28.

The latter are commonly found on **beakers**, either defining zones of decoration or completely covering the whole vessel, when the type is referred to as **All-over combed** (Clarke 1970). Impressions of both rectangular- and round-toothed combs are found widely on pottery of the second millennium and combs were also used on Iron Age ceramics. Actual combs for decorating pottery have been found at Northton, Isle of Harris (Simpson 1976, 230), Gwithian, Cornwall (Megaw 1976, 62), Bishops Cannings Down and Dean Bottom, Wiltshire (Gingell 1980, 217), all of which probably date to the second millennium (Fig. 19).

Concertina bowls (Fig. 83)
A type of bowl found in Surrey, particularly at Hawk's Hill, named after its multiple carinations, which result in a sharply multi-angled form.
    See also Harding 1974; Hastings 1965.

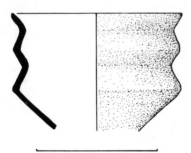

Fig. 83 Concertina bowl from Hawk's Hill, Surrey. After Harding 1974. Scale = 10 cm.

Cord impressions (Figs. 78, 84, 85, 86)

Cord decoration is perhaps the most commonly used decorative technique other than **incised decoration** on pottery of the third and early second millennia. Cord is a generic term used to describe any collection of twisted fibres but, in reality, impressions labelled 'twisted cord' vary greatly from soft and blurred, as if wool has been used, to very thin, sharp and well-defined, suggesting the use of sinew. Sometimes impressions of individual fibres can be seen (Gibson 1986a, 55).

Simple twisted cord impressions can take the form of short lengths (Fig. 78: 1, 5, 6) or encircling lines (Fig. 84). In the case of **Beaker** pottery, the whole vessel may be covered with encircling lines of twisted-cord impressions and the style known as **All Over Cord** (Clarke 1970).

Twisted cord wrapped around itself or another core is termed **whipped cord** and similarly appears in a variety of thicknesses, lengths and degrees of

Fig. 84   Twisted cord decoration on a sherd from Brackmont Mill Farm, Fife. Sherd size 3.5 cm.

Fig. 85   Whipped cord maggot impressions on a sherd from Risby Warren, Lincs. Sherd size 5 cm.

Fig. 86 Very fine whipped cord impressions on the inside of the rim of a food vessel from Seamer Moor, Yorks. Scale = 10 cm.

definition (Figs. 85, 86). Short lengths of whipped cord are usually called '**maggots**' (Fig. 85) after their short, segmented appearance and they occur frequently on **Peterborough ware**, **food vessels** and early **collared urns** but were rarely used after *c.* 1400 bc.

Double cord is found on some pottery of the **Trevisker** tradition and is simply, as the name suggests, two lines of cord placed close together to form a double line. It is a technique that is quite rare outside the south-western peninsula (ApSimon 1957-8).

Plaited cord impressions are also found, particularly on pottery of the early second millennium in the south-west, such as the Trevisker style, and appear almost as a narrow **herring-bone motif**. Plaited cord in Britain is, however, comparatively rare.

Cordon

A device, usually either **raised** from or **applied** to the body of the vessel, but occasionally **incised** and flush with the surface, used to break the body of the pot into distinct sections . The cordons may be decorated with incisions at right angles to or diagonally on the line of the cordon; these are often called **slashed cordons**. On **grooved ware** (Fig. 131), cordons may be multi-directional (Wainwright and Longworth 1971), though normally they occur horizontally on other ceramics.

Cordoned bowls and jars

Iron age vessels decorated with multiple, horizontal cordons dividing the vessel into distinct segments. They are particularly common amongst the **haematite-coated wares** and **Belgic wares** but are not restricted to these. See also **cordoned urn**.

Cordoned urns (Fig. 87)

Large vessels with **raised** or **applied cordons** running horizontally on the body of the vessel. On iron age ceramics, the term is used simply descriptively (Birchall 1965; Harding 1974, 164-6) but in second millennium contexts it refers to a specific ceramic type (Fig. 87).

The bronze age cordoned urn is either a **barrel-shaped** or, less frequently, **bucket-shaped** urn with at least one cordon situated in the upper third of the vessel. In the case of vessels with two cordons, the second is usually placed a short distance below the first but still within the upper third of the pot (Gibson 1986a, 48; Savory 1980). These cordons are either raised or applied and are usually undecorated. Cordoned urns may resemble **collared urns**, to which they are closely related, single cordoned urns resembling bipartite and double resembling tripartite collared urns.

Cordoned urns are generally restricted to the highland zone, and particularly to northern Britain. They are associated with cremation burials but are also found on domestic sites. Decoration may be either impressed or incised, and there is some use of **twisted cord** impressions; a similar range of motifs to that used on collared urns is found. Multiple cordons are also

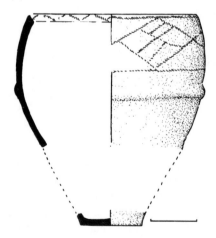

Fig. 87   Cordoned urn from Moralee Farm, Northumberland. Scale = 10 cm.

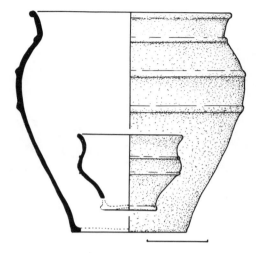

Fig. 88 Cordoned ware of the later Iron Age from Caloggas, Cornwall. After Threipland 1957. Scale = 10 cm.

found, occasionally decorated with applied roundels or rosettes, but vessels of this type are generally rare and are related to **food vessel urns**.

See also Burgess 1980; ApSimon 1972.

Cordoned ware (Fig. 88)
A general term used to describe **wheel-thrown** jars, bowls and *tazza*-like vessels decorated with horizontal **cordons**. They are found in the south-west of the country and date from the late first century BC and later (Raleigh Radford 1951). The forms are rounded and have flaring necks. The vessels are often grey in colour and are in a fine, well-made **fabric**. The pottery bears a strong resemblance to that from Brittany and north-western France and probably represents contacts between the two countries. See also **cordoned bowls and jars**.

Corky fabric (Fig. 89)
A term used to describe pottery from which **inclusions** have either burned out or, more commonly, been dissolved out during burial, leaving a pitted and vesicular fabric. Pottery with **calcareous** or organic inclusions is particularly susceptible to this degeneration, the former being adversely affected by acidic soils. The term is frequently used to describe pottery in the **Grimston–Lyles Hill** or **Mildenhall** traditions. It should be noted that, in the case of calcareous inclusions, this effect is created by burial conditions and not by firing: calcareous inclusions cannot be burned out in the firing process but may frequently be attacked and dissolved out by an acidic burial environment.

Fig. 89   Sherds of Huntcliff pottery from which the calcareous inclusions have been leached during burial. Scale in centimetres.

Cornish urns (Fig. 90)

Large **biconical urns** from the south-western peninsula which are decorated on the upper third with impressed techniques, such as **twisted** or **plaited cord,** occurring in chevron or herring-bone motifs (ApSimon 1957-8, 1972; ApSimon in Pollard and Russell 1969). These urns also often have handles or **lugs** on the side of the vessel, sometimes spanning a shoulder **cavetto zone.** These are sometimes called ribbon-handled urns and are usually found with cremations.

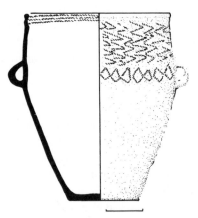

Fig. 90   Cornish handled urn from Tregaseal, Cornwall. After Patchett 1944. Scale = 10 cm.

Corrugated jars or urns (Fig. 42:2)
Large, open-mouthed vessels of the **Aylesford-Swarling** complex named after their multiple but slack, horizontal **carinations** covering the entire body of the vessel and resembling strongly the corrugated iron after which modern researchers have named them (Birchall 1965).

Countersunk handles (Fig. 102:1)
Handles found on late iron age pottery, particularly **Durotrigian ware**, which are flush with the profile of the vessel, being set into depressions in the actual wall of the pot.

Covesea ware (Fig. 91)
A north-eastern Scottish variant of what is generally termed **flat-rimmed ware**, which Benton (1931) suggested was based on Continental prototypes from the lower Rhine area. The fabric is usually fine with abundant, finely crushed **fillers**, which give it a smooth but sandy texture. The surface of the pot may have a **slip**. Rim forms may be bevelled, rounded or flat.

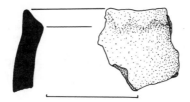

Fig. 91   Barrel urn rim of Covesea ware from Tentsmuir. After Longworth 1967. Scale = 5 cm.

Cranbourne Chase style (Fig. 98)
Local style in the **Deverel–Rimbury** tradition.

Croft Ambrey-Bredon Hill style (Fig. 92)
A style of pots, as identified by Cunliffe (1974, 43), in the **saucepan pot** tradition and centred on the Cotswold and Herefordshire region in the fifth to fourth centuries BC. They are decorated below the rim with bands of **duck-stamp** impressions or with **incised** linear decoration. Peacock (1968, 419) has shown by study of the **inclusions** that these pots were made in three areas in the Malvern region.

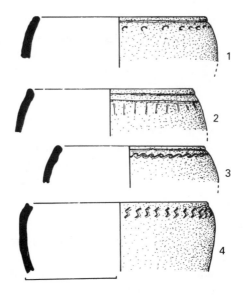

Fig. 92   Croft Ambrey-Bredon Hill style pottery, as identified by Cunliffe. 1-3, Sutton Walls, Hereford; 4, Cleve Hill, Glos. After Cunliffe 1974. Scale = 10 cm.

Crowsfoot impressions (Fig. 93)

A term used to describe paired **fingernail** impressions which produce a splayed V effect. The technique is not related to **bird bone impressions**.

Dales ware (Figs. 94, 95)

Coarse pottery of the third and fourth centuries, probably produced in northern Lincolnshire (Loughlin 1977, 102). The vessels are uniform in shape and are characterized by their 'high, outspringing rim with thickened extremity and well developed internal ledging' (Gillam 1951) (Fig. 94). Most appear to have been used for cooking. Although there is evidence on some vessels that the rims were **wheel-thrown**, the vessels are essentially hand-made in a **fabric** containing abundant fragments of shell added by the potters (Fig. 95). They were produced in **open firings**. The ware represents an adaptation by the Romans of the local potting tradition, similar to the way in which they took on **black-burnished wares**. 'Dales ware types' were also produced in the same area; while still intended as cooking pots, these were wheel-thrown in a sandy fabric.

Dane's Graves-Staxton style (Fig. 96)

A group of coarse, thick-based, **bucket-shaped** pots of the third to first centuries BC, as identified by Cunliffe (1974, 47). They are invariably

Fig. 93 Crowsfoot impressions on a sherd from Fengate. Sherd size 9 cm.

undecorated, fairly uneven in their profiles and may or may not have internal rim **bevels**.

Darmsden–Linton group (Fig. 97)
Style of fifth to third century BC pottery identified by Cunliffe (1974, 39) and centred on eastern England from the Thames to the Wash. The style is influenced by Continental, **La Tène** I types and is characterized by bowls made of a black and **burnished fabric** and having a pronounced shoulder and an upright or slightly everted rim. Deep grooves frequently decorate the shoulders; the bases may have **foot rings**. **Shouldered jars** are also present in the assemblage.

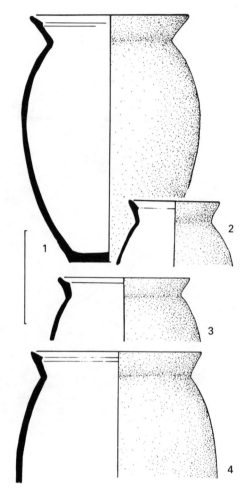

Fig. 94   Dales ware. 1, Doncaster, Yorks; 2-4, Flaxfeet, Yorks. After Loughlin 1977. Scale = 10 cm.

Deverel–Rimbury (Fig. 98)

The name given to a complex series of pottery dating to the second half of the second millennium. It is a southern British tradition but has equivalents in other parts of the country and is characterized by heavy, **barrel-** and **bucket-shaped** urns, as well as smaller and finer, **globular urns**. The barrel urns are decorated with vertical and horizontal **cordons** and with **fingernail** and **fingertip impressions**, often highlighting the cordons and the rim. **Applied** zig-zags may also decorate the upper third of some vessels: barrel urns with these rarer elements and with vertical ribs are termed **South Lodge urns**. The bucket urns are generally in a coarser **fabric** than the barrel urns,

Fig. 95 Photomicrograph of a thin section of Dales ware, showing abundant shell fragments. XPL, × 28.

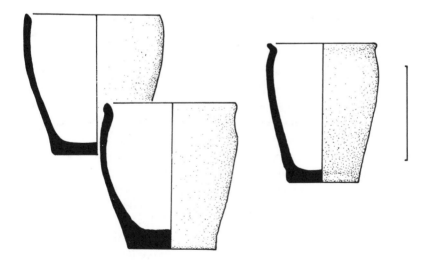

Fig. 96 Barrel-shaped vessels of the Dane's Graves–Staxton group, as identified by Cunliffe. After Brewster 1963. Scale = 10 cm.

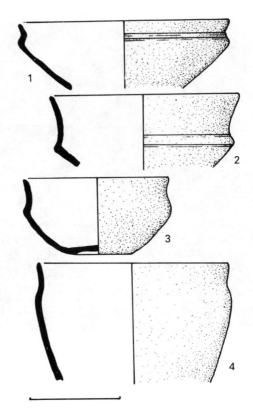

Fig. 97   Pottery of the Darmsden–Linton group, as identified by Cunliffe. 1, Linton, Cambs; 2, Hindersby, Suffolk; 3, Cobham, Surrey; 4, Darmsden, Suffolk. After Cunliffe 1974. Scale = 10 cm.

often with **calcined** flint **fillers**. (Vessels from cemeteries in the East Midlands have been examined in thin section (Allen *et al.* 1987, 213 ff) and shown to contain grog as the main filler; other opening materials present include shell and quartz.) The sides of the vessels are straight and occasionally vertical. The vessels may be decorated with fingertip impressions on the rim and shoulder or on the cordons or base angle. **Lugs** and **horseshoe handles** are also found.

Globular urns may be divided into two main styles:

Class I pots are found in a vesicular fabric and are poorly fired. The decoration consists of lightly **tooled** triangles or filled chevrons above encircling tooled lines. Circular stabs may occur below this, as might lugs.

Class II pots are in a better fabric with smooth or **burnished** surfaces.

Class II globular urns have been subdivided into type II*a*, recognized by five to ten fingertip furrows round the neck and occasionally with **fingernail** decoration, and type II*b*, decorated with a sharp point, so that the ornamentation consists usually of **incised decoration** or occasionally **comb**

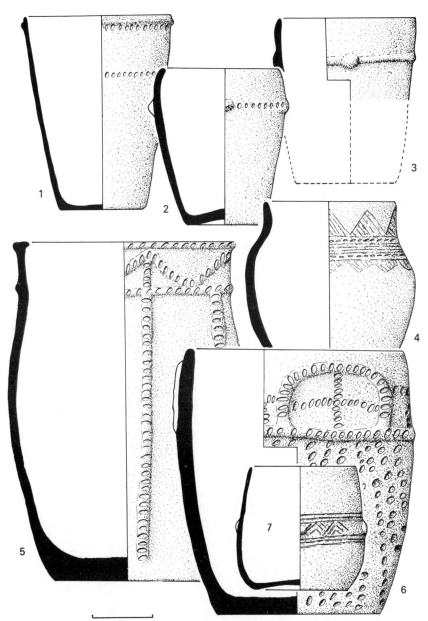

Fig. 98   Pottery from the Deverel-Rimbury tradition. 1, 3, bucket urns; 2, 5, 6, barrel urns; 4, 7, globular urns. 1, Pokesdown, Dorset; 2, Stourfield, Hants; 3, Puddletown Heath, Dorset (all after Calkin 1962); 4, Salisbury, Wilts. (after Langmaid 1978); 5, Bower Chalke, Wilts. (after Annable and Simpson 1964); 6, Ardleigh, Essex (after Burgess 1980); 7, Hill Brow, Hants. (after Calkin 1962). Scale = 10 cm.

impressions, mainly in bands of horizontal lines alternating with filled triangles.

The pots occur both in cremation cemeteries and on settlements and have been divided by Calkin (1962) and by Erith and Longworth (1960) into regional groups:

The South Dorset group is characterized by bucket urns and type II, globular urns.

The Cranborne Chase group is composed of bucket, barrel and type I, globular urns.

The South Downs group is represented mainly by bucket urns with a rather 'baggy' profile and by globular urns with prominent lugs.

The Ardleigh group centres on Suffolk and Essex and is characterized by bucket urns with cordons and abundant fingertip decoration (Fig. 39).

The Deverel–Rimbury pottery has been demonstrated as being derived from the early second millennium pottery styles (Barrett 1976; Barrett *et al.* 1978) and to date between 1400 and 1000 bc.

Diatom analysis (Fig. 99)

A technique whereby the provenance of a clay can be determined by examining the remains of microscopic plants in the **fabric** of pots. These

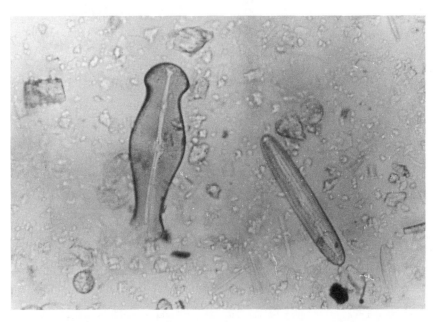

Fig. 99 Diatoms extracted from a clay sample from the River Glen, Milfield Basin. × 650.

plants lived on the surface of the water and, as they died, their valves (or frustules) sank to the bottom of the lake or stream and became incorporated in the sediments, which might later have been used as a potting clay. The frustules of the diatoms are made of silica and are durable, surviving even the potting and firing processes. As a result, they can be found within the fabric of pots made from diatomaceous clay (Gibson 1986b).

The technique was first used extensively in the Netherlands by Jansma, who examined the ratios of salt, brackish and fresh water diatom species in clays and in Protruding Foot Beaker sherds from the coastal areas Netherlands (Jansma 1977). He observed that the local clays contained salt water species, while the potsherds contained fresh water species and therefore concluded that the pottery had been imported to the coast from the areas of fresh water clays in the interior.

Because diatoms are environmentally sensitive, different species and combinations of species live in different conditions; by examining the ratios of different species within a sediment, a diatom 'fingerprint' for a particular clay can be constructed and displayed in a manner similar to a pollen diagram. Fingerprints from local pottery can be matched against this to determine whether or not the local clay source has been utilized in the manufacture of the pottery (Gibson 1986b). The technique is, however, still in its infancy and in need of great refinement. Contamination factors prove the greatest hindrance and it must also be stressed that not all clays, and hence not all pots, need be diatomaceous.

Drag marks (Fig. 100)
Lines and scratches created on the surface of a vessel during **turning**, when the turning tool picks up inclusions from within the clay and drags them along the surface.

Dragonby sequence (Fig. 202)
Pottery from Dragonby in Lincolnshire has been identified by Cunliffe (1974, 46) as a regional style which he termed the **Sleaford–Dragonby style**, but May (1964; 1976, 184-90) has recognized a sequence of pottery from Dragonby which can be described as follows:

Phase 1: Hand-made pottery in a variety of forms and **fabrics**. Angular jars and bowls are present, as are **bucket-shaped** pots and **globular** vessels with upright, elongated necks with **incised** and/or **rouletted** decoration, occasionally accentuated by **burnishing**. The pottery of this phase probably dates from the third century BC.

Phase 2: Vessels exhibit a greater homogeneity of fabric and are rather better made in many cases. Large vessels with **cordons** and **pedestalled bases** are found, as are angular, bipartite jars and bowls. Incised decoration is

Fig. 100 Drag marks created during turning. The smooth surface texture created by turning, visible on the lower part of the vessel, is quite distinct from the untreated, lattice-decorated section above it. Vessel height 16 cm.

common, as are burnished zones. The pottery is probably datable to the first century BC.

Phase 3: This pottery dates to the beginning of the first century AD and consists of locally made, bipartite, shouldered vases and jars. Cordons and burnishing are generally less common than in Phase 2 and in addition there are **Belgic** forms, such as **pedestalled bowls** and **butt beakers**.

Drinking cup

Old-fashioned name for a **beaker** of the second millennium bc, used mainly in the late nineteenth and early twentieth centuries and especially by the barrow diggers, such as Greenwell, Bateman and Thurnham (see above, pp. 8–11.

Drying shrinkage (Figs. 4:2, 129)

All clays shrink as they dry. After a pot has been made, it is left to dry before firing; the **water of plasticity** evaporates from the surfaces of the vessel and the clay particles are gradually brought into contact with one another. The finer the clay (i.e. the smaller the particles), the greater will be the shrinkage on drying. Thin parts of a vessel obviously dry more quickly than thick parts, creating stresses that cause cracks. The drying rate can be made more even and drying shrinkage reduced by the addition of **opening materials**.

Duck-stamped pottery (Fig. 92:4)

Later iron age pottery from the south and west of England, noted for the rounded, S-shaped impressions running round the top of the vessel, immediately below the rim and vaguely resembling swimming ducks (Harding 1974, 91 and 200). Hencken (1938) suggested that these stamps were derived from a duck motif originating in the Aegean and reaching north western Europe via Italy. Peacock (1968; 1969a) traces the British origins of this pottery to the gabbroic outcrops of the Lizard Peninsula, though there is a considerable concentration of this type of pottery in Hereford and Worcester. **Bucket** and bowl forms are the usual vessel types displaying this ornament. See also **Croft Ambrey-Bredon Hill style**.

Dunting (Fig. 101)

Cracking that occurs when a fired body is cooled too quickly. It is thought to be caused by the change in volume of free silica as it cools through the α-β **inversion**, and therefore vessels that contain abundant quartz are most at risk. Typical dunting cracks run vertically down from the rim and horizontally around the vessel.

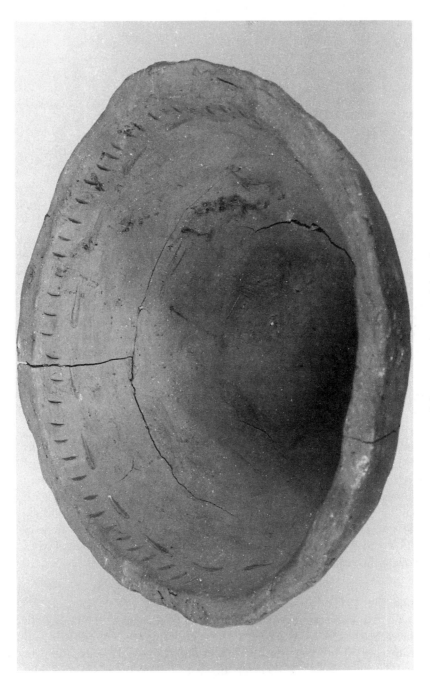

Fig. 101 Typical dunting cracks. Vessel diameter 13.5 cm.

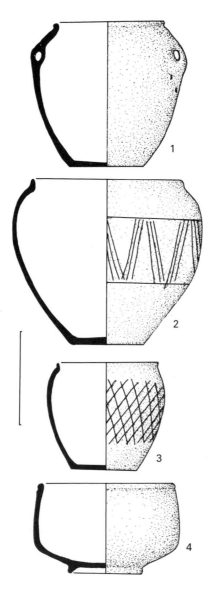

Fig. 102   Durotrigian ware from Hengistbury Head, Dorset. After Cunliffe 1974.
Scale = 10 cm.

Durotrigian ware (Fig. 102)
A well-made pottery from the area of the Durotriges, the iron age tribe of the
Dorset area. It was hand-made in a sandy **fabric** (similar to that illustrated in
Fig. 10) and **open-fired**. The materials (Williams 1977) and methods of its

production were adapted by the Romans for the manufacture of **black-burnished 1 wares**.

Durrington Walls style (Fig. 131:2)
Sub-style of **grooved ware**.

East Anglian ware
Style of decorated neolithic pottery identified by Piggott (1954, 72-4) and now termed **Mildenhall ware** (Fig. 165).

Ebbsfleet ware (Fig. 180:1)
Stylistically earliest style of **Peterborough ware** in the **later neolithic, impressed ware** tradition.

Encrusted urns (Figs. 103, 115:4)
The name is now rather old-fashioned, as it is recognized that this type of vessel is a variant of the **food vessel urn** associated mainly with cremation burials and characterized by abundant **plastic decoration**, from which Fox (1927) derived its name.

Fig. 103   Food vessel urn with plastic decoration ('encrusted urn') from Penllwyn, Cardigan. After Fox 1927. Scale = 10 cm.

Enlarged food vessel (Fig. 115)
See **food vessel urn**.

Fabric
The term used to describe the clay and inclusions of a vessel. Synonymous with **body** and paste (U.S.).

Fig. 104   False relief on sherds from Dalmore, Lewis.

False relief (Figs. 104, 114:3)
A technique of decoration involving the impressing of an alternating and opposing, triangular point into plastic clay to produce a raised zig-zag. The technique is called false relief, as it is a result of **impressed decoration** rather than **raised** or **applied decoration**. It is commonly used on **food vessel** pottery, and on northern and western styles in particular.
  See Burgess 1974; 1980, 84 ff; Simpson 1965; Gibson 1976.

False rim (Figs. 15, 105)
A term formerly used by archaeologists to describe sherds which had broken along the junction between the rings or straps of clay from which the pots were constructed and which revealed rounded edges that resembled rims. See also **join void**.

Fenestrated cups
See **perforated wall cups**.

Fengate style (Fig. 180:3)
Final stylistic component of **Peterborough ware**.

Fengate–Cromer group (Fig. 106)
A decorated style, identified by Cunliffe (1974, 40-1), centring on the Fens

Fig. 105 'False rims' on sherds from Dalmore, Lewis.

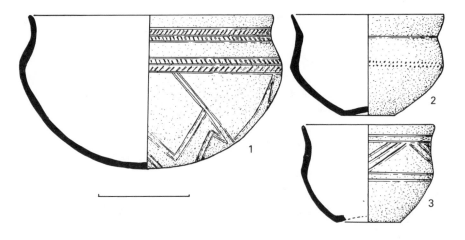

Fig. 106 Pottery of the Fengate–Cromer style as identified by Cunliffe. 1, Cromer, Norfolk; 2, 3, Fengate, Northants. After Cunliffe 1974. Scale = 10 cm.

and Norfolk and datable to the fifth to third centuries BC. **Globular** bowls with flaring rims are present in the assemblages and they are decorated with encircling grooved lines above and below the point of maximum diameter. Large jars with everted rims are also present. Shoulders and rims are decorated with **fingertip impressions** and, occasionally, neck **cordons**.

See Hawkes and Fell 1945.

Filler (Figs. 212, 213, 215, 216, 217)
Inclusions deliberately added to the clay by the potter. See also **opening materials** and **temper**.

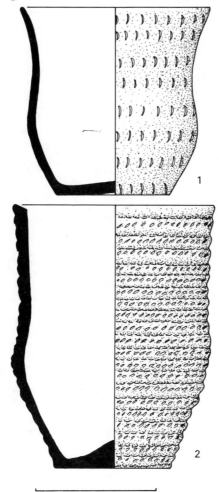

Fig. 107   Fingernail-impressed beakers. 1, Bury St Edmunds, Suffolk; 2, East Tuddenham, Norfolk. After Clarke 1970. Scale = 10 cm.

Fingernail impressions (Figs. 93, 107, 108)
A common decorative technique. The name is quite self-explanatory but is included here as the term is frequently misused. These impressions are made by pushing a fingernail into the wet clay and may either be crescentic or lanceolate, the latter produced by a slight movement of the finger. Both of

Fig. 108   Fingernail impressions and incised lines on beaker sherds from
Northton, Harris. Scale in centimetres.

these may be arranged randomly or in often complex, geometric patterns;
they may be arranged singly or in pairs.

Paired, fingernail impressions often produce a splayed-V shape, known by
the ungainly term of **crowsfoot impressions** (Fig. 93), and may be arranged
randomly or in vertical or horizontal rows forming **herring-bone** (Fig. 189)
motifs. Such regular pairing may also have the effect of raising horizontal or
vertical **cordons**; this may often have been intentional.

Fingernail impressions may also be used to accentuate features of a pot,
particularly cordons, but also rims and **carinations**. Accidental fingernail

impressions can also be seen on some vessels as a result of the forming of the pot or the application of decoration.

Some fingernail-impressed pottery is often described simply as rusticated, but this fails to acknowledge the full meaning of the term: fingernail impressions are simply one form of **rustication** and the terms are not interchangeable. The description of a pot as 'fingernail-rusticated' would in this case be the accurate and only acceptable description.

Fingernail decoration is found on pottery of all periods but particularly on Neolithic and Bronze Age pottery. The profusion, complexity and quality of fingernail decoration on large **beaker** vessels indicate that this decorative technique can be far from being as crude as its name suggests (for example, Fig. 107:2).

See also Barrett *et al.* 1978; Brewster 1963; Clarke 1970; Cunliffe 1974; Gibson 1982 and 1986*a*; Harding 1974; Robertson-Mackay 1961.

Fingertip impressions (Figs. 43:5, 98:5, 6)
Like **fingernail impressions**, this term is self-explanatory yet often misused. They are used in the same way as fingernail impressions, but in this case appear as large, oval depressions. They may be paired, sometimes resulting in raised **cordons**, or may also be arranged in complex patterns. The term should not be confused with **rustication**, a surface treatment of which fingertip impressions are just one form. 'Fingertip rustication' would be the correct usage.

Fingertip impressions are found on pottery of all periods, but profuse fingertip decoration is most common on pottery of the second millennium. On later pottery, it is most often used to accentuate formal features of a pot, such as the rim, base angle, cordon (Fig. 43:5) or **carination**. For references and further reading, see **fingernail impressions**.

Fire clouds (Figs. 28, 109, 110)
Black patches on the surfaces of vessels produced in **open firings**. They are characteristic of this type of firing and are the result of the deposition of carbon on the pot; they frequently occur where the pot has been in direct contact with the smoky part of the flame or with incompletely burnt fuel.

Fire spalls (Figs. 5, 25, 111, 112)
The round flakes of clay that are blown out of the walls of clay vessels when the temperature is raised too quickly during the early stages of firing. Corresponding scars are left on the surfaces of vessels. Such **wasters** occur in all types of firings. See also **open firing** and **water smoking stage**.

Fig. 109   Fire clouds on an open fired vessel from Caprivi, Namibia. Scale in centimetres.

Firing
The process whereby clay is converted to ceramic. A temperature in excess of 550°C is required to drive off chemically combined water from the clay molecules and make them ceramic (i.e. go through the **ceramic change**); when this process has occurred, the clay will be hard and will not become plastic when in contact with water. See **plasticity**.

Flat-rimmed ware (Fig. 113)
A term originally devised to describe the **bucket-**, **barrel-** and flowerpot-shaped vessels of early first millennium northern Britain, of which a

Fig. 110   Fire clouds on an open-fired vessel from Kavango, Namibia.

flattened rim was the only distinctive feature (Feacham 1961; Jobey 1976). The term is no longer suitable as a chronological indicator, as third millennium, 'flat-rimmed ware' is also known from that region. This pottery is usually fairly coarse. It is typically found on settlement sites of the late second and first millennia, particularly north of the Tees but also extending into Yorkshire. Long recognized as inadequate, the term has resisted abandonment due to the otherwise generally featureless nature of the pottery.

Fluting (Fig. 60)
Decorative technique involving covering the surface of a pot with shallow

Fig. 111   An open fired vessel from Kavango, Namibia, showing fire-spalling and a small fire cloud.

grooves, executed when the clay is in a plastic state. It is found on pottery of all periods and is not a chronological indicator, occurring on **Boghead bowls** (Fig. 60) of the early Neolithic and domestic pottery of the late first millennium, as, for example, on **flat-rimmed ware** at Green Knowe in Peebleshire (Feacham 1961; Jobey 1976).

Food vessel (Fig. 114)
As **beakers** were termed **drinking vessels** because of their fine fabric and generally simple rims, food vessels were named as a result of their coarser **fabric** and generally thickened or elaborated rims, considered unsuitable for drinking from. Food vessels are frequently found in graves yet are very different in character from beakers: a term was accordingly devised to

Fig. 112 Fire spalling on a bowl fired in an experimental bonfire. Vessel height 9.5 cm.

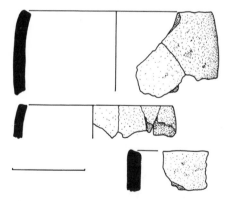

Fig. 113 Flat rimmed ware from Green Knowe, Peebles. After Jobey 1978. Scale = 10 cm.

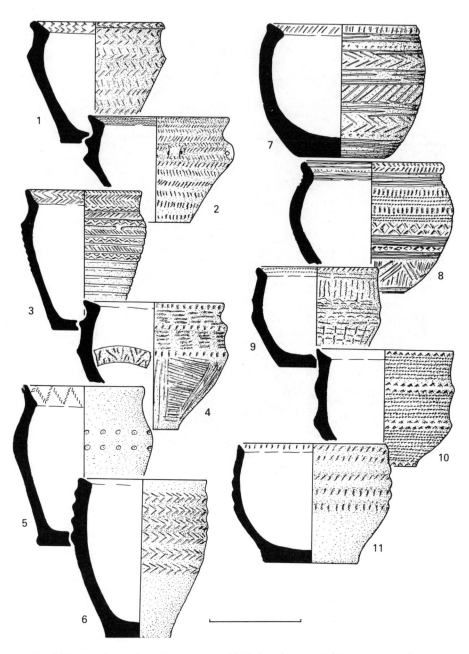

Fig. 114 Food vessels, 1-6, vase types; 7-11, bowl types. 1, bipartite vase, Great Tosson, Northumberland; 2, Yorkshire vase, Denton Hall, Northumberland; 3, Irish vase, Craigbirnoch, Wigtownshire; 4, tripartite vase, Haugh Head, Northumberland; 5, southern bipartite vase, Belle Toute, Sussex; 6, ridged vase, Knocken, Lanarkshire; 7, globular British bowl, Ford, Northumberland; 8,

express a relation in function, in terms of sepulchral accessory, while differentiating form and fabric. Food vessels are found with individual inhumations or cremations, either in flat graves or beneath round barrows, and either as a primary or secondary interment. Food vessel burials may be found in a context secondary to a beaker, but the reverse has not yet been encountered. Food vessels are also, however, found in domestic contexts, often in surprisingly large quantities, at sites such as Dalmore on Lewis or Ardnave on Islay (Ritchie and Welfare 1983).

Food vessels are directly related to the **later neolithic impressed wares** and particularly to the northern variants such as the **Meldon Bridge** (Fig. 163) or **Rudston** (Fig. 196) styles, with which they have stark similarities of form and decoration, particularly **impressed decoration**, such as **twisted** or **whipped cord** (Gibson 1984, 81; 1986a, 35-40). Like the Rudston style, and possibly like the Meldon Bridge style, food vessels have flat bases in proportion to the maximum diameters and heights of the vessels. They often retain a **cavetto zone**, which regresses into a deeper neck, more in keeping with the **Grimston-Lyles Hill** (Fig. 127) Series, and the heavy, moulded rim of the **Peterborough** tradition.

Food vessels are often richly decorated and overlap in their form and decoration with other second-millennium types, such as **collared urns, accessory vessels** and, of course, **food vessel urns,** all of which have a broadly common ancestry. They range from roughly 10 to 20 cm in height. They are distributed widely over the British Isles, occurring chiefly in northern Britain but with a dramatic decrease in popularity and degree of ornamentation south of the Severn—Wash line.

There is no accepted typology or classification for food vessels, although this was attempted by Abercromby in 1912 and later by Manby in 1957. Neither scheme is now used. Instead, a number of formal traits can be recognized and used for descriptive purposes; some broad, regional styles have also been identified. Both are described in detail below.

There are two main distinctive forms of food vessel, the vase (Fig. 114:1-6) and the bowl (Fig. 114:7-11). The vase is upright, with at least one **carination,** and has a height greater than the maximum diameter. Bowls, on the other hand, are more squat, have their maximum diameter equal to or slightly greater than their heights but may also be carinated; as with vases, bipartite and tripartite forms are found. The decoration is impressed or **incised** and exhibits the range of techniques and motifs found on later neolithic impressed wares,

---

Hiberno-Scottish vase, Jesmond, Tyne and Wear; 9, waisted bowl, Portpatrick, Wigtownshire; 10, tripartite bowl, Lochinch, Wigtownshire; 11, ridged bowl, Cambuslang, Lanarkshire; 1 and 7 after Gibson 1978, 2, 4 and 8 after Hurrel in Gibson 1976, 3, 6 and 9-11 after Simpson 1965, 5 after Musson. Scale = 10 cm.

though sometimes there are motifs with a geometry inherited from **beakers**. The decoration usually covers the whole vessel, even extending into the interior, particularly on a rim bevel. Sometimes even the bases are decorated. To the south and east of the country, however, the abundance of decoration drops dramatically and generally only the upper third of the pot is ornamented. ornamented.

The simplest form of vase food-vessel is the bipartite vase with moulded rim, concave neck, carination and truncated body (Fig. 114:1). It resembles a flat-based, **Mortlake** bowl and is not greatly dissimilar to vessels in the **Rudston** or **Meldon Bridge** styles. A variant of this has a shoulder **cavetto zone** and a further variant, known as a **Yorkshire vase** (Kitson Clark 1937), has stop ridges in the cavetto zone. These **stops** may or may not be perforated (Fig. 114:2). The term 'Yorkshire vase' does not, however, mean that this type of food vessel is restricted to that area; it simply highlights an area of abundance and Yorkshire vases are found widely in northern Britain (Burgess 1980, 86-9).

South of the Severn–Wash line, the **southern bipartite vase** is very similar to the simple bipartite form already described but tends to be sparsely decorated with, perhaps, short incisions accentuating the rim and/or the pronounced carination. It is generally more angular in form (Fig. 114:5).

Ridged vases, as the name suggests, are recognized by horizontal encircling ribs running round the body of the vase, thus dividing the vessel into numerous, slack and shallow cavetto zones (Fig. 114:6). These encircling **cordons** usually appear to be **raised**; they may be highlighted by decoration and appear to be derived from northern **grooved ware**.

Perhaps the most widely distributed food vessel type is one that is also simplest in shape, the **bucket**-shaped food vessels which are simple, upright vases without carinations or changes in direction in the profile.

As with the vase food vessels, regional styles and variations in profile are also found amongst the bowl food-vessels. Such is the variety, however, that many vessels will fall between two distinct types, exhibiting traits from more than one regional style and causing the types to appear to merge. The simplest of the bowl types is the **globular British bowl** (Fig. 114:7), which has a national distribution, mainly as a result of the simplicity of the form. The globular British bowl is an open, flat-based pot with the rim diameter either equalling or being slightly less than the maximum diameter. They are decorated in a rich variety of motifs, which decrease in complexity as one moves south and east. Elaborately decorated bowls, particularly with **false-relief** decoration, and often tripartite or with waists, are termed **Hiberno-Scottish** bowls (Fig. 114:8). This denotes their main areas of distribution, though they are also found in northern England (Gibson 1976) and Wales (Savory 1980). They also have vase equivalents.

Waisted bowls have a **cavetto zone** about midway up the profile of the vessel (Fig. 114:9) and this may or may not be stopped with solid or perforated lugs in the same manner as Yorkshire vases. This cavetto zone may be deep enough to give the bowl a tripartite appearance (Fig. 114:10) developing into the **northern tripartite** bowl—a term once more denoting regionality. Multiple carinations and cavettos lead to ridged vessels (Fig. 114:11), the bowl equivalent of the ridged vase.

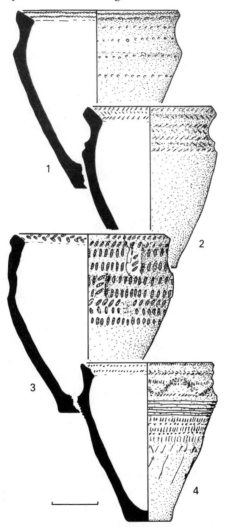

Fig. 115 Food vessel urns. 1, bipartite vessel, Catcherside, Northumberland; 2, bipartite with shoulder cavetto zone, Houghton-Le-Spring, Tyne and Wear; 3, bipartite with shoulder cavetto zone and stop ridges, Goatscrag, Northumberland; 4, 'encrusted urn' with plastic decoration, Ryton, Tyne and Wear. Scale = 5 cm.

Food vessel urns (Fig. 115)

These are also known as **enlarged food vessels**, though this term is rather out of vogue at present and 'food vessel urn' is favoured, as it describes the **food vessel** form and the **cinerary urn** function of the pottery (Cowie 1976). Food-vessel urns are essentially food vessels over 20 cm high and are found in both sepulchral and domestic contexts. Vase and bucket forms are found, but never bowls, probably as they would result in over-bulky vessels. The forms, decorative motifs and techniques are exactly paralleled in the smaller vessels, as is their generally northern and western distribution.

The food vessel urns are generally bipartite (Fig. 115:1), with or without shoulder **cavetto zones**, which may appear singly or in multiples (Fig. 115:2). As with **Yorkshire vases**, these cavettos may be interrupted by solid or perforated **lugs** (Fig. 115:3). Other vessels may have distinctive **plastic decoration**, most typically in the form of zig-zagging **cordons** in the neck of the pot (Fig. 115:4). These were formerly called **encrusted urns** (Fox 1927), the name being taken from the distinctive **applied** or **raised** decoration, but now their affinity with the other food-vessel-urn types is acknowledged and they find themselves under the more general heading. These cordons may be accentuated by incisions or impressions, either on or flanking them, and may be augmented by the application of plastic **rosettes** or roundels, often forming elaborate decorative schemes. The decoration rarely extends much below the shoulder of the pot and is once more derived from the later neolithic, impressed wares with, perhaps, **grooved ware** influence visible in the cordons and applied decoration.

See also ApSimon 1972; Gibson 1986*a*.

Foot ring bases (Fig. 34:2, 42:4*a*, 50:2, 52:1)

A foot ring consists of a ring of clay on the underside of the base angle. This gives the base a profile resembling the base of a modern teacup. It would appear to be decorative rather than functional and is most common on pottery of the first millennium BC and later.

Ford style (Fig. 116)

Regional style of later neolithic impressed ware found in the border-land of northern Northumberland and recognized by its heavy, semi-circular rims with profuse **impressed** and **incised decoration** (Longworth 1969; Kinnes and Longworth 1985, UN 18). **Twisted cord impressions** and short incisions are particularly common decorative techniques. The vessels are found in a heavy, coarse **fabric**, though the surface condition is good. They have a marked and deep **cavetto zone**, sharp **carination** and a splayed and almost straight-sided profile, which suggests that the vessels may have had flat, rather than rounded, bases.

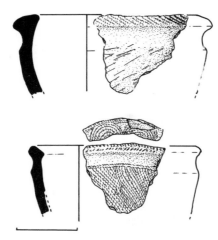

Fig. 116 Ford style pottery from Ford, Northumberland. Scale = 10 cm.

Frilford bowls (Fig. 117)
Southern English style of **La Tène** pottery within the **globular bowl** series. Recognized by **incised decoration** in curvilinear motifs. A southern equivalent of the **Hunsbury bowls** (Fig. 140) of the Midlands.

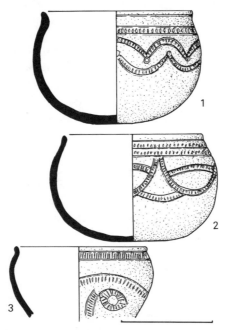

Fig. 117 Frilford bowls. 1, 2, Frilford, Berks.; 3, Iffley, Oxon. After Cunliffe 1974. Scale = 10 cm.

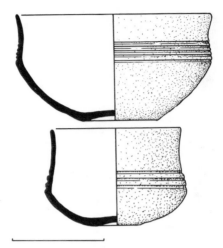

Fig. 118   Furrowed haematite-coated bowls from All Cannings Cross, Wilts.
After Harding 1974. Scale = 10 cm.

Furrowed bowls (Fig. 118)
Haematite-coated bowls with multiple horizontal grooves above the
carination. They are found particularly in Wessex and date from the late
seventh century BC. There are two basic forms, those with U-sectioned
grooves and a short neck above the shoulder, and those with a longer and
somewhat concave neck. They appear to be chronologically sequential. Some
vessels may also have **omphalos bases** (Fig. 166) and it is thought that they are
derived from metal prototypes, though the rarity of such metal forms has led
Harding (1974, 150-1) to suggest that the relationship may have been
reciprocal.

Furrowing (Fig. 118)
Surface treatment formed by repeatedly dragging a blunt and broad-ended
instrument through the soft or **leather-hard** clay to produce multiple, parallel,
shallow grooves. See **furrowed bowls** and **tooled decoration**.

Gabbroic wares (Figs. 119, 120)
Pottery made from the gabbroic clays of the Lizard Peninsula in Cornwall.
The distinctive **inclusions** in this clay make it readily identifiable in **thin
section** (Figs. 119, 120) and pottery made from this clay has been found
widely distributed over south-western England and has been taken to
represent a 'trade' in pottery in the Neolithic and later periods. See also
Hembury ware (Fig. 135).

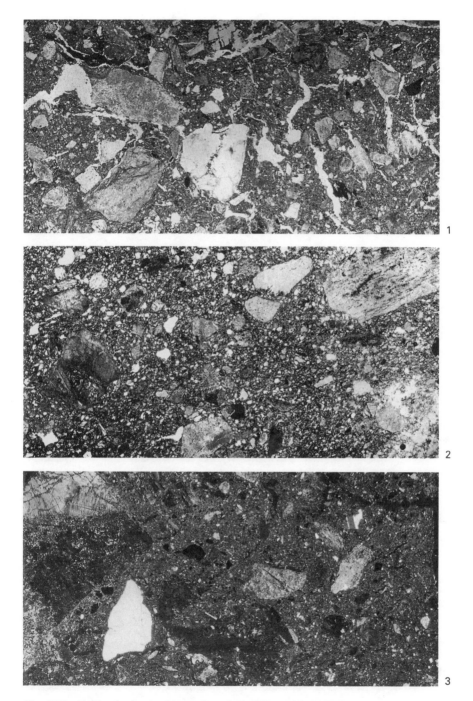

Fig. 119   Gabbroic clay in thin section. 1, 2, PPL, × 20; 3, XPL, × 20.

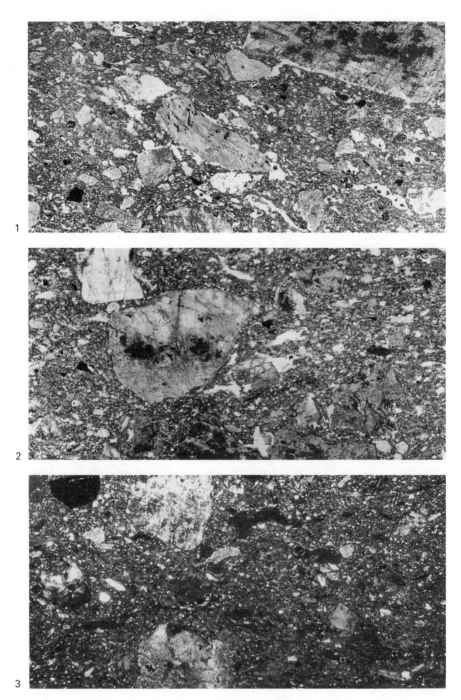

Fig. 120   Gabbroic pottery in thin section. 1, 2, PPL, × 20; 3, XPL, × 20.

Gallo-Belgic imitations (Fig. 121)

See also **Belgic wares, butt beakers** and **Aylesford–Swarling**. These imitations, as defined by Thompson (1982), are **grog**-filled, indigenously made copies of imported Gallo-Belgic and Roman types, first recognized in the Camulodunum sequence of Hawkes and Hull (1947). The classification is based very much on the original Camulodunum sequence and is too detailed to be within the scope of this work, but the basic subdivision, as devised by Thompson, is as follows:

G1 Plates
G2 Bowls
G3 Cups
G4 **Girth beakers** with strongly accentuated waists
G5 **Butt beakers**
G6 Jugs

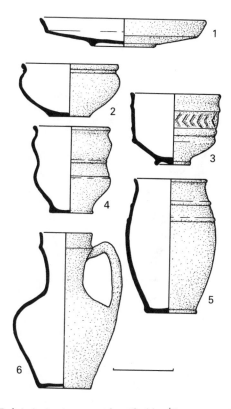

Fig. 121 Gallo-Belgic imitations, as identified by Thompson. 1, platter from Colchester; 2, bowl from Colchester; 3, cup from Puddlehill; 4, girth beaker from Kempston; 5, butt beaker from Arlesey; 6, jar from Colchester. After Thompson 1982. Scale = 10 cm.

Girth beakers (Fig. 121:4)
Drinking cups of the first century BC, named after a distinctive constriction at the waist. These are **Belgic wares** and often locally made copies of Roman or Continental types. See **Gallo-Belgic imitations.**

Glastonbury style (Fig. 122, 123)
A pottery style of the later Iron Age restricted to south-western England and dating from *c.* 200 BC (Cunliffe 1974, 43). The style is represented by necked bowls, often with an internal groove, **saucepan pots** and simple **bead-rimmed** jars, which are decorated with filled and lightly **incised decoration** consisting of curvilinear or geometric designs. Peacock (1968; 1969*a*) has shown that there was a number of centres of manufacture for these pots in northern Somerset, indicated by Old Red Sandstone, Mendip or Jurassic limestone **inclusions,** and in the Lizard Peninsula and the Exe valley. Finds of Cornish-made pottery with **gabbroic** inclusions in Devon and Somerset indicate a trade in pottery of this style, which has also been called the **La Tène** south-western style (Grimes 1952).

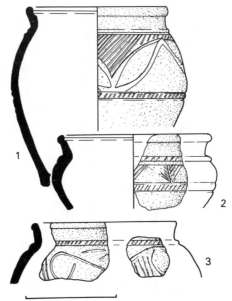

Fig. 122 Selected pottery of the Glastonbury style. 1, 3, Castle Dore, Cornwall; 2, Caerloggas, Cornwall. After Cunliffe 1974. Scale = 10 cm.

Glastonbury–Blaise Castle Hill style (Fig. 123)
A Somerset style of **saucepan pot,** tentatively identified by Cunliffe (1974, 43) and dating from the second century BC. The vessels are characterized by

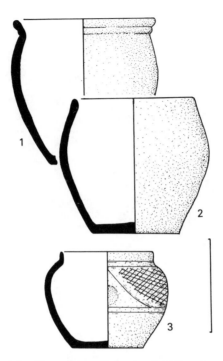

Fig. 123   Pottery of the Glastonbury-Blaise Castle Hill style, as identified by Cunliffe. 1, 2, Worlebury, Somerset; 3, Read's Cavern, Somerset. After Cunliffe 1974. Scale = 10 cm.

curvilinear and linear geometric **incised decoration**. Everted rim bowls are also found in the assemblage. The style, however, is not closely defined.

Glaze (Fig. 124)

Glazes are vitreous coatings consisting of a glass former (usually silica) with the addition of a glass modifier, or flux, to lower its melting point. Typical modifiers are lead, sodium and potassium. Colour is achieved by the addition of metallic oxides, such as copper and iron.

Glazing was used in the Near East as early as the fifth millennium BC, when alkaline glazes coloured with copper were applied firstly to steatite and later to ground silica bodies to produce what is known as Egyptian faience. Although glaze itself was never used on British prehistoric pottery, glazed materials, such as faience beads, are found in Bronze Age contexts; they have been subjected to extensive programmes of chemical analysis, but their origin has as yet not been positively determined. Recent experimental work, coupled with scanning electron microscope studies and ethnographic reports on the manufacture of modern faience, indicates that there are three principal

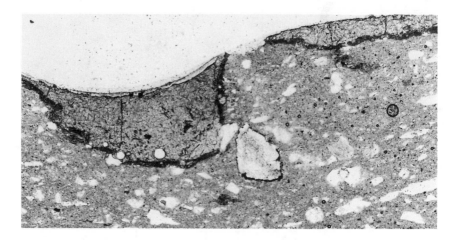

Fig. 124   Thin section of a medieval glazed vessel. The glaze is filling a shallow depression in the pot surface. The round holes are typical of glazes and other vitrified materials. PPL, × 25.

methods that might have been used in antiquity for the production of the beads (see, for example, Wulff *et al.* 1968, Vandiver 1982, Tite and Bimson 1986), viz. efflorescence, dipping of the beads in a glazing mixture or the cementation method, involving the use of a dry glazing powder, in which the beads were buried for firing (Vandiver 1982, 168). Whichever method was employed, the technology was considerably more advanced than that involved in contemporary pottery production, suggesting that they may have been produced as an offshoot of metal-working.

Early glazes on pottery in western Europe were lead-based and arrived in Britain with the Romans. This type of glaze, which was again used in the medieval period, is easily prepared by applying crushed lead sulphide or oxide to the surface of a **leather-hard** vessel; during firing, the lead reacts with the silica present in the clay to form a glaze. In thin section, glazes are transparent in plane polarized light, inactive under crossed polars, and frequently exhibit highly rounded voids, a characteristic of molten material (Fig. 124).

Globular bowls and jars

These are not indicative of date but are simple bowls or jars with bulbous but otherwise generally unelaborated profiles. The rim diameter is much narrower than the maximum diameter, resulting in a **closed vessel**. The maximum diameter usually occurs around midway in the vessel's height. For examples of globular bowls, see Figs. 51:4, 114:7 and 117:1-3; for jars, see Figs. 51:2, 52:3, 58:2.

Globular urns (Fig. 98:4, 7)
Fine ware urns of the **Deverel–Rimbury** complex, characterized by a globular body and an upright neck.

Grain impressions (Fig. 125)
Impressions left in pottery by cereal grains. They are found either in the surfaces of vessels or occasionally also in the **fabric** itself, only showing in the breaks, and are usually accidental inclusions in British prehistoric pottery. Impressions attest the manufacture of pottery within the bounds of an agricultural settlement and have been important indicators for palaeo-environmental studies (for example Helbaek 1952). It has been suggested (for example, Howard 1981, 25) that the presence of grain impressions in pottery may provide evidence for the seasonality of pottery production; however, it is likely that grains and seeds would probably have been lying around throughout the year at an agricultural settlement site and too much credence should not be attached to this argument.

Fig. 125   Grain impression on the base of a cordoned urn from Fan y Big, Brecknock, identified as *Triticum dicoccum*. Length of impression = 6 mm. Photo by Jenny Britnell, courtesy of Clwyd-Powys Archaeological Trust.

Grape cups (Fig. 126)
A type of small **accessory vessel** of the early second millennium with distinctive pellets of clay applied to the exterior of the pot to give a 'knobbly'

surface resembling a bunch of grapes. These vessels are simple cups with the rim diameters usually equalling the maximum diameter and with flat bases. They accompany cremations in varying types of **cinerary urn**, particularly in the Wessex region. The **applied decoration** is probably derived from **grooved ware.**

See Annable and Simpson 1964; Burgess 1980.

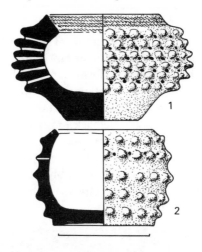

Fig. 126   Grape cups. 1, Wilsford G7, Wilts.; 2, Preshute G1, Wilts. After Annable and Simpson 1964. Scale = 5 cm.

Grimston-Lyles Hill ware (Fig. 127)
An insular variant of a wider western European style of the fourth and third millennia. This is the earliest dated pottery tradition in Britain but is also one of the longest-lived. Lasting for over half a millennium, ^{14}C dates indicate the appearance of the tradition *c.* 3500 bc (Green 1976). The pottery is distributed widely over Britain, particularly in the east and the north (Manby 1975). It is characterized by plain hemispherical bowls and everted-rim bowls with shoulder **carinations,** from which many of the later traditions develop. The vessels are invariably round-based and the rim forms are rarely elaborate, tending to be simple, everted or slightly thickened and rolled (Fig. 127:3) (Smith 1974, 106-8). Occasionally **lugs** may be found on the exterior of the pots but these are generally rare. The **fabric** varies considerably from region to region but commonly is a **corky fabric** resulting from the burning-out of organic **inclusions** or the dissolution of **calcareous inclusions,** giving the clay a pitted and open texture. Fine and **burnished** fabrics are also found.

Regional variations have been recognized in this geographically widespread tradition. In Yorkshire, vessels with a very slack S-shaped profile

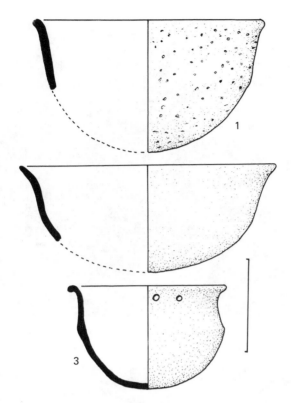

Fig. 127   Grimston ware from Thirlings, Northumberland. After Hurrel in Miket 1976. Scale = 10 cm.

are known as **Heslerton ware** (Piggott 1954, 114), but as this style is represented only by vessels from the type site, it may be that we are looking at poorly produced vessels rather than a distinct style *sensu stricto* (Fig. 138). Also in Yorkshire, and widely distributed enough to be regarded as a true local style, are **Towthorpe bowls**, which are simple hemispherical bowls, occasionally with lugs, but typically with sharply out-turned rims (Fig. 222).

In south western England, carinated bowls known as **Hembury ware** (Fig. 135) constitute a regional equivalent, if not a local sub-style, while, in northern Scotland, **Boghead bowls** (Fig. 60) are recognized by their distinctive internal and external vertical **fluting** and good, burnished fabric closely similar to vessels from the type site of Lyles Hill in Co. Antrim. A reassessment of Grimston ware is currently being undertaken (Herne 1988).

Grog (Figs. 128, 129, 130)
Crushed, previously-fired ceramic used as an **opening material**. Macroscopically, a difference in colour between the grog and the

Fig. 128   Grog fragments in a thin section of bronze age pottery from Thailand. PPL, × 15.

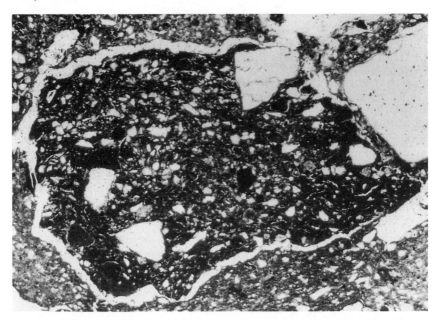

Fig. 129   Grog fragment in a thin section of bronze age pottery from Skendleby, Lincs. The void around the outside of the fragment is the result of drying shrinkage. PPL, × 20.

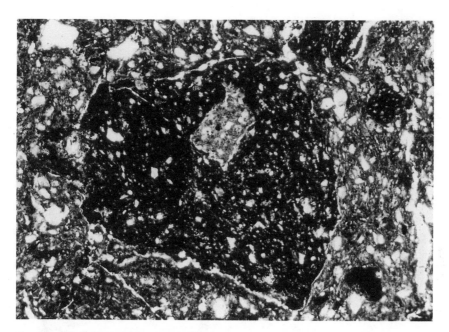

Fig. 130   Recycling of raw materials: the large grog fragment in the middle of the photomicrograph contains a smaller, lighter-coloured piece. (Bronze age sherd from Skendleby, Lincs.) PPL, × 40.

surrounding matrix often serves to facilitate its identification. In **thin section,** grog is usually angular and is often surrounded by **voids** created when the wet and **plastic** clay shrinks away from the inert grog during the drying of the vessel (Fig. 129). Grog may be of clay similar to or different from the matrix, and this can also be seen in thin section. Frequently, grog within grog, indicating recycling and continuity of ceramic tradition, can also be observed (Fig. 130). (See Whitbread 1986 for a fuller description of the properties of grog in thin section.)

Grooved ware (Fig. 131)

Grooved ware was first recognized by Piggott (in Warren *et al.* 1936), principally from sites on the Essex coast but also from Skara Brae and Woodhenge. Later, Piggott (1954, 321) suggested that the term 'grooved ware' be abandoned in favour of **Rinyo–Clacton ware** to illustrate the geographical distribution of this tradition. Recently, the term 'grooved ware' has been reinstated to describe the main decorative technique employed on the pottery of this tradition. Grooved ware is the first flat-based pottery type in Britain, being established in the Orkney Islands at the neolithic village of Skara Brae by 2700 bc (Clarke 1976). The dates for southern English

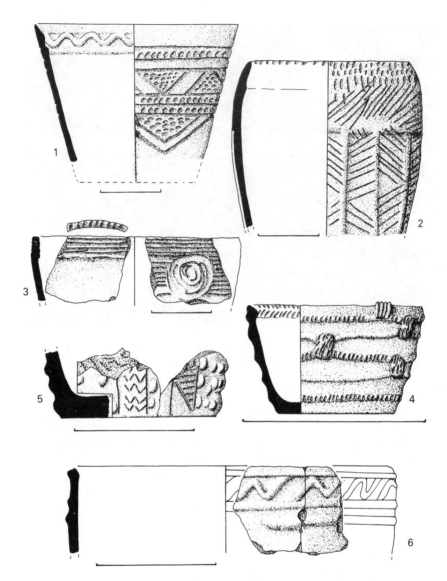

Fig. 131   Grooved ware. 1, Clacton style from Clacton, Essex; 2, 3, Durrington Walls style from Durrington Walls, Wilts.; 4, Woodlands style from Woodlands, Wilts.; 5, 6, Rinyo style from Skara Brae, after Longworth *et al.* 1971, 2, 3, after Wainwright and Longworth 1971, 4, after Stone 1949; 5, after Childe 1931, 6, after Fraser 1982. Scales = 10 cm.

grooved ware are much later, at around 2200 bc. However, the corpus of grooved ware in the borders and central Scotland and, more importantly, absolute dating of the finds within that region, are insufficient to allow any diffusion theories to be formulated. Finds of grooved ware have been made in Ireland but they are few and some local equivalents may yet await study.

The origins of grooved ware are unknown. There are no convincing Continental parallels, but some of the motifs used in the decoration of this tradition are so close to motifs found in the art of the Irish, British and Breton passage graves that some symbolic interchange must be at least co-influential.

In 1956, Smith identified three styles of grooved ware, as follows:

Clacton style: Characterized by the use of grooves and **impressed decoration** with recurring motifs, such as multiple lozenges or chevrons filled with circular impressions or **stabs**. **Comb impressions** and internal decoration were also present. The main corpus of material was from the Essex coast.

Woodlands style: Consisted of fine, small pots with perforated **lugs** and with pellets of clay standing proud on the rim. The bodies of the vessels were decorated with converging **cordons** and 'knots' of clay.

Woodhenge style: Noted for its **fingernail impressions** and the presence of round and flat rims, vertical cordons and panelled decoration.

Using a much greater corpus than was available to Smith, grooved ware was reviewed by Wainwright and Longworth in 1971 and the following four styles were identified:

Clacton style: Follows Smith's classification and is characterized by simple rims with internal grooved decoration, rims with internal **plastic decoration**, dot-filled **incised decoration** in single and multiple chevrons and lozenges, and oval impressions (Fig. 131:1).

Woodlands style: Also basically that outlined by Smith and characterized by horizontal or converging, **raised** or **applied** cordons. These may be either **slashed cordons** or undecorated (Fig. 131:4). There may also be external ladder-patterning, pellets of clay on the rim, incised **herring-bone** on the rim and applied or raised 'knots' at the convergence of the cordons.

Durrington Walls style: Extends Smith's Woodhenge style and comprises large **bucket-** or **barrel-shaped** pots, which are richly decorated (Fig. 131:2). The use of **whipped** and **twisted cord** is peculiar to this style. Internally bevelled or concave rims and the frequent presence of incised decoration below the rims are also characteristic. Externally incised or grooved, concentric circles and/or spirals are present as are vertical, plain or decorated cordons. Single or multiple, incised vertical lines and filled chevron decoration are also common.

Rinyo style: Restricted to the Northern Isles and recognized by internally stepped or scalloped rims, applied pellets and roundels of clay, applied lozenges or converging cordons, grooved, diagonal cordons and cordons with dot-impressed decoration (Fig. 131:5, 6).

Wainwright and Longworth's groups have received a mixed response, basically because, with the exception of the Rinyo style, they lack geographical cohesion. Recently, Richards and Thomas (1984) have advocated a hierarchical ordering of grooved ware decoration from undecorated at the lower end of the range, rising through gradual increases in the amount of decoration to highly ornate pots with decorated cordons at the upper end. They have interpreted the hierarchical ordering as being significant when combined with the structured deposition of vessels, as at Durrington Walls. These conclusions, however, have not yet been widely applied.

Haematite (Fig. 132)
Red iron (ferric) oxide, Fe_2O_3. It is the iron oxide that is most commonly responsible for the yellow, red or brown colour of clays and of fired pottery. The characteristic liver-red colour of the mineral is easily recognized and it was extensively used in antiquity, in particular, during the Iron Age, to colour the surface of pottery. Most frequently, the pulverized pigment was applied to the surface of a **leather-hard** pot and then **burnished** (Fig. 132), but it was also sometimes applied as a **slip**.

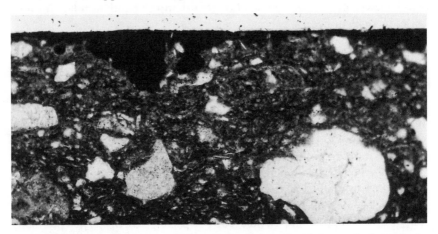

Fig. 132 Photomicrograph of a thin section of a vessel with haematite burnished into the surface. The haematite appears as a black line of varying thickness along the surface; some larger pigment particles, which have been pushed into the pot body underneath by the burnishing, can also be seen. PPL, × 100. The effect should be compared with that of slip (Figs. 203, 206) and smudging (Fig. 205).

Haematite-coated wares (Figs. 34:1, 2; 118)
Late bronze age and early iron age pottery, found particularly in southern England, with a distinctive red, often **burnished** surface. The two main groups, cordoned and furrowed bowls, have been discussed by Harding

(1974, 153 ff.). Recent research, involving X-ray diffraction and scanning electron microscopy studies (Middleton 1987), has shown that haematite was not always used to create the red surface and that the wares were produced in three ways: firstly by the application of crushed iron oxide, secondly by the application of a clay slip, and finally by simple burnishing of the surface of a vessel, without the application of any surface coating.

Hardness test

This may be used to help identify **opening materials** in sherds, as the hardness of mineral and rock fragments may be diagnostic. It is particularly useful in distinguishing between white or cream-coloured inclusions, in that **calcareous inclusions** are softer than siliceous ones. See **Mohs' Scale**.

Hawk's Hill-West Clandon style (Fig. 133)

A Surrey style of **saucepan pot** identified by Cunliffe (1974, 43). Upright tub-shaped and **barrel-shaped** forms are both present, with simple **incised decoration** in curvilinear or multiple chevron motifs.

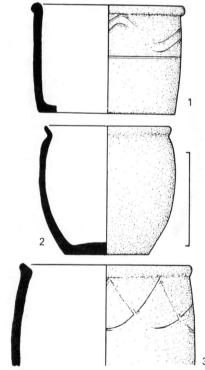

Fig. 133 Pottery from the Hawk's Hill-West Clandon style, as identified by Cunliffe. 1, Hawk's Hill, Surrey; 2, 3, West Clandon, Surrey. After Cunliffe 1974. Scale = 10 cm.

Heavy mineral analysis (HMA)

A technique most applicable to the analysis of sandy **fabrics**, heavy mineral analysis has been used with some success in provenance studies of **black-burnished wares** in Britain (Williams 1977). It is a destructive technique, involving the sampling of between 20 and 30 grams of pottery and the use of unpleasant and dangerous chemicals; consequently, it is not used frequently. The sample is crushed and floated on a liquid of known specific gravity (Bromoform); the light minerals, such as clay and quartz, float, while heavy minerals, such as garnet, kyanite, tourmaline and zircon, sink and can be removed and mounted on a slide for identification, using a **polarizing microscope**. Comparison of the suite of heavy minerals with assemblages from known localities may allow the identification of a source for the sand or sandstone **inclusions** present in the pottery.

Hebridean bowls (Fig. 134)

A type of pottery dating to the later third millennium and restricted in its distribution to the western isles of Scotland (McInnes 1969; Simpson 1976). They are recognized by their rather baggy and multi-carinated profiles; the **carinations** often interrupt the **incised decoration**, which forms a **herring-bone motif**. The mouths of these bowls are often closed, though never severely constricted, and the rim forms may be heavy and moulded.

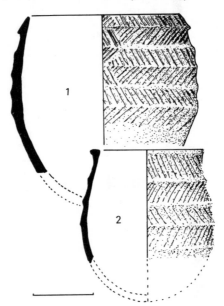

Fig. 134   Hebridean neolithic bowls. 1, Eilean an Tighe (after Scott 1951); 2, Northton, Harris (after McInnes 1969). Scale = 10 cm.

Hembury ware (Figs. 119, 120, 135)

A style of round-based bowl distributed widely in south-western England and related to the **western Neolithic** tradition and to **Grimston–Lyles Hill ware**. This pottery dates to the third millennium and is named after the pottery found at the causewayed enclosure of Hembury in Devon. This name can be confusing, however, as the source of the raw materials for the pottery has been shown by Peacock (1969*b*) to be at the gabbroic outcrops of the Lizard Peninsula in the far south-west of Cornwall. This pottery provides one of the most concrete pieces of evidence for the 'trade' in Neolithic pottery at this time. It is not only found in the area around the clay outcrops but as far east as Wiltshire (Windmill Hill, where local, inferior imitations were also found) (Smith 1965) and Dorset (Maiden Castle) (Wheeler 1943). The pottery is well made and conforms to strict shapes and styles, suggesting perhaps that professional potters were at work. Both simple open and everted-rim bowls with shoulder **carinations** are found, with simple or rolled-out rims. The **fabrics** are usually well finished and sometimes **burnished**. The vessels may carry external **lugs** which may or may not be perforated, and also **trumpet lugs** (Fig. 226), which occur only on this style of pottery and its imitations at this period (Mercer 1981).

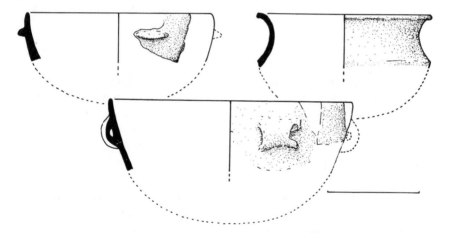

Fig. 135   Hembury ware from Carn Brea, Cornwall. After Mercer 1981. Scale = 10 cm.

Hengistbury assemblage (Fig. 136)

The broad name for the pottery from Hengistbury Head, Dorset, given by Cunliffe (1978) to cover Bushe-Fox's classes B–L (Bushe-Fox 1915) and datable to the first centuries BC and AD. Cunliffe divides the assemblage into seven classes:

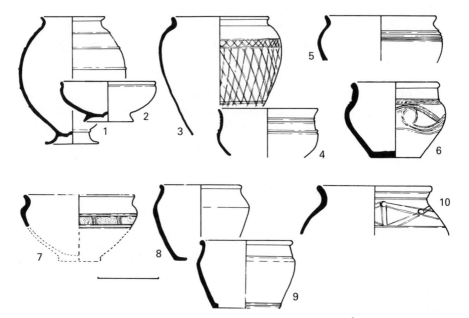

Fig. 136   Pottery in the Hengistbury sequence from Hengistbury Head, Dorset. 1, 2, Class 1; 3, 4, Class 2; 5, Class 3; 6, Class 4; 7, Class 5; 8, 9, Class 6; 10, Class 7. After Cunliffe 1974. Scale = 10 cm.

Class 1: **Wheel-thrown** vessels decorated with multiple but widely spaced **cordons**, whose **fabric** is black and frequently **burnished**. Some vessels may have **pedestalled bases** or **omphalos bases**. Bowls and jars are both represented and have close parallels in northern France.

Class 2: Jars with lattice decoration, bowls with neck cordons and shouldered bowls; all are coated with graphite. They are probably imported from France.

Class 3: **Globular bowls** with everted rims. This style is further characterized by deeply **incised** grooves on and below the point of maximum diameter. Micaceous **inclusions** suggest that these vessels were also imported from France.

Class 4: **Glastonbury ware** and vessels from Hengistbury Head examined petrologically show them to have been imported from the Lizard, the Exe valley, and the Mendip production centres.

Class 5: A small class represented by bowls and jars with encircling, incised lines, between which is a roughened area.

Class 6: Jars with upright or everted rims in a smooth, grey and burnished fabric. Decoration is restricted to the shoulder and consists of **impressed** dimples between incised, encircling lines or **roulette** decoration in a variety of decorative motifs.

Class 7: Shouldered jars and bowls with beaded rims and sometimes with shallow, shoulder grooves. These are probably local copies of French types.

Following Cunliffe's reworking of the material, some seventy sherds of cordoned and graphite-coated pottery from Hengistbury Head, from Bushe-Fox's Classes B and H, were subjected to examination in thin section; results from forty of the sherds have been published (Freestone and Rigby 1982). On typological grounds, the sherds were considered to be imports from the Armorican peninsula. The thin-section study allowed the pottery to be divided into nine fabric groups, of which Groups 1-7 contained igneous and metamorphic inclusions and were considered to have been imported into the site, and Groups 8 and 9 contained grog and sand respectively as the main inclusion type and were probably locally produced. Nineteen of the vessels examined were found to be of Group 1 fabric. The rock inclusions in Groups 1-7 could have come from Devon and Cornwall, but an origin in Brittany or Normandy is thought to be more likely. Results from the thin sections were not sufficient to prove this, however, and so a microprobe analysis of Group 1 and some gabbroic sherds from south-western England was carried out. This also showed the fabrics to be similar, but statistical discriminant analysis of the amphibole analysis was able to separate them, reinforcing the argument for a non-British origin.

The fabric groups determined by the analysis cover a range of vessel types and, similarly, the typological classifications of both Bushe-Fox and Cunliffe (1978) were found to contain different fabrics. For example, Bushe-Fox's Class B included fabrics from at least five, and probably six, different sources, while, of the eleven vessels illustrated by Cunliffe as his Class 1 (roughly the same as Bushe-Fox's Class B), probably only seven are of the Group 1 fabric. In addition, the graphite-coated wares (Bushe-Fox's Group H, Cunliffe Class 2) also include two different fabrics.

The analytical programme therefore confirmed the suggestion, on typological grounds, that the wares were imports to the site of Hengistbury but also indicated that, as well as coming from a variety of sources, the wares may not have been contemporary, a prospect that had not previously been considered.

Herring-bone motif (Figs. 108, 114, 121, 137)
Decorative motif consisting of opposing rows of short, oblique linear impressions or incisions. The motif may be horizontal (Fig. 137:1) or vertical (Fig. 137:2); it is most commonly found on neolithic and bronze age pottery (Fig. 114:1, 6) but is not exclusive to those periods (Fig. 121:3).

Fig. 137   Herring-bone motif which can be executed in a number of techniques, such as twisted cord, whipped cord, comb, incision, etc. 1, horizontal; 2, vertical. Not to scale.

Heslerton ware (Fig. 138)

A local Yorkshire variant of **Grimston-Lyles Hill ware** recognized by Piggott (1954, 114), though now doubted. As defined, Heslerton ware comprises S-shaped bowls with very slack **carinations** and out-turned rims. These are now considered to be poorly made carinated bowls, as commonly found in other Grimston-ware assemblages elsewhere, and they are only found at the type site (Manby 1975).

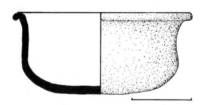

Fig. 138   Heslerton ware from West Heslerton, Yorkshire. After Piggott 1954. Scale = 10 cm.

Hiberno-Scottish bowls (Fig. 114:8)

Variant of **food vessel** named after its Scottish and Irish distribution.

Hiberno-Scottish vase (Fig. 114:3)

Variant of **food vessel** named after its Scottish and Irish distribution.

Horseshoe-handled urns (Fig. 139)

Variant of **biconical urns** and related to the **food vessel urns** of the early second millennium (ApSimon 1972). They are particularly common in the Wessex area and are recognized by the horseshoe-shaped handles on the upper third of the vessel, occasionally below the shoulder but more usually in the concave neck. **Impressed** and **incised decoration** is used to ornament the vessels with a variety of motifs. The techniques are derived from the

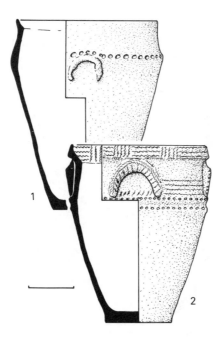

Fig. 139 Horseshoe-handled urns. 1, Roke Down, Dorset (after Calkin 1962); 2, Corfe Castle, Dorset (after Longworth 1984). Scale = 10 cm.

later neolithic impressed wares and are also common on food vessel pottery. pottery.

Hunsbury bowls (Fig. 140)

A local, south-east-Midlands form of iron age globular bowl named after those from the iron age settlement at Hunsbury in Northamptonshire (Fell 1936). They are decorated in horizontally encircling panels of incised decoration in curvilinear designs, rather open in effect (Harding 1974, 198). Rosettes and rosettes with a central dot (Fig. 140:1), often filling the open ends of spirals, are also common on this style.

Hunsbury-Draughton style (Fig. 140)

Style of bowl in the saucepan pot tradition identified by Cunliffe (1974, 46) and identical with the Hunsbury bowls above.

Huntcliff ware (Figs. 68, 141, 142)

Coarse ware widely distributed in Yorkshire from AD 370. Developed from the native Knapton ware, the fabric typically features abundant crushed calcite opening material (Fig. 68). In contrast to the earlier wares, however, some vessels are wheel-thrown, while others have rims that appear to have been made or finished on the wheel. The cooking pot (Fig. 142) is the most characteristic shape, featuring a sharply in-turning shoulder and a thick, everted and turned-over rim with a pronounced groove on the inside (Fig. 142) (Hull 1932).

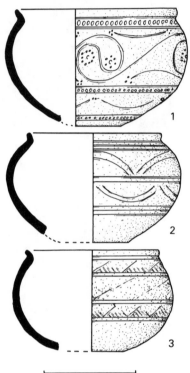

Fig. 140   Hunsbury bowls from the type site. After Cunliffe 1974. Scale = 10 cm.

Hurdling or hurdle motif (Fig. 143)
Decorative motif composed of alternating panels of multiple, vertical then horizontal lines. This motif is commonly found on **collared urns** (Figs. 78:1, 5; 79:5).

Hydrochloric acid (HCl)
This is used, in conjunction with a **hardness test,** to assist in the macroscopic identification of **opening materials** in pottery fabrics. **Calcareous materials** will react with hydrochloric acid and decompose, accompanied by effervescence; this indicates the evolution of carbon dioxide and therefore that the material was calcareous. Siliceous materials, such as quartz or flint, which may be similar in colour, are not affected by HCl. Vinegar can also be used for this test if HCl is not available.

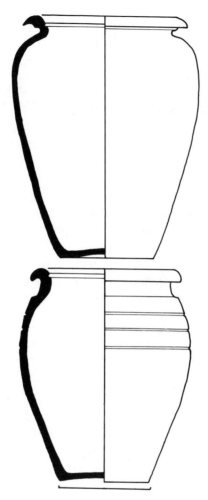

Fig. 141 Huntcliff cooking pots. After Gillam 1957. Scale = 10 cm.

Fig. 142 Huntcliff ware rims. After Newbold 1912. Scale = 10 cm.

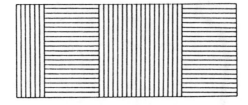

Fig. 143 Hurdle (or hurdling) motif which can be executed in a variety of techniques. Not to scale.

Impressed decoration

Surface treatment carried out by pressing an object or utensil into the clay of a newly fashioned vessel while the clay is still soft. This technique is common throughout prehistory but especially in the third and second millennia on **later Neolithic impressed wares** and their derivatives. Most commonly found techniques include **whipped cord, twisted cord, bird bone, reed, shell** and **comb impressions. Fingernail impressions** and **fingertip impressions** are common on pottery of all periods from *c.* 2500 bc. **False relief** is also an impressed technique.

Incense cups (Figs. 32, 126, 179, 181)

Small **accessory vessels** of the early second millennium commonly found with **cinerary urns** and also called **pigmy cups** (Fig. 181), **perforated wall cups** (Fig. 179), **Aldbourne cups** (Fig. 32) or **grape cups** (Fig. 126). Perforated wall cups were most commonly called incense cups, as it was believed that they were used for burning incense at funerals and that the vapour escaped through the perforations in the sides of these small vessels. The term is now rather antiquated and subjective and has generally been abandoned.

Incised decoration (Figs. 144, 145)

A very common **surface treatment** used throughout prehistory and indeed later. It involves dragging a sharp instrument (Fig. 18:2) through **leather-hard** clay (Fig. 144). The technique can vary considerably in sophistication, attaining high degrees of complexity in some first millennium pottery, such as the **Glastonbury wares** or the **saucepan pots**.

Inclusions

The term used to describe all non-clay and/or non-plastic materials present in a clay **body** or fired **fabric**. They may be naturally occurring or added by the potter. See also **filler, opening materials** and **temper**.

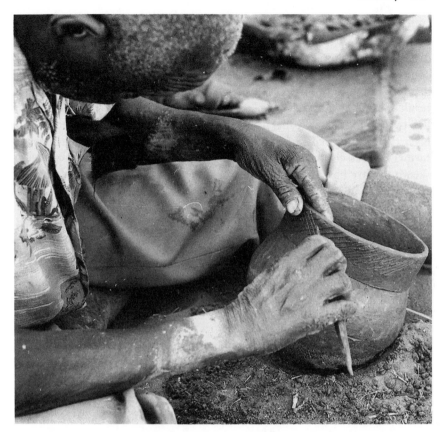

Fig. 144 A contemporary potter in Kavango, Namibia, using a wooden tool (illustrated in Fig. 18) to incise lines on a clay vessel.

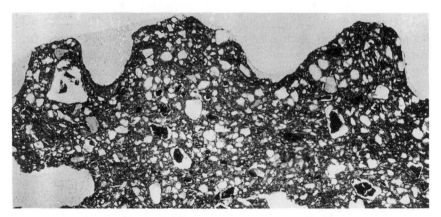

Fig. 145 Photomicrograph of a thin section taken through incised lines on an iron age sherd from Namibia. The rounded grooves indicate that the clay was in the leather-hard state when the incision was executed. PPL, × 16.

Inlay

A decorative technique rare on prehistoric pottery and one that has caused controversy. The finding of **beakers** from the Wessex chalklands with white deposits in the comb impressions was at first claimed to be inlay, then the result of burial in a chalk subsoil, and once more inlay. Clarke (1970, 10-11) lists two inlaid beakers from Fife and Aberdeenshire from which the inlay had been chemically analysed and shown to be derived from burnt bone. A further two vessels from Norfolk and another two from Cambridgeshire were shown to have had a crushed chalk inlay which was deliberate and not the result of natural chalk precipitation. An **accessory cup** from Breach Farm in Glamorgan was found to have had red colouring in the decoration (Clarke *et al.* 1985, 297-8) and white inlay is well attested on the **haematite-coated wares** of first millennium Wessex (Cunliffe 1974, 275-6; Harding 1974, 153). In both the haematite-coated wares and the beakers, the white inlay would have contrasted with the red surface of the pots.

Irish bowls (Fig. 114:8)

Variant of the **food vessels** named after its predominantly Irish distribution, but also found in Britain. See also **Hiberno-Scottish bowl**.

Irish vase (Fig. 114:3)

Variant of the **food vessels** named after its predominantly Irish distribution, but also found in Britain. See also **Hiberno-Scottish vase**.

Iron oxides

These are responsible for the colour of most clays, fired vessels, and, on occasions, of **glazes**. They are usually derived from the breakdown of ferruginous minerals, such as biotite, amphiboles or pyroxenes in the parent rock. Ferric oxide (**haematite**, Fe_2O_3) is the most usual, but others, such as ferrous oxide (FeO) or magnetite (Fe_3O_4), are also important. If firing is carried out under **oxidizing conditions**, the iron oxides will be brought to their highest state of **oxidation** and the fired product will be yellow, red or brown; if, however, a **reduction** firing is carried out, the wares will be dark brown, black or grey. The actual colour obtained depends on the original iron content of the clay and the degree of oxidation or reduction achieved.

Haematite was used extensively for **slips** and for other surface coatings; it was either powdered and **burnished** into the surface (Fig. 132) or applied as a coating after being mixed with water (see Middleton 1987). Iron was also a frequent glaze colourant in antiquity, particularly in the medieval period; under oxidizing conditions, it yields yellow or brown, but green under reducing conditions. Refiring experiments indicate that, for many vessels, it

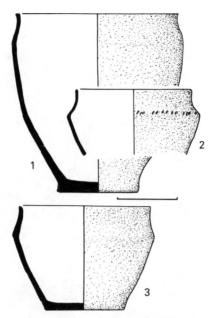

Fig. 146 Pottery of the Ivinghoe–Sandy group, as identified by Cunliffe. 1, Grantchester, Cambs.; 2, Sandy, Beds.; 3, Chippenham, Cambs. After Cunliffe 1974. Scale = 10 cm.

was not added to the glaze mixture and the potters instead relied on reducing the iron in the clay to obtain a green glaze.

Ivinghoe–Sandy group (Fig. 146)
A local group of **shouldered jar** and bowl identified by Cunliffe (1974, 35) and datable to the sixth century BC in southern England. The fabric is coarse, often decorated with **fingertip impressions** and occasionally carries **applied** cordons on the shoulders. The pottery is a local equivalent of the nationwide shouldered jar tradition of the early Iron Age.

Jar
Upright vessel usually with a shoulder and sometimes an everted rim. The rim diameter is invariably narrower than the maximum diameter, which occurs at the shoulder of the vessel. See, for example, **Kilellan jars** (Fig. 148) and **situla jars** (Fig. 201).

Join void (Figs. 3, 11, 12, 13, 14, 15, 16, 147)
The gap between two **coils** or **rings** of clay that have not been thoroughly joined in the manufacturing process. During drying, any gaps left will increase in size as the clay shrinks. They can frequently be detected in **thin**

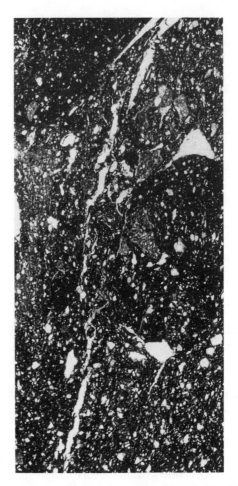

Fig. 147   Photomicrograph of a thin section showing a join void between two rings of clay in a bronze age sherd from Pilismarot, Hungary. PPL, × 20.

section (Figs. 3, 14, 16, 147) and can sometimes be seen with the naked eye in the walls of vessels that have been **ring-** or **coil-built** (Fig. 11). Vessels tend to break along these planes of weakness (Fig. 13), leaving rounded edges exposed, frequently referred to in the past as '**false rims**' (Figs. 15, 105).

Kilellan jars (Fig. 148)
Upright plain or decorated **shouldered jars** named after the type site of Kilellan Farm on Islay (Burgess 1976*b*) and datable to the early second millennium. Though tall and upright, these vessels appear to have had rounded bases and would doubtless have been unstable unless seated in a

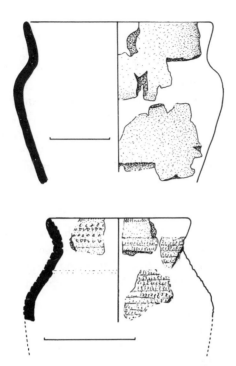

Fig. 148 Plain and decorated shouldered jars from Kilellan Farm, Islay. After Burgess 1976*b*. Scale = 10 cm.

concavity or in a stand. Both decorated and plain wares have flaring rims and the plain wares especially are in a comparatively thick **fabric**. The vessels display both **impressed** and **incised decoration** and **shell impressions** are particularly favoured. The decoration is also zoned and extends to the inside of the rim. It is probable that the decorated versions were strongly beaker-influenced.

Kiln

A structure for firing ceramics. Kilns are almost invariably associated with wheel-thrown pottery, as the finer clay bodies required for that process contain few opening materials and must therefore be fired slowly at first, so that the **water of plasticity** can be removed gradually and thus prevent **fire spalls** and explosions. Kilns consist of a firebox, a flue, a firing chamber, a dome (which may or may not be permanent) and an exhaust vent. The raw clay vessels are placed in the firing chamber, thereby being separated from direct contact with the flames from the fire.

In contrast to open firing, kiln firing utilizes hot gases rather than direct contact with the flames to fire the pots. It is a much slower and less economical process, as much time and fuel are expended in heating the kiln structure itself. However, the end products are generally of higher quality, because finer bodies are used and higher temperatures may (but were not always in antiquity) be reached.

Although kilns and the potter's wheel were used in the Near East from an early period, they did not really appear in Britain until the Roman invasion; a few wheel-thrown wares were produced in the first century BC, but it is likely that they were imports or made by immigrants. Romano-British kilns have been extensively studied by Swan (1984) and their medieval counterparts by Musty (1974).

Kimmeridge–Caburn group (Fig. 149)

Shouldered jar and bowl tradition of the sixth century BC, identified by Cunliffe (1974, 3-4) and occurring along the south coast. As well as marked shoulders, the vessels may have **beaded rims** and upright or everted necks, often carrying **cordons. Fingertip** or **fingernail impressions** may be used to

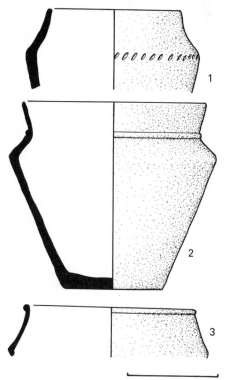

Fig. 149   Pottery of the Kimmeridge–Caburn group as identified by Cunliffe. 1, 3, Kimmeridge, Dorset; 2, The Caburn, Sussex. After Cunliffe 1974. Scale = 10 cm.

decorate the rims or shoulders. The pottery is probably ultimately derived from the preceding pottery of the **Deverel–Rimbury** complex and is a local variant of a widespread, shouldered-jar tradition.

Knapton ware (Fig. 150)

Hand-made, coarse native pottery produced in Yorkshire and featuring **calcite opening materials** (Fig. 68). It developed into **Huntcliff ware** in the fourth century AD.

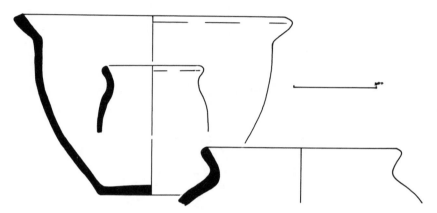

Fig. 150   Knapton ware. After Corder and Kirk 1932. Scale = 10 cm.

La Tène pottery (Figs. 151, 152, 153, 154, 155)

Generic name for pottery of the fifth to first centuries BC with distinctive, curvilinear decoration similar to that from Europe and, in particular, the areas of Armorica and the Marne (Avery 1973; Grimes 1952). The curvilinear decoration is also parallelled on metalwork of the period. Generally Eastern and Western styles can be recognized. The Eastern style has broadly geometric patterns based on arcs, chevrons and lozenges in a single zone and highlighted by circular **stamp** impressions. The Western style uses **scroll** designs more extensively; patterns are usually filled with **incised** cross-hatching or diagonal lines and may be in two zones covering a large proportion of the vessel surface. The Eastern style has been further divided into five regional sub-styles by Elsdon (1975)—the Upper Thames, Thames Estuary, Sussex, East Anglia, and Lincolnshire, as follows:

The Upper Thames group (Fig. 151) in the early La Tène period often utilizes simple arc and chevron motifs, either incised or **rouletted** and which may often contain **inlay**. Circular stamps are also used within the motifs. Small bowls with shoulders and flaring rims are the most common vessel type with **pedestalled**, dished or **foot-ring bases**. In the middle La Tène period, the

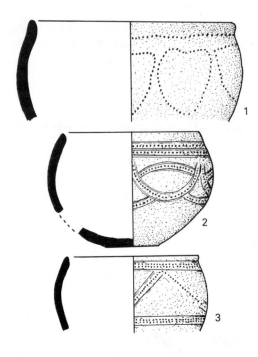

Fig. 151   La Tène pottery from the Upper Thames. 1, Blewburton, Berks.; 2, 3, Frilford, Berks. After Elsdon 1975. Scale = 10 cm.

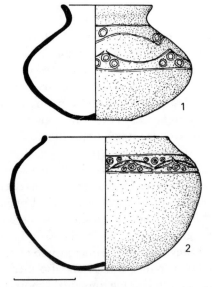

Fig. 152   La Tène pottery from the Thames Estuary. 1, Mucking, Essex; 2, Canewdon, Essex. After Elsdon 1975. Scale = 10 cm.

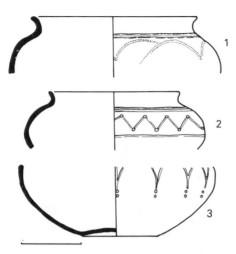

Fig. 153 La Tène pottery from Sussex. 1, 3, Horsted Keynes; 2, Charleston Brow. After Elsdon 1975. Scale = 10 cm.

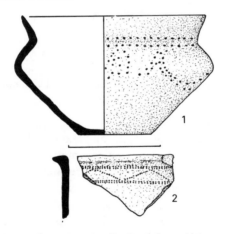

Fig. 154 La Tène pottery from East Anglia. Both from Abington Pigotts, Cambs. After Elsdon 1975. Scale = 10 cm.

most common design is the arc, which is normally **tooled** rather than rouletted and which is usually combined with circular impressions. Curvilinear designs predominate over rectilinear, and **globular bowls** are the most distinctive vessel form, though **saucepan pots** are also common. The decoration is confined to a single, albeit extensive, zone.

The Sussex region (Fig. 153) La Tène pottery utilizes most frequently the simple standing arc motif. Scroll patterns are rare. Large **globular jars** with **omphalos** bases, **pedestalled urns** and foot-ring jars are all common and saucepan pots are also present in the assemblage.

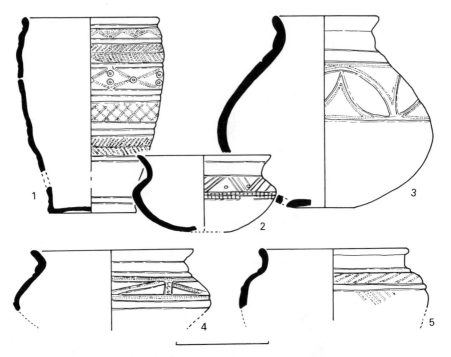

Fig. 155   La Tène pottery from Lincolnshire. 1, 2, 4, Dragonby; 3, Ingoldmells; 5, Ancaster. After Elsdon 1975. Scale = 10 cm.

The Thames Estuary (Fig. 152) and Lower Thames region group extensively exploits the interlocking-arc motif, with circular, stamped impressions also forming an important decorative element. Patches of **burnish** may be incorporated within the decorative scheme. Foot-ring or **globular jars** are most common in the assemblages and the decoration is usually restricted to a zone on the shoulder of the pots.

The East Anglia sub-style (Fig. 154) represents something of a lacuna, though Cunliffe's **Darmsden** style includes plain and decorated pottery from this region.

The Lincolnshire group (Fig. 155) makes abundant use of a double, square-toothed roulette as the main decorative tool, in contrast to the incised or tooled lines used elsewhere. Burnishing is also common and used to highlight aspects of the vessels' shapes or decoration. Circular and non-circular stamps are used and the variety of motifs is larger than in any other region. Both curvilinear and rectilinear styles are used, the former particularly on **globular jars** and bowls. S-profiled jars and bowls with **foot-ring** base are also common in the region. See also **Ancaster bowls** (Fig. 37).

Later neolithic impressed wares
Generic term given to a large variety of ceramics dating to the late third and early second millennia. They are broadly related by the abundant impressed decoration. See **cord, comb** and **bird-bone impressions**, and also **Peterborough ware, Meldon Bridge style, Ford style, Hebridean bowls** and **Rudston style**.

Leather-hard (Fig. 4:2)
The stage reached in the drying of clay when most of the **water of plasticity** has evaporated off, maximum **shrinkage** has occurred and the clay particles have come into contact with each other (Fig. 4:2). It is at this stage that most **surface treatments** and some secondary manufacturing techniques, such as paddling (see **paddle**), are executed, because the clay is still moist enough to allow alteration. Also known as green-hard.

Lime blowing (Figs. 72, 156, 157, 158)
Post-firing defect normally taking the form of small **spalls** pushed out of the walls of vessels containing **calcareous inclusions** (Fig. 157). When fired between 650° and 890°C, and in particular at temperatures in excess of 750°C, calcium carbonate decomposes to lime:

$$CaCO_3 \rightarrow CaO + CO_2 \uparrow.$$

After firing, the lime so formed will absorb water from the atmosphere to form slaked lime:

$$CaO + H_2O \rightarrow Ca(OH)_2.$$

In doing so, it undergoes an increase in volume which forces flakes out of the surface of the fired clay. In extreme cases, for example, high temperature or excess calcareous material, complete disintegration of the vessel may result (Fig. 156). Lime blowing is readily recognized by the presence of pits in the surface of a vessel, each containing a soft, white or yellowish **inclusion** (Fig. 157).

Lime blowing can be reduced or prevented by firing at a low temperature (below 750°) or in a **reducing atmosphere** (Letsch and Noll 1983) or by the addition of common salt (Fig. 158). (See Laird and Worcester 1956; Rye 1976; and Woods 1986, for a fuller discussion of this.) There is almost no evidence for the use of salt in British pottery and it therefore appears likely that disintegration of vessels containing calcareous inclusions was prevented by firing them at low temperatures. This is reinforced by the results of thermal expansion measurements carried out by Tite (1969, 140), which, although a largely unsuitable method for calcareous wares, indicated that the original firing temperature of a Romano-British **calcite-gritted** vessel from Yorkshire had been below 800°C.

Fig. 156   Lime blowing: calcareous inclusions have caused these six experimental bricks, fired to 900°C, to disintegrate. Scale in centimetres.

Fig. 157   Lime-blowing: after firing, the limestone inclusions have pushed small flakes (spalls) out of the surface of the sherds. Scale in centimetres.

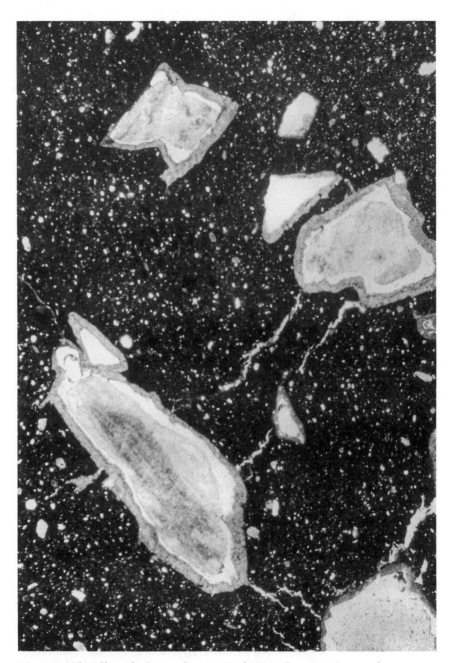

Fig. 158   The effect of salt on calcareous inclusions. Reaction rims can be seen surrounding the shell fragments in this experimental vessel; salt added to the clay has reacted with the shell during firing, attacking some of it but then forming stable compounds, so that it will be unaffected by lime blowing. PPL, × 28.

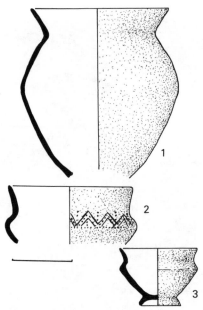

Fig. 159   Pottery of the Long Wittenham–Allen's Pits group, as identified by Cunliffe. 1, Long Wittenham, Berks.; 2, Dennis Pit, Oxon.; 3, Chinnor, Oxon. After Cunliffe 1974. Scale = 10 cm.

Long Wittenham-Allen's Pit group (Fig. 159)
Fifth- to third-century pottery from the Cotswold and Upper Thames Valley region, as identified by Cunliffe (1974, 38-9), consisting of sharply **shouldered jars** and bowls with wide, flaring rims. The pots are well made and often **burnished**. Decoration on the shoulder may be lightly **tooled** or consist of **fingertip impressions**. The style is related to the **All Cannings Cross–Meon Hill group** (Fig. 34).

Lugs
Projections, either **raised** or **applied**, protruding from the sides of vessels and which may or may not be functional. Some lugs, as found on third millennium pottery, such as **Windmill Hill ware** (Fig. 238) or **Hembury ware** (Fig. 135:1), may be either vertically or horizontally perforated (Smith 1965; Mercer 1981), and it has frequently been suggested that the perforations are to allow the suspension of the pots. Other lugs may be solid and their function is more difficult to speculate upon; a cord could still have been tied beneath the lugs to allow suspension. Equally, they may have been to aid the lifting of the vessel or have been skeuomorphic or even purely decorative. Small lugs, which again may or may not be perforated, are found on **food vessels**, particularly **Yorkshire vases** (Fig. 114:2) (Kitson-Clarke 1938) and on **grooved ware** (Fig. 131:4) (Wainwright and Longworth 1971). See also **trumpet lugs**.

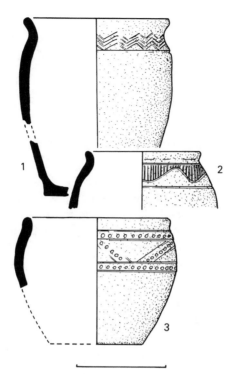

Fig. 160   Pottery of the Lydney–Llanmelin style as identified by Cunliffe. 1, Llanmelin, Monmouth; 2, 3, Lydney, Glos. After Cunliffe 1974. Scale = 10 cm.

Luting
The process whereby two pieces of clay are joined and, in particular, where extra parts, such as handles or **lugs**, are added to vessels. It is normally done when the vessel and the part to be added are in the **leather-hard** stage, and a clay **slip** or slurry is used as adhesive to ensure that the two parts are joined securely.

Lydney–Llanmelin style (Fig. 160)
Southern-Welsh variant of the **saucepan pots** identified by Cunliffe (1974, 43) and restricted in distribution to the coastal plain of South Wales. Chevrons and oval stabs, which tend not to appear in other groups, are distinctive of this style.

Maggots (Figs. 85, 161)
This term is described under **cord impressions**, but segmented **stamps** also occur on **La Tène** pottery from Lincolnshire and may be termed 'maggot stamps'.

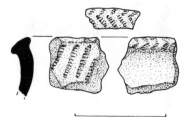

Fig. 161   Maggot impressions executed in whipped cord on pottery from Skendleby, Lincs. Scale = 5 cm.

Maiden Castle–Marnhull style (Fig. 162)

Dorset regional variant of the **saucepan pot** tradition, as identified by Cunliffe (1974, 44-5) and dating to the third to first centuries BC. The tradition is characterized by ovoid jars with **beaded** or slightly everted rims (Fig. 162:1). Occasionally, **countersunk handles** (Fig. 162:3), similar to those of **Durotrigian ware**, may be found. Grooved **scrolls**, wavy lines, arcs or dimples are used to decorate the vessels.

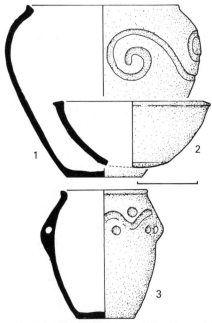

Fig. 162   Pottery from the Maiden Castle–Marnhill style, as identified by Cunliffe. After Cunliffe 1974. Scale = 10 cm.

Meldon Bridge style (Fig. 163)

Local Borders style of northern **later neolithic impressed wares** named after the pottery from the enclosure of Meldon Bridge in Peeblesshire (Burgess 1976*a*). The style is characterized by large vessels with open mouths, shallow concave necks, **carinations** and rounded bodies. No bases have been found and it is uncertain whether round or flat bases were used; however, the

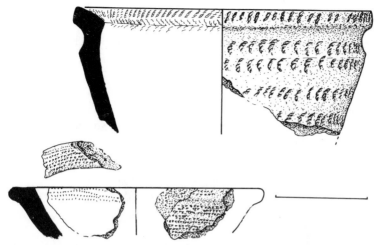

Fig. 163 Meldon Bridge style pottery from the type site. After Burgess 1976*a*. Scale = 10 cm.

profiles of published vessels suggest that the former may be more likely. The rim forms of these bowls are angular with external moulding and internal **bevel**, both of which may be **impressed** with **bird bone** and **twisted cord** decoration.

See also Gibson 1984, 1986*a*.

Metope motifs (Fig. 164)

Term used to describe panels of decoration which occur in bands or friezes and which are usually separated from each other by vertical lines. This type of

Fig. 164 Metope decoration on a beaker sherd from Burnt Fen, Cambs. Sherd height 13 cm.

decoration is particularly common on **beaker** pottery of the early second millennium and derives its name from the metopes of Greek architecture, viz. panels on the architrave of a building which are separated from each other by vertical triglyphs.

Mildenhall ware (Fig. 165)
A quite elaborately decorated, regional style of the **southern neolithic decorated bowl tradition** centring on East Anglia and eastern England

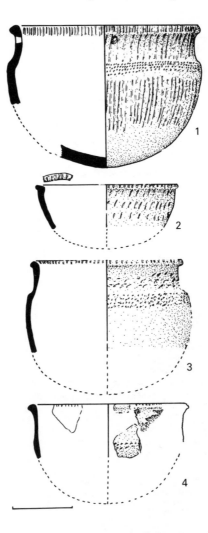

Fig. 165   Mildenhall ware. 1-3, Hurst Fen, Norfolk (after Clark 1960); 4, Briar Hill, Northants. (after Bamford 1975). Scale = 10 cm.

(Whittle 1977) and originally termed **East Anglia ware** by Piggott (1954, 72-4) to reflect its distribution. The style consists of bowls with shoulder **carinations** and with concave necks and everted rims, though some closed rims are also present (Clark *et al.* 1960; Clark and Godwin 1962). The pots are often deep and the rim forms may be thickened or rolled slightly, almost in anticipation of the heavier rims of the later neolithic **Peterborough ware**. The decoration is usually confined to the rim, extending sometimes into the interior of the vessel, and the neck; only occasionally does it extend to the lower body of the pot. Decorative techniques and motifs are simple, comprising simple **stabs, incision** or **fingernail impressions**, usually in vertical parallel lines. Multiple stabs frequently decorate the shoulder of the pots and they may be arranged in **metopes** or continuously. **Lugs** are rare and, if present, are almost vestigial.

Mohs' Scale
A scale of relative hardnesses of selected minerals which can be employed to help identify **inclusions** in pot **bodies**.

Hardness	Mineral	Comments
1	Talc	
2	Gypsum	Easily scratched with a fingernail
3	Calcite	Easily scratched by metal, distinctive rhombic shape, reacts with HCl
4	Fluorite	
5	Apatite	
6	Orthoclase	Difficult to scratch with metal
7	Quartz	Too hard to be scratched with metal, no reaction with HCl
8	Topaz	
9	Corundum	
10	Diamond	Extremely hard, will scratch glass

From this, it can be seen that the important hardnesses, from the point of view of trying to identify inclusions in archaeological ceramics, are 3 and 7. The degree of difficulty required to scratch inclusions, particularly those that are white or cream in colour, supplemented by a test with **hydrochloric acid**, is usually sufficient to distinguish **calcareous** from siliceous inclusions.

Mortlake ware (Fig. 180:2)
Second stage in the **Ebbsfleet–Mortlake–Fengate** progression of **Peterborough ware**, as defined by Smith (1956).

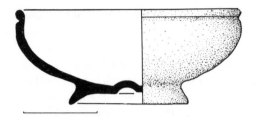

Fig. 166   Bowl with omphalos base from Hengistbury Head, Dorset. After Bushe-Fox 1915. Scale = 5 cm.

Omphalos (Fig. 166)
Small and internally convex boss on the base of a vessel, particularly of the first millennium. This device is a deliberate feature and not to be confused with **foot rings** or otherwise convex bases.

Open firing (Figs. 20-27, 167, 168)
Methods of firing vessels without a proper **kiln** structure. The most common methods are bonfires (Figs. 24-27, 167) or pits (Figs. 20-23). Open firings are rapid and economical of fuel. They are characterized by a rapid rise in temperature (Figs. 6, 7) and frequently last less than one hour, though the duration of the firing is largely determined by the type of fuel used (Woods 1983). Pit firings normally last longer than surface bonfires (Fig. 168): firstly, they are usually ignited from the top or side and the fire takes longer to burn to the bottom of the stack of fuel and, secondly, the walls of the pit retain heat and so ensure a lengthier cooling period than occurs in a surface firing. (See, for example, Lauer 1972, Woods 1983.) Temperatures in the range 650°-900°C are commonly attained, quite sufficient to ensure that the clay minerals have been through the **ceramic change**. Open-fired vessels can usually be recognized by the blotchy, multicoloured appearance of the surface, the presence of **fire clouds** (Figs. 109, 110), and of unburned **carbonaceous matter**, indicative of a short firing time, in the centre of sherds (Figs. 29, 69).

The use of the term **clamp** should be reserved to describe the structures used for the firing of brick and should not be applied to pottery.

Opening materials (Figs. 169, 170, 171)
Any **inclusions**, whether naturally occurring or added by the potter, that occur in a clay **body**. When added by the potter, they may also be called **filler** or **temper**. A great variety of materials, both mineral (Figs. 169, 170) and organic (Fig. 171), has been used. When a vessel is being constructed and the clay is in the wet, plastic state (see **plasticity**), such materials strengthen the clay and prevent the walls from collapsing in on themselves. However, in the

Fig. 167 Experimental open firing. The economical use of fuel should be noted.

fired product, they interrupt the bonding of the clay particles with one another and therefore have a weakening effect: a very coarse pot is much more easily broken than a fine one (see Fig. 8).

They also serve to facilitate drying by allowing water to evaporate more easily from the clay vessel and reduce **drying shrinkage**. However, the main function of opening materials in open-fired pottery (see **open firing**) is to open the body, allowing remanent **water of plasticity** to escape in the form of steam during the early stages of firing (see **water smoking**).

Overhanging-rim urn
Antiquated term, no longer in current use, for **collared urn.**

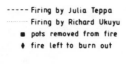

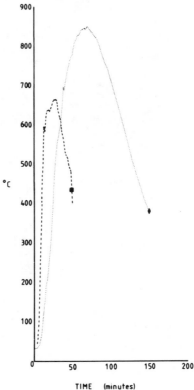

Fig. 168   Firing curves obtained in two firings using cow dung in Kavango, Namibia. The longer firing was a pit firing, the shorter one a surface bonfire.

Oxidation

Under **oxidizing conditions, iron oxides** present in clay will be brought to their highest state of oxidation and, depending on the amount present, will give a yellow or, more commonly, a red or reddish-brown colour to the fired clay. See **reduction**.

Open-fired vessels are usually not completely oxidized, because the atmosphere fluctuates during firing and the firing time involved is too short to allow for the total combustion of the organic matter present in the clay (Fig. 29) and for the iron oxides to be affected.

Fig. 169 Photomicrograph of a thin section of a prehistoric sherd from the long barrow at Skendleby, Lincs. Most of the large, angular, grey and mottled fragments are chunks of calcined flint. PPL, × 20.

Fig. 170 Photomicrograph of a thin section of an early neolithic sherd from Skendleby. Shell, including bivalve and brachiopod fragments, is the main inclusion present. XPL, × 20.

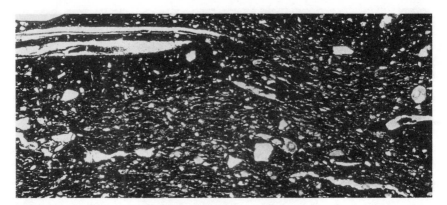

Fig. 171 Traces of vegetal matter, probably grass, in an Anglo-Saxon sherd. The elongated voids in the upper left-hand corner are characteristic and both contain charred traces of the original material. PPL, × 10.

Oxidizing conditions
Firing atmosphere characterized by the presence of excess oxygen. Under such conditions, the fire burns cleanly and total combustion results:
$$C + O_2 \rightarrow CO_2.$$
Pottery fired in such an atmosphere will be subject to **oxidation**.

Paddle (Figs. 17, 18:3, 49, 172)
A tool used in conjunction with an **anvil**, usually as a secondary method of manufacture. It can also be called a **beater**. There is little evidence for the use of the paddle and anvil technique in British prehistory, possibly because it has not been looked for. Signs of the method may be detected by **X-radiography** (Rye 1977), because it can impart characteristic **particle orientation** (Rye 1981, 85). Macroscopically, laminar fracture may indicate the use of a paddle (ibid.).

Park Brow–Caesar's Camp group (Fig. 173)
Jars and bowls with strongly everted necks and defined shoulders and which have been identified by Cunliffe (1974, 38) as occurring on settlement sites of the North and South Downs. The pottery is usually in a well-made **fabric** and may be **burnished**. Occasionally it may be decorated with **fingertip impressions** on the rim and shoulder. **Pedestalled bases** may be found.

Particle orientation (Figs. 174, 175)
The methods employed in the manufacture of pottery push clay particles, **voids** and **inclusions** present in the clay into positions such that their long axes are perpendicular to the direction of the forces employed. Elongated particles

Fig. 172   A paddle being used by a contemporary Gciriku potter in Kavango, Namibia.

(for example, shell fragments, mica laths, etc.) and voids only will be affected: equidimensional particles (for example, rounded sand grains) will not be subject to the forces in the same way. This orientation can be detected in a tangential **thin section** and **by X-radiography** and is characteristic of the manufacturing method employed. In **wheel-thrown** vessels, the characteristic orientation is diagonal; the faster the wheel is rotating, the steeper will be the angle of orientation away from the horizontal (Fig. 174). In **ring-** or **coil-built** pots, the particles become aligned with their long axes running horizontally and parallel to the rim and base of the vessel (Fig. 175).

See Lawrence and West 1982, 92 ff., Rye 1977 and Woods 1985 for fuller descriptions.

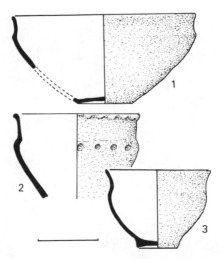

Fig. 173 Pottery of the Park Brow–Caesar's Camp group as identified by
Cunliffe. 1, St Catherine's Hill, Surrey; 2, Caesar's Camp, Surrey; 3, Chertsey,
Surrey. After Cunliffe 1974. Scale = 10 cm.

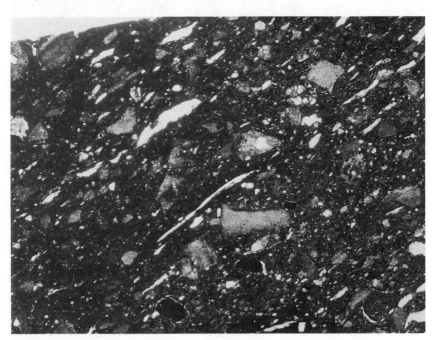

Fig. 174 Characteristic diagonal particle orientation revealed by a tangential thin
section of a wheel-thrown pot. The elongated white areas are voids and the
mottled inclusions are shell fragments. Medieval cooking pot from Bedford, PPL,
× 20.

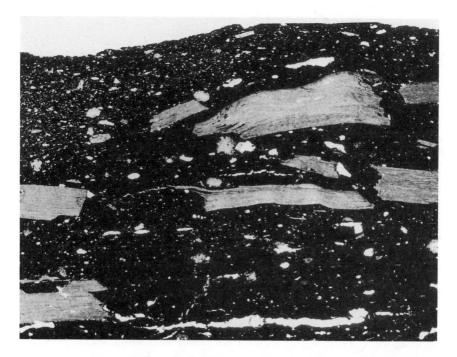

Fig. 175 Particle orientation in a ring-built vessel. The striated inclusions are cross-sections of shell plates, indicating that they have become aligned with their flat surfaces parallel to the rim and base. PPL, × 20.

Pedestalled base

A type of base common on late iron age pottery, particularly **Belgic** pottery, which, in essence, consists of an inverted cone of clay forming an elaborate stand for the vessel. Pedestals resemble the bell of a brass instrument. They vary considerably in height and degree of elaboration. See **pedestalled bowl, pedestalled jar or urn, Aylesford–Swarling, Belgic wares** and **Tazza.**

Pedestalled bowl or cup (Fig. 176)

See also **Belgic wares, Aylesford–Swarling** and **Tazza.** According to Thompson (1982), these are pedestalled variants of standard bowl and cup forms in a **grog**-filled **fabric**. As a class, they are difficult to recognize, since a large proportion needs to survive to allow positive identification. Thompson has subdivided this class as follows:

F1 Plain pedestalled vessels.
F2 Squat pedestalled bowls with **cordons.**
F3 Vessels with **carinations.**
F4 Small, splayed-rim vessels.
F5 Pedestalled bases not from **pedestalled urns.**

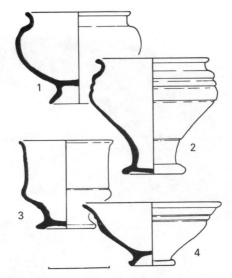

Fig. 176 Pedestalled bowls as classified by Thompson. 1, type F1, Broxbourne; 2, type F2, Billericay; 3, type F3, Lexden; 4, type F4, Harrold. After Thompson 1982. Scale = 10 cm.

These classes may be further subdivided, but such minutiae are beyond the scope of this work. F5 is also dubious as a class, representing, at best, portions of vessels whose survival is too poor to allow them to be positively assigned to any particular group.

Pedestalled jar or urn (Fig. 177)

Tall jars of the final pre-Roman Iron Age, recognized by the distinctive, **pedestalled bases** from which their name derives (see **Belgic pottery** and **Aylesford–Swarling**). The jars are tall, with narrow mouths. They sometimes have horizontal **cordons** and it has been suggested that the jars and pedestalled bases were made separately and bonded together, Thompson (1982) has divided these vessels into ten categories:

A1: Plain, pedestalled urns with ordinary feet, in which the pedestal profile is essentially flat, rounded and often dished on the underside.

A2: Pedestalled urns with 'dice-box' feet, in which the foot is deeper than the A1 type and has a triangular profile.

A3: Elaborately cordoned, pedestalled urns which, as the name suggests, are decorated at intervals over the exterior of the vessel with **raised**, encircling **cordons**.

A4: Pedestalled urns with dished feet, in which the underside of the base rises gently in a shallow arc.

A5: Urns with 'trumpet' pedestals, represented by pedestals with strongly dished bases and with an out-turned lip at the edge of the foot resembling the bell of a brass instrument.

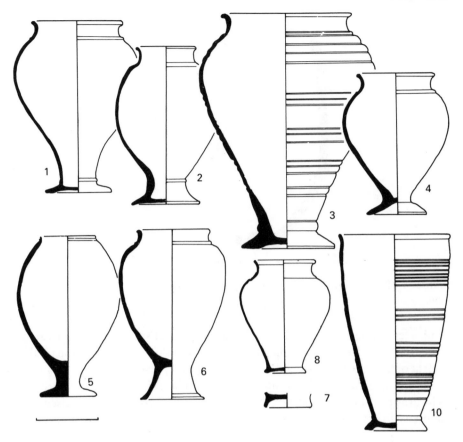

Fig. 177 Pedestalled urns. Types A1–A10 as classified by Thompson 1982. Scale = 10 cm.

A6: Urns with stunted pedestals, in which the pedestal is represented by little more than a **foot ring**.

A7: Urns with hollow, stunted pedestals and which are represented only by a few base sherds and may prove to be simply variants of other classes.

A8: Urns with flat-footed pedestals, and which are represented by vessels with strongly protruding feet and otherwise flat bases.

A9: Urns of unknown base type.

A10: Tall, conical jars with pedestals.

Of these types, A9 can clearly not be a type *sensu stricto* and the validity of type A7 is also open to question, as both may be badly damaged examples of other types.

Pennine urn (Fig. 178)

Regional variant of **collared urn,** as identified by Varley (1938). They are restricted in distribution to the Pennine and north-western region of England

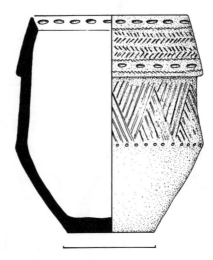

Fig. 178   Pennine urn from Bleasdale, Lancs. After Longworth 1984. Scale = 10 cm.

with a few outliers in the Yorkshire Wolds, Wales and Somerset. The urns are tripartite with deep necks, which take up about a third to a half of the total height of the vessel. The shoulder **carination** may be very slack and decorated with multiple circular depressions called 'necklace decoration' by Varley. The urns have an internal **bevel** and are frequently decorated with **incised** or **impressed** chevron or cross-hatched decoration on the collar and in the neck.

Perforated wall cups (Fig. 179)
Type of richly decorated **accessory vessel** named after the perforations in the wall of the pot. These may be simple holes punched through the wet clay of the newly formed pot or may be elaborate geometrically-shaped sections of clay actually cut from the vessel wall. These perforations were formerly thought to enable incense to escape from the vessel and the term **'incense cup'** was once used to refer to this type of pot. The term 'incense cup' is now rather antiquated.

Longworth (1983) has subdivided these cups into five categories:
A Cups with triangular and/or lozenge-shaped perforations.
B Cups with broad, rectangular perforations.
C Cups with broad, oval perforations.
D Cups with round perforations greater than 10 mm in diameter.
E Cups with narrow, vertical perforations.
Of these, A and E show marked regional distributions, A occurring in an Irish Sea province, and E restricted mainly to southern England. The decorative repertoire on these cups consists of **incised** and, though more rarely,

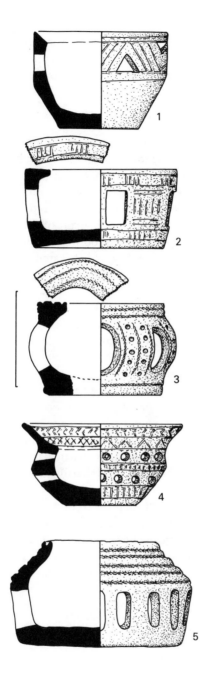

Fig. 179 Perforated wall cups. 1, type A, Stanton Moor, Derbys.; 2, type B, West Ayton Moor, Yorks.; 3, type C, Great Shefford, Berks.; 4, type D, Wylye, Wilts.; 5, type E, Portsdown, Hants. After Longworth 1983. Scale = 5 cm.

impressed geometric motifs, derived mainly from **grooved ware, beaker** and **collared urn** influence. The last type of pottery is frequently, though not exclusively, associated with these vessels. Perforated wall cups may also be called fenestrated cups.

Peterborough ware (Fig. 180)

This style of pottery once gave its name to the entire **later neolithic impressed ware** tradition (Piggott 1954, 302-16) but has now been relegated to a regional style covering mainly southern and eastern England. Terms such as 'Peterborough northern ware' were, at one time, used to describe the material north of Yorkshire, but this term has been abandoned in favour of later neolithic impressed ware and with local styles recognizable within that greater tradition (Manby 1975). Peterborough ware was defined by R. A. Smith (Wyman-Abbott 1910) and named after finds of elaborately decorated pottery with **impressed decoration** found at a multiple-pit site at Fengate near Peterborough.

I. F. Smith (1956) divided the tradition into three chronological steps based on the development of form and decoration. The distinctive **carination** on Peterborough vessels is developed out of the carinated-bowl forms of the earlier third millennium and this can be most clearly seen in the earliest of the styles:

The **Ebbsfleet** style (Fig. 180:1), named after a valley-bottom site in Kent. In this style, the rim is developed but no more so than, say **Mildenhall ware**, and is certainly not over-accentuated. The carination is usually quite sharp and the neck is wide. The decoration is simple, consisting mainly of **incised** decoration and with some **impressions**, particularly the advent of **twisted-cord** decoration. Cross-hatching and **herring-bone motifs** are the most commonly occurring.

The **Mortlake** style (Fig. 180:2) is the second style and sees a development of the rim, which becomes heavy, rounded and sometimes even angular. The neck becomes thinner vertically but pronounced in depth to the extent that it is almost a deep **cavetto zone**. Decoration is profuse, involving a multitude of decorative techniques, though the motifs are usually simple, such as herring-bone or encircling lines. Decorative techniques used on this style include **whipped cord, twisted cord, bird bone, fingernail, fingertip, reed and quill impressions.** In both this and the Ebbsfleet style, decoration may extend into the vessel but if this occurs, it rarely extends below the neck. These bowls are round-based.

The **Fengate** style (Fig. 180:3) is the third style, named after the site at Peterborough, and at first sight appears to be very different from the preceding styles, as it has a heavy collar, a tapering body and a flat base which seems to be more closely related to **collared urns** than to round-based bowls.

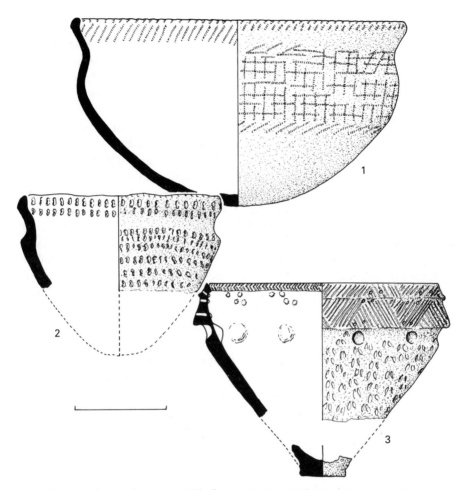

Fig. 180 Peterborough ware. 1, Ebbsfleet style, Windmill Hill, Wilts. (after Smith 1965); 2, Mortlake style, West Kennet, Wilts.; 3, Fengate style, West Kennet, Wilts. (2, 3, after Piggott 1963). Scale = 10 cm.

In fact, however, the development is clear. The rim of Mortlake ware slips down at an angle to create the collar; the cavetto zone beneath this collar is derived from the neck of Mortlake ware and then the body slopes down to an impractically small base. This is an unusual development and the reasons for it are hard to explain (see Chapter 2). It may be that the base is influenced by **beaker** and **grooved ware** pots which were in contemporary use and which had flat bases, or else it may have been derived from flat-based, northern styles, such as the **Rudston style**. The base is always tiny in relation to the maximum diameter and the height of the pot. This means that each pot was invariably unsteady, even on a flat surface. It is unlikely that this base was ever intended to be functional, so vessels may have been suspended by a cord, either passed through holes in the neck or wrapped round the neck, held in place by the collar. As yet, the reason for the flat base is uncertain. The decorative repertoire of the Mortlake style continues in the Fengate style, with the addition of geometric motifs such as filled triangles, especially on the collar and heralding the collared urn tradition which evolves from it.

The chronology of these three styles cannot be given precisely as many finds were made before radiocarbon dating or are from dubious contexts, and though the stylistic progression from Ebbsfleet ware to Fengate ware is unequivocal, this development must be chronological in only the broadest terms. Ebbsfleet, Mortlake and Fengate wares were all found in the same context at the West Kennet long barrow (Piggott 1962) and there was certainly a period around 1800 bc in which all three styles were in contemporary use (Smith 1974, 111-3). Nevertheless, radiocarbon dates suggest that Ebbsfleet ware was in use by the beginning of the second half of the third millennium, that Mortlake ware was in use by the end of the third millennium and that Fengate ware was developed shortly afterwards and continued in use until about 1700 bc.

Pigmy cups (Fig. 181)
A blanket term for the small **accessory cups** frequently found accompanying cremation burials of the early second millennium. See also **Aldbourne cups**, **grape cups** and **perforated wall cups**.

Pinch pottery (Fig. 182)
The simplest method of pottery manufacture, involving the opening out and expanding of a ball or cone of clay by squeezing the clay between the fingers, while the shape is supported by and turned in the potter's hand. It tends to result in small, round-based, open shapes (such as bowls), in which the method of manufacture can be recognized by the indentations in the vessel walls left by the pressure of the potter's hands. It can, however, be used as a preliminary method of manufacture, the shape so formed being added to later by the addition of coils or rings of clay: present-day Gciriku potters in the Kavango region of Namibia start all their vessels by forming the base in this way (Fig. 182), adding flattened rings, or straps, of clay and finishing the vessels by using a tool known as a rib (Fig. 18:1 shows an example) and paddle to join the rings and smooth and expand the walls (Figs. 17, 172). (See Woods 1984b, 303-7, for a detailed description of this technique.) It has generally been thought that pinch pottery was probably not used in antiquity or, if the technique were employed, it was purely for the manufacture of small vessels (see, for example, Howard 1981, 25), but this is to deny the possible use of the technique as a preliminary method of manufacture, to be

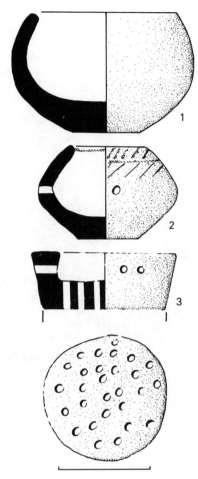

Fig. 181 Pigmy cups. 1, Forgan, Fife; 2, Musselburgh, East Lothian; 3, Wilsford, Wilts.; 1, 2, after Longworth 1984, 3, after Annable and Simpson 1964. Scale = 5 cm.

supplemented by other methods, as in the African example given above; as with other less immediately obvious methods of manufacture, it may have been missed because researchers have not known what to look for.

Plaited cord impressions (Fig. 223:1, 2)
See **cord impressions**.

Plastic
See **plastic decoration** and **plasticity**.

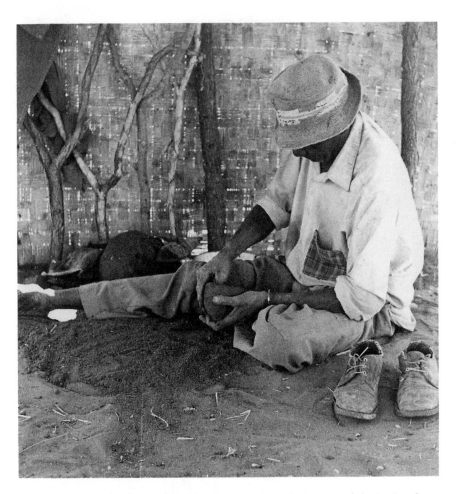

Fig. 182 A contemporary Namibian potter opening out a cone of clay, using the pinch-pottery method. The shape is subsequently enlarged by the addition of vertically rolled clay rings.

Plastic decoration
Decoration that is modelled on the wall of a vessel, being either **applied** (Fig. 38) or **raised**. Particularly common are **cordons** on pottery such as **grooved ware** and zig-zag decoration on the necks of **food vessel urns**. See also **plasticity**.

Plasticity
The property of clay which allows it to be deformed by pressure and to retain the shape created once the pressure has been removed. It is the result of water being present between the clay particles, which allows them to glide over each

Fig. 183 Pleochroism of biotite mica in thin section (1). When the crystal is aligned with its cleavage traces parallel to the north–south cross-wire, it appears light in colour. PPL, × 40.

other. The smaller the clay minerals involved, the more water can be adsorbed between the particles in a given volume of clay; therefore, **sedimentary clays**, the particles of which have been physically broken down by transport, are more plastic than **residual clays**.

Pleochroism (Figs. 183, 184)
An optical property shown by some minerals when examined in **thin section** with plane polarized light in the **polarizing microscope**. Pleochroic minerals are coloured and change colour when the microscope stage is rotated. A typical example of a pleochroic mineral is biotite; when its cleavage traces are parallel with the north–south crosswire in the microscope, it is typically yellow or light brown in colour (Fig. 183), but when the crystal is turned through 90°, so that the cleavage is parallel with the east–west crosswire, it usually exhibits a dark brown colour (Fig. 184).

Polarizing microscope (Fig. 185)
The microscope used for the examination of **thin sections** of rock and pottery and of **heavy mineral** samples. It employs transmitted light, but its distinguishing features are a rotating stage and a pair of polarizing filters; the

Fig. 184   Pleochroism of biotite mica in thin section (2). When the microscope stage is turned so that the cleavage traces are parallel to the east–west cross-wire, the crystal appears dark in colour. PPL, × 40.

latter limit the vibrations of light to one plane and are mounted in the microscope at right angles to each other. When both are in position (crossed polars, cross polarized light, XPL), the field of view is black until a thin section is placed on the microscope stage; many of the minerals present will have the ability to rotate the light so that it can pass through the top polarizer (the analyzer) and so will appear coloured (Fig. 186). When the stage is rotated, minerals or clay matrices that are anisotropic (or optically active) will change colour, going black at intervals of 90°, while isotropic (optically inactive) minerals and clay matrices will always appear dark. Such properties (isotropism, anisotropism) may help in the identification of the minerals present. When the lower polarizer only is in position (plane polarized light, PPL), the field of view is white and many of the minerals present will be transparent (Fig. 187). Others, however, may show colour and will exhibit **pleochroism,** i.e. they will change colour when the stage is rotated (Figs. 183, 184).

Polish
See **burnish.**

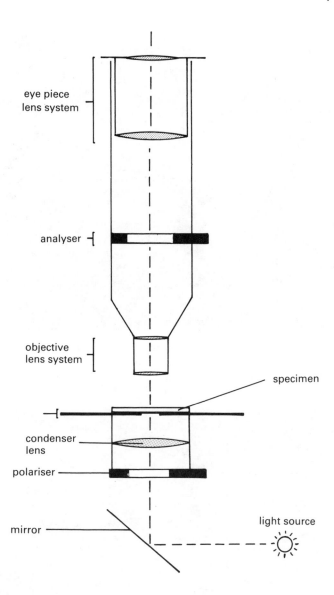

Fig. 185 Diagrammatic section through a polarizing microscope. After Tite 1972, 216. Not to scale.

Fig. 186 Photomicrograph of a thin section of neolithic pottery from the Philippines. This view has been taken with both polarizer and analyser in position (XPL), so many of the crystals show colour. The striped and white grains are feldspars and the grey fragments are amphiboles. × 15.

Fig. 187 The same view taken with only the polarizer in position (PPL). Most of the amphiboles still appear grey but are rather lighter in colour (in reality they are green), but the feldspars are transparent. × 15.

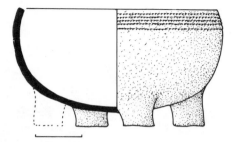

Fig. 188 Beaker polypod bowl from Inkpen Hill, Berks. After Clarke 1970. Scale = 10 cm.

Polypod bowl (Fig. 188)
A shallow, open bowl with a rounded base and three or more small feet on which it stands. This type of vessel is notable in the **beaker** assemblages of the second millennium BC and has close Continental parallels (Clarke 1970). See also **tripod vessels.**

Potbeaker (Figs. 107:2, 189)
Large variant of early second millennium **beaker** which is usually decorated with **fingernail** or **fingertip impressions** (Clarke 1970; Gibson 1980). The type is commonly found on domestic sites (Gibson 1982) and may be up to almost 1 m in height. The fabric is correspondingly thicker than the fine ware beakers.

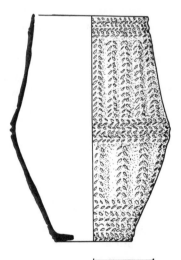

Fig. 189 Potbeaker with fingernail impressions from Butley, Essex. After Clarke 1970. Scale = 10 cm.

Fig. 190   Clay vessels being preheated prior to firing, Kavango, Namibia.

Preheating (Fig. 190)
A process sometimes used to warm clay vessels prior to **open firing**. It is aimed at heating them gently through the **water smoking** stage, thereby driving off remanent **water of plasticity** before firing proper is commenced. Archaeologically, it is unlikely to leave any remains different from those of an ordinary hearth and will probably always be impossible to recognize. However, there is much ethnographic evidence for the use of this technique and archaeologists should be aware that it might have been used.

Primary clay
See **residual clay**.

Raised decoration
Plastic decoration which is raised up from the body of the pot and thus differs in technique from **applied decoration**, which superficially is often identical in effect. **Cordons** and/or knobs are the most frequently used raised decorative motifs and are particularly common on **grooved ware** (Fig. 131:2) and later pottery of the second and first millennia.

Reducing conditions

Firing atmosphere characterized by the shortage or absence of oxygen. Under such conditions, combustion will be incomplete and carbon monoxide will be created.

$$2C + O_2 \rightarrow 2CO.$$

Reducing conditions are almost impossible to maintain in an **open firing** because the atmosphere is constantly changing, but if such conditions are sufficiently stringent in a **kiln**, **reduction** of the **iron oxides** in clay bodies will occur.

Reduction

The carbon monoxide evolved under **reducing conditions** has an affinity for oxygen (i.e. it is oxygen-hungry) and will attempt to obtain it from any available source; if none is present in the firing atmosphere, it will take it from the **iron oxides** in the clay bodies being fired, removing some of the oxygen (not all, as is the case in metal smelting) and reducing them to lower oxides which are dark (brown, grey or black) in colour.

$$Fe_2O_3 + CO \rightarrow 2FeO + CO_2$$

or
$$3Fe_2O_3 + CO \rightarrow 2Fe_3O_4 + CO_2.$$

For this reason, properly reduced wares usually exhibit one or more of these colours, depending on the amount of iron oxide present in the clay and the stringency of the reducing atmosphere. Other factors can intensify the colours. For instance, if the atmosphere in the kiln is reducing, some of the fuel and the **carbonaceous matter** present in clay will not be burned during the firing and a smoky atmosphere, with plenty of free carbon, will result; this carbon, in the form of soot, may be deposited on the pots or within the pores of the fabric, intensifying the dark colour. (This is also what happens in **smoking** or **smudging**.)

Reduction is as yet not fully understood, even by those in the ceramics industry. Unfortunately, archaeologists have an even less comprehensive grasp of the problem, to the extent that the literature is full of statements to the effect that, if a pot is black, it has been reduced. This is particularly true of many reports on prehistoric pottery. However, although superficial, patchy surface reduction can sometimes be achieved, it is not possible to produce completely reduced wares in an open firing, as the atmosphere fluctuates rapidly and constantly within the fire and cannot be controlled for any length of time. Consequently, black patches and surfaces of pottery produced in such firings are usually the effects of smudging and not of reduction. Black colouration in the centre of open-fired sherds (Figs. 29, 69) is the result of incomplete oxidation, not reduction. Proper reduction only occurs when the iron oxides are affected, usually over quite lengthy periods of time and at temperatures in excess of 850°C.

Reed impressions

Small circular impressions found on late third and early second millennia pottery and thought to have been formed by a hollow reed pressed into the clay to give a ring-shaped impression. Often this reed has been impressed diagonally into the clay to form a crescentic impression. Little work has been done on the authenticity of the identification; cut quills, straw or the scar from a shed leaf will produce similar impressions, and thus the name 'reed' must be regarded as a convention. The circular impressions in the food vessel in Fig. 30 may be reed impressions.

Repair holes (Fig. 191)

These can sometimes be seen in the wall of a pot, usually high up in the profile, and consist of a pair of drilled holes made after the pot has been fired and has broken in use. Through these holes, cord or sinew could be passed and pulled tight to bind together a crack or fracture in the vessel wall. Where only a single hole exists, signs of wear can often be seen on the side of the repair hole to indicate the direction of binding. Care must be taken in the identification of these features, as they may also be confused with holes designed to facilitate the fastening of a cover over the pot or to allow the suspension of the vessel.

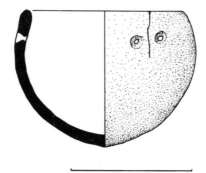

Fig. 191   Repair holes either side of a crack in a small cup from Windmill Hill, Wilts. The section shows the typical 'hour-glass' profile, indicating that the holes have been drilled through the fabric of the pot from both sides. After Smith 1965. Scale = 10 cm.

Residual clay

A **clay** which has not been transported from its site of formation. Also known as primary clays, such clays generally consist of relatively large particles and are accordingly less **plastic** than **sedimentary clays**. The china clay deposits around St Austell in Cornwall provide an excellent example of a residual clay; they are very pure, consisting almost entirely of kaolinite, and contain little colouring matter and few organic impurities. As a result of this purity and large size, they are not very plastic and require a very high firing temperature; they were not utilized in prehistory for the manufacture of pottery. At Legis Tor on Dartmoor, however, the Dartmoor Exploration Committee found that a cracked pot sunk into the floor of a hut circle had been sealed with china clay (Baring Gould 1896); from this, it can be seen that the clays were at least known to prehistoric populations, even if they did not possess the technology to use them for potting purposes.

Residue analysis
Analysis of the residues found within a pot, in the form of either carbon encrustations or organic residues absorbed by and surviving within the fabric of the pot, in order to try to determine the former contents and thus the use of the vessel.
See Evans 1984, Hill 1984.

Ribbon-handled urns
See **Cornish urns** (Fig. 90).

Ridged bowls
Bowls with multiple **carinations** on the outside of the body, giving them a corrugated effect (Fig. 114:11). This characteristic is most commonly found on **food vessels** of the early second millennium. Contemporary **ridged vases** (Fig. 114:6) are also found.

Ridged vases (Fig. 114:6)
See **ridged bowls** and **food vessels**.

Rilling (Fig. 192)
Grooves and ridges found particularly on the inside surfaces of **wheel-thrown** vessels, created by irregularities in the clay catching on the potter's hands as the walls of the vessel are drawn up and expanded during manufacture. They tend to be more pronounced in **closed vessels**, as the shape of the pot prevents the potter from reaching inside to smooth them out or remove them. They can be an indicator of the direction in which the wheel was turning during manufacture: the vessel should be held and turned in a horizontal plane; if the rilling grooves are a spiral from top right to bottom left, the wheel was rotating in an anticlockwise direction.

Fig. 192   Rilling grooves on the inside of a Romano-British wheel-thrown pot.
Scale in centimetres.

Rim moulding (Fig. 78)

Any elaboration of rim design found either externally or internally. In pottery
of the late third and early second millennia, the moulding is usually angular
and complements the **bevel**. See, for example, Fig. 78:2, 3.

Ring-building (Figs. 193, 194)

A method of vessel construction involving the use of rings of clay. It is similar
to **coiling**, except that a ring is only long enough to go once around the
diameter of the clay vessel (Fig. 193), while a coil is frequently applied as a
longer roll of clay spiralling around the vessel (see, for example, Litto 1976,
158–9). Vessels tend to break along the joins between the rings if they are
not securely bonded because the junctions provide planes of weakness (see

Fig. 193   A modern potter ring-building a pot in Kavango, Namibia. The join in the ring can be clearly seen below the potter's left wrist.

false rim, join void). A stronger bond should be achieved by applying the rings or coils on a diagonal (Fig. 16) or by using a tongue-and-groove technique, as these result in a greater surface area for bonding (Fig. 11:2, 4, 5, 9). Both methods were extensively used in the manufacture of European prehistoric pottery (see Stevenson 1953, Woods 1989). The beaker in Fig. 194 is a good example of the diagonal bonding technique: the rings visible to the eye are illustrated in the section on the left-hand side of the drawing and can be seen to be about 3 cm in height, including the diagonal facets, and the fact that the diagonals in the upper half of the vessel slope in the opposite direction suggests that the vessel may have been made in two parts that were joined together.

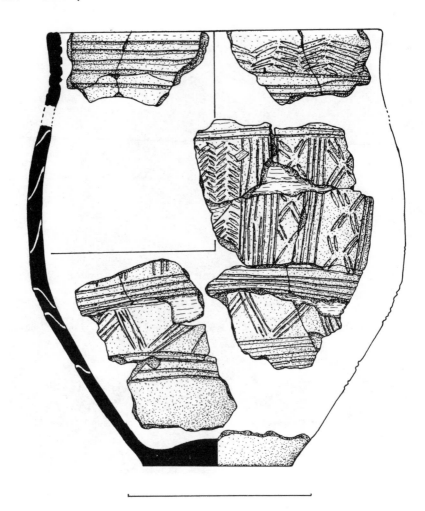

Fig. 194   A ring-built beaker from Northton, Harris, clearly showing diagonal bonding. Scale = 10 cm.

Rinyo–Clacton ware (Fig. 131)

A name often applied to **grooved ware** to denote the geographical distribution of the style (Piggott 1954, 321 ff.). Though occasionally still used, the term is rather antiquated and does not take into account the western distribution of the tradition into Wessex and even Ireland. Grooved ware is now the more acceptable term.

Rinyo style (Fig. 131)

Northern sub-style of **grooved ware**.

Roseisle bowls (Fig. 60)
Scottish regional style of **Grimston–Lyles Hill ware**. See **Boghead bowls**.

Rosettes
A circular motif common in the **La Tène** decorated pottery groups and recognized by a circle of **impressed** dots (Fig. 140:1) or dimples, often around a central depression. Grimes (1952) suggested that these motifs represent a reverse imitation of metal bosses. On earlier pottery, the name may be used to describe decorative roundels of clay usually **applied** to the surface of the vessel and elaborated with incised decoration (Fig. 103).

Rothesay style (Fig. 195)
Deep, baggy-profiled pots of the third millennium in western Scotland (McInnes 1969). They are associated with Clyde tombs (Scott 1964) and have heavy, T-sectioned rims, which are either left undecorated or have simple, obliquely **incised decoration**. **Lugs** may be found around the upper portion of the vessel.

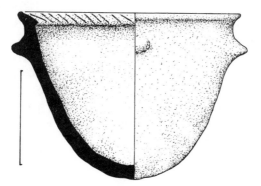

Fig. 195 Bowl in the Rothesay style from the type site. After Piggott 1954. Scale = 10 cm.

Rouletting
Decoration resembling **comb impressions** but apparently formed by a circular toothed wheel, which is rolled along the surface of the wet clay, leaving small separate impressions. No such roulettes have yet been found, however. The technique is most commonly used on pottery decorated in the **La Tène** style of the late first millennium, either to form linear decoration or as infilling of geometric motifs. See Fig. 155:1, 3, 4, 5.

Rudston style (Fig. 196)
Style of **later neolithic impressed ware** from the Yorkshire Wolds and recognized by simple incised decoration, a T-sectioned rim and a straight-

Fig. 196   Rudston style of later neolithic impressed ware from the type site. After Manby 1975. Scale = 10 cm.

sided body, which tapers to a flat base (Manby 1975). This is one of the few flat-based styles of the impressed tradition, but the base may be rather uneven, causing the vessel to stand unsteadily, and it is not very practical. The pottery may be decorated all over, usually with **incised decoration** forming a **herring-bone motif** or with **fingertip impressions**; this decoration may extend over the rim and into the interior of the vessel. This style may be regarded as a proto-**food vessel** similar to the **Meldon Bridge** style of southern Scotland and the Borders (Gibson 1984).

Running scroll (Fig. 140:1)
Decorative motif of the later Iron Age found on both metalwork and pottery. See **La Tène pottery, scroll, Glastonbury ware, Hunsbury bowls, Frilford bowls, Dragonby sequence**, etc.

Rustication
A general term given to any roughening of the surface of a vessel for either functional or decorative purposes. For example, in the case of **butt beakers** (Fig. 42:6), the surface may be roughened by either incision or thick **slip** or by rolling the vessel in sand before drying; it is thought that this may have been to facilitate handling of the vessel in general use. Vessels with **fingernail** and **fingertip impressions** from the early second millennium are frequently called rusticated but this is a slight misuse of the term; such descriptions should always be qualified, for example, as fingertip or fingernail rustication).

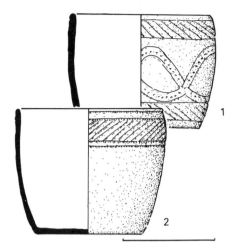

Fig. 197 Saucepan pots. 1, curvilinear design, Blewburton Hill, Berks.; 2, geometric design, Maiden Castle, Dorset. After Cunliffe 1974. Scale = 10 cm.

Saucepan pot (Fig. 197)
A tradition of decorated pots with upright or slightly bulging sides and simple or **beaded rims**, dating from the third to the first centuries BC. The decoration on these pots can either be rectilinear or curvilinear, the latter tending to cover the entire outer surface of the vessel while the former is normally restricted to a zone in the upper third of the vessel. The tradition is a southern one, distributed from Surrey and Sussex in the east to Somerset in the west, the vessels being extremely rare north of the Thames (Harding 1974, 194-6; Cunliffe *et al.* 1964).

St Catherine's Hill–Worthy Down style (Fig. 198)
A local style of **saucepan pot,** as identified by Cunliffe (1974, 43), centred on Hampshire. It is recognized by a zone of decoration consisting of oblique, **incised** lines bordered by **impressed** dots, considered by Cunliffe to imitate stitching. Jars are also found in this style and may also be decorated with the characteristic motif. Encircling incised lines and wavy incised lines are also found on the bodies of these pots.

Scored ware
Also known as Ancaster–Breedon ware. The predominant middle iron age, pottery type of the East Midlands area, ranging from Northamptonshire to Lincolnshire but centred around Breedon-on-the Hill, Leics., the upper Nene and the Trent Rivers. It continued in use into the Roman period. The surface treatment from which it derives its name consists of rough, random **incised**

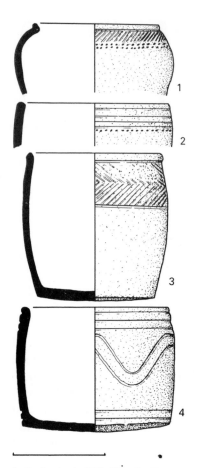

Fig. 198 Pottery of the St Catherine's Hill–Worthy Down style. 1, Worthy Down, Hants.; 2, Twyford Down, Hants.; 3, St Catherine's Hill, Hants.; 4, The Trundle, Sussex. After Cunliffe 1974. Scale = 10 cm.

decoration. (See Elsdon 1989, 22 and 37.) The incision is sometimes shallow, so that the vessels resemble **wiped wares**, and often has raised edges, indicating that it was executed when the clay was relatively wet.

Scroll (Figs. 136:6; 140:1)
A curvilinear motif on **La Tène** decorated pottery of the third to first centuries BC (Grimes 1952; Elsdon 1975). It normally takes the form of two circles linked by a curving line from the top of one circle to the base of the other (Fig. 136:6), resembling a partly unrolled scroll, after which the motif is named. **Running scroll** (Fig. 140:1) is a continuous variation of the simple scroll, in which a circle will be in effect the start of one scroll and the end of the

previous motif. Interlocking horizontal-S designs have a similar effect. The motif may be executed using **roulette** or **incised decoration**, and may be open or filled with cross-hatching.

Secondary clay
See **sedimentary clay**.

Sedimentary clay
A clay which has been transported from its site of formation. Movement of the clay (for example, by water, wind or glacial action) brings about a physical breakdown of the clay particles, with the result that sedimentary clays have greater **plasticity** than **residual clays**. They usually also contain more organic material and mineral and rock **inclusions** as a result of being moved. Although there are some exceptions (see **gabbroic wares**), sedimentary clays are the types of clays that would normally have been used for the manufacture of prehistoric pottery: **residual clays** are usually too pure, contain too few inclusions and require too high a firing temperature to be used for open firing.

Shell impressions (Fig. 199)
Impressions formed when the edge of a shell has been used to decorate pottery. The resulting impressions are similar to **comb impressions** and indeed the finding of **beaker** pottery of the early second millennium with such shell impressions suggests that shells were used as a substitute for combs. Shell impressions are most commonly found on pottery of the early second millennium from the coastal sites of northern Britain (Simpson 1976; Gibson 1982).

Shetland neolithic house ware (Fig. 200)
Highly decorated pottery of the late third millennium associated mainly with the stone houses and settlement sites of Shetland (Calder 1956; Whittle 1986). The pottery is flat-based and decorated with geometrically arranged **incised** lines and **comb impressions**. The vessels may be either simple or bipartite with upright necks and bulbous bodies. The change in direction may be slight and may be marked by a shallow waist groove. The forms with upright necks and geometric decoration may be imitations of northern-British **beakers** (Gibson 1984).

Shouldered jars
Generally upright jars with sharply angled shoulders in the upper third of the vessel. See **Kilellan jars, Darmsden-Linton group, Ivinghoe-Sandy group, situla jar**, etc.

Fig. 199 Cockle shells and shell impressions on sherds from Northton, Harris. The impressions are different because the shells have been pressed into the surfaces at different angles; yet another effect can be seen on the experimental vessel in Fig. 112. Scale in centimetres.

Shrinkage

Clay shrinks during drying and, at temperatures in excess of about 900°C, during firing (Fig. 231). During drying, it is a direct result of the amount of free water present and fine clays will shrink more than coarse ones: the smaller the clay particles, the greater the amount of water that can be adsorbed between the particles to make the clay **plastic**, and therefore the greater will be the shrinkage as the clay dries. Drying shrinkage can be reduced by the addition of **opening materials**, which effectively take the place of clay in a given volume. Less water will therefore be needed to produce a workable body and, as a consequence, less shrinkage will occur as the clay dries. Drying shrinkage frequently results in voids around opening materials (see, for example, Fig. 129).

Firing shrinkage occurs as the clay particles begin to melt at high temperatures. It rarely occurs at temperatures below about 900°C; in contrast, most clays actually expand by small amounts, becoming increasingly porous, during the early stages of firing up to about 800°C. (See Grimshaw 1971, 803-5, Hamer 1975, 124, and Woods (in press) for fuller

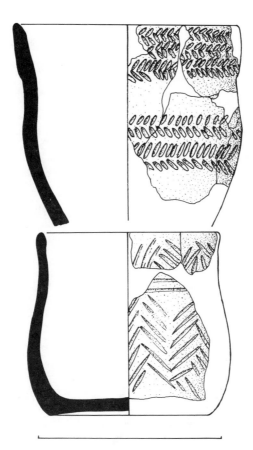

Fig. 200   Neolithic pottery, obviously beaker-influenced, from the Shetland stone houses. Ness of Gruting, Shetland. After Henshall 1956. Scale = 10 cm.

discussions of this.) Few vessels produced during prehistory are likely to have been affected by firing shrinkage.

Sintering
The stage in firing when the edges of the clay particles begin to soften and melt and stick together. It represents the initial stage in the **vitrification** process and results in a harder, denser and more rigid body.

Situla jars (Fig. 201)
Upright jars with sharply angled shoulders and upright or slightly flaring necks, thought to be pottery copies of metal situla prototypes of the seventh century BC (Clark and Fell 1953). Pottery from **West Harling** is typical of this style, in which even the **fingertip** decoration on the rims, shoulders and bodies

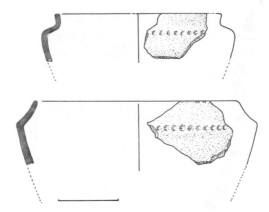

Fig. 201   Situla jars from Staple Howe, Yorks. After Harding 1974. Scale = 10 cm.

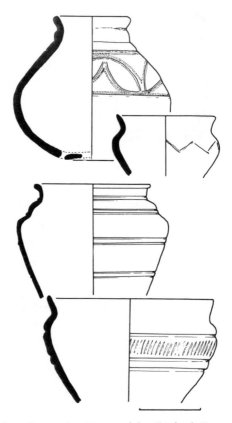

Fig. 202   Pottery from Dragonby, Lincs., of the Sleaford–Dragonby style as identified by Cunliffe. After May 1963. Scale = 10 cm.

is thought to imitate the rivets of sheet bronze vessels. Harding (1974, 139-40) suggests that large bipartite vessels, but without the extended neck, may likewise be copies of the Meppen–Gladbach situla type.

Slashed cordons (Fig. 131:4)
Cordons decorated with short strokes of incised decoration placed at right angles to, or obliquely across, the direction of the cordon. Commonly found on grooved ware (Fig. 131:4).

Sleaford–Dragonby style (Fig. 202)
Lincolnshire variant, as identified by Cunliffe (1974, 46), of the saucepan pot tradition of the third to first centuries BC. Bowl forms with everted necks or extended, upright necks are common and are usually black, well-finished and burnished. Coarse, shouldered jars are also found. Decoration usually consists of stamped circles linked by incised, tooled or rouletted arcading. This type of pottery influences the later Aylesford–Swarling complex. A Dragonby sequence has been identified by May (1976).

Slip (Figs. 203, 206)
Surface treatment involving the application of a suspension of clay in water to a vessel in the leather-hard stage. It can be both decorative and functional: it is most usually employed to change the colour of a vessel (for example, Romano-British wares from the Nene Valley, which frequently have a creamy-yellow fabric covered with a brown or black slip) but may also be used to reduce the permeability of food and drinking vessels by partially sealing the surface.

Slips are applied in a viscous state by dipping, pouring or painting. They are not absorbed to any great extent by the clay body and in thin section are easily distinguished as an optically inactive, separate layer on the surface (Figs. 203, 206).

Slip-trailing, a technique akin to icing a cake, was also used, at least during the Roman period, to build up plastic features on the surface of a vessel or to add different coloured slips.

Smoking or smudging (Figs. 204, 205)
A technique used to deposit carbon on and immediately below the surface of a vessel in order to turn it black (Fig. 204). Although macroscopically similar to slip, in thin section it can often be seen to be a much thinner and less regular layer (Figs. 205, 206).

South Lodge urns (Fig. 207)
Type of barrel urn of the Deverel–Rimbury complex.

Fig. 203   Slip, as shown in a thin section of a Romano-British fine ware vessel.
The black layer on both surfaces is slip and additional white slip decoration,
applied on top of the dark slip on the external surface of the vessel, is visible on the
far right-hand side. PPL, × 30.

Fig. 204 Smoking or smudging on the surface of sherds from a modern vessel from Swaziland. Although it has given the pot a black and glossy external surface, the carbon has not penetrated far into the walls, remaining as a thin layer on the surface which is hard to detect in the sections of the sherds. Scale in centimetres.

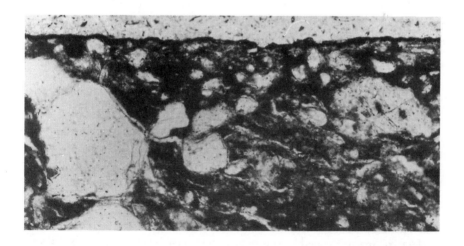

Fig. 205 Photomicrograph of a thin section of the smudged vessel shown in Fig. 204. The thin layer of deposited carbon can be seen on the surface and should be compared with the layers of slip shown in Figs. 203 and 206. PPL, × 175.

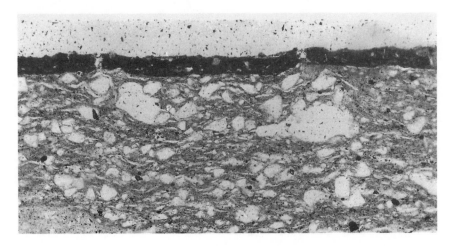

Fig. 206   Another photomicrograph of slip in thin section. The slip layer is discrete and is much thicker than the smudged carbon layer shown in Fig. 205. PPL, × 100.

Southcote–Blewburton style (Fig. 208)

Style of **saucepan pot** of the late first millennium, identified by Cunliffe (1974, 43) and restricted to the Berkshire Downs area. The main decoration employed is of rectilinear zones or panels filled with lightly **incised** lines in a variety of motifs. The style is not homogeneous.

Southern decorated bowl tradition

Generic term used to describe the tradition of middle neolithic decorated bowls in southern England. See **Abingdon ware, Mildenhall ware, Whitehawk ware** and **Windmill Hill ware**.

Spalls

Flakes of clay pushed or blown out of the surface of a vessel. See **fire spalls** (Figs. 5, 111, 112) and **lime blowing** (Fig. 157).

Stab and drag

Surface treatment formed by stabbing a point into the clay while it is still soft and then pulling the point along and out. The result is usually a roughly triangular depression in the vessel surface. The technique is particularly common on pottery of the late third and early second millennium but is not exclusive to that period.

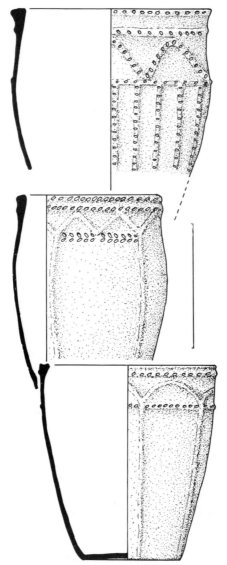

Fig. 207   South Lodge urns of the Deverel–Rimbury complex. All from Dorset. After Calkin 1962. Scale = 20 cm.

Stamped decoration or stamped impressions

Impressed decoration which is found mainly on iron age pottery and which is made by a pre-formed die or stamp. Dot **rosettes** (Fig. 140:1) are examples of this, but other, more complex, patterned stamps are also found (Elsdon 1975).

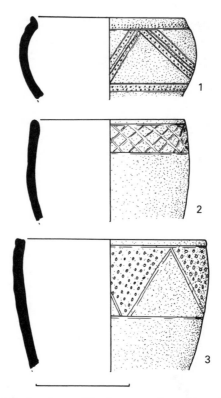

Fig. 208   Pottery of the Southcote–Blewburton style, as identified by Cunliffe. 1, 2, Blewburton, Berks.; 3, Knighton Hill, Berks. After Cunliffe 1974. Scale = 10 cm.

Stanton Harcourt–Cassington style (Fig. 209)

Pottery style identified by Cunliffe, dated to the third and second centuries BC and distributed in the Upper Thames region. It is characterized by undecorated bowls and loosely S-profiled jars in a coarse **fabric**. Cunliffe (1974, 46) sees this as intermediate between the **Long Wittenham–Allen's Pits style** and the later, highly decorated, **Hunsbury bowls**.

Stops

Small vertical ridges of clay, either **raised** or **applied**, which are placed in **cavetto zones** to interrupt them. Two or four arranged regularly round the vessel are usual, but numbers can vary. These may also be called stop-ridges and may be solid or perforated. They are most common on **food vessels**, particularly **Yorkshire vase** (Fig. 114:2) types. See also **lugs**.

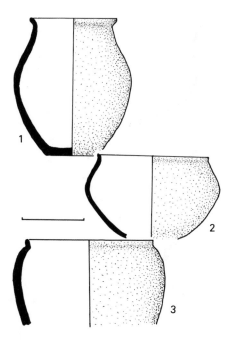

Fig. 209   Pottery of the Stanton Harcourt–Cassington style, as identified by Cunliffe. 1, Frilford, Berks.; 2, Yarnton, Oxon.; 3, Mount Farm, Oxon. After Cunliffe 1974. Scale = 10 cm.

Strainers (Fig. 210)

Shallow, wide-mouthed bowls with multiple perforations in the base, so fine as to allow only a liquid to flow through. They are classed by Thompson (1982) as in the **Belgic** tradition of **grog**-filled pottery, though they are essentially native types in a thick and heavy **fabric**. Thompson further suggests that the perforations were formed by using thin wooden pegs, which were left *in situ* and burned out during firing.

Strainer-spouted bowls (Fig. 210:3)

These are related to the **strainers** and are also regarded by Thompson (1982) as part of the **grog**-filled **Belgic** tradition. They are in a hard, grey **fabric**, occasionally mica-dusted and recognized by their equally proportioned, bipartite shape and the presence on the vessel of a short, stubby spout, behind which is a perforated panel or strainer not dissimilar to that found in a modern teapot.

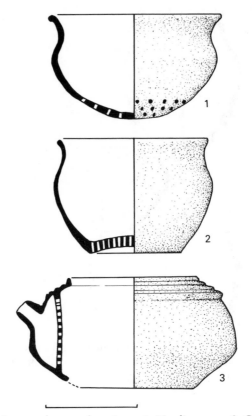

Fig. 210 Strainers and spouted strainers. 1, Hardingstone; 2, Colchester; 3, Ardleigh. After Thompson 1982. Scale = 10 cm.

Surface treatment
Any decorative or functional method used to alter the surface of the vessel, for example, **burnish, slip, glaze, rustication, impressed** and **incised** patterns.

Swags
Decorative motif found on **La Tène** decorated pottery, consisting of either incised or rouletted pendant semicircles (Fig. 140:2). Occasionally they may be interlocking to form a leaf motif (Fig. 202:1) (Grimes 1952).

Tazza (Fig. 211)
Cordoned bowl of the first century BC with a wide mouth and moderately tall **pedestalled base** (Birchall 1965; Harding 1974, 211). The shoulder of the pot is low down, just above the top of the pedestal, and the type is commonly found in graves of the **Aylesford–Swarling** tradition in Hertfordshire and

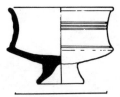

Fig. 211   Pedestalled *tazza* from Welwyn, Herts. After Birchall 1965. Scale = 10 cm.

north of the Thames (Birchall's vessel type X). The vessel is an imported form, having close parallels in northern France and the Low Countries.

Temper (Figs. 212, 213, 214, 215, 216, 217)
One of the terms used to describe **opening materials** added to clay by the potter. Synonymous with **filler**, the term has become subject to misuse in recent years (for example, see above, Chapter 2, p. 30, *re* Maggetti's usage of the term).

Examination of pottery fabrics in **thin section** is the best way to determine whether inclusions have been added or are naturally occurring in the clay: the nature, shape and size of the inclusions in relation to the clay matrix may yield results. For example, the highly angular rock fragments in Figs. 212 and 213 consist of crystals of several minerals, including quartz (clear in Fig. 212, white or grey in Fig. 213) and feldspar (mottled grey in Fig. 212, often striped or more heavily mottled in Fig. 213), and they are much larger than most of the (white and grey) inclusions in the surrounding matrix: as a result of this size difference, the fabric would be described as bimodal and the larger inclusions regarded as deliberate additions. Their nature (granite fragments), composition (polymineralic) and shape (highly angular) further reinforce this classification. In contrast, Fig. 214 shows a unimodal composition, consisting of rounded, poorly sorted inclusions all of which would be classed as naturally occurring.

Unfortunately, interpretation of pottery fabrics in thin section is not always so simple and many confusing cases arise. Rounding of inclusions is sometimes thought to indicate that they are naturally occurring, the argument behind this being that transportation of clay (see **sedimentary clay**) not only breaks down the clay particles, but also abrades the rock and mineral fragments present. However, there are obvious problems with this argument, one of which is created by sand grains which, as they may occur in deposits formed by the action of wind and water, have been subjected to considerable rounding; they may subsequently be added to clays by potters. Comparison with the background matrix may, however, help to solve this problem. For example, the large inclusions in Figs. 215 and 216 would also be classed as

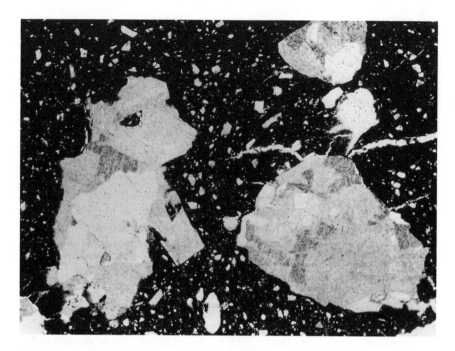

Fig. 212 Angular, polymineralic granite fragments that have been crushed and added to clay. PPL, × 15.

Fig. 213 The same granite fragments photographed under crossed polars. XPL, × 15.

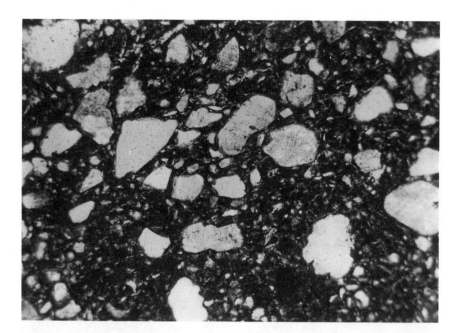

Fig. 214 Poorly sorted inclusions in a unimodal fabric. PPL, × 50. Boulder clay, Enderby, Leics. × 50.

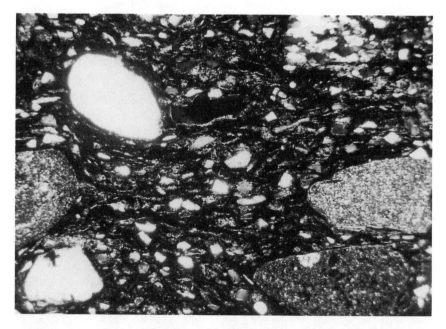

Fig. 215 The larger opening materials in this fabric are very different in size and rounding from the smaller inclusions in the matrix; because of these differences they would be called temper and the fabric would be described as bimodal. Medieval cooking pot from Southampton, XPL, × 40.

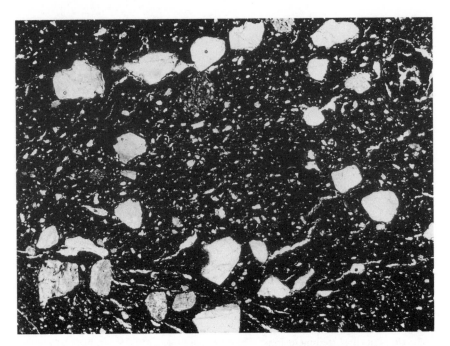

Fig. 216 The larger grains present in this fabric would also be regarded as deliberate additions. Medieval vessel from Nottingham. PPL, × 20.

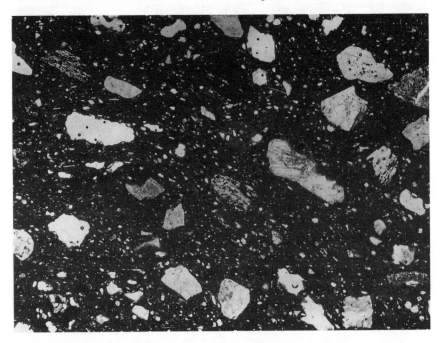

Fig. 217 Another example of deliberately added opening materials. Italian medieval tile. XPL, × 20.

temper (or added **opening materials**) because, even though they are highly rounded, they all occur in a similar size range, exhibit the same degree of rounding and are different in both size and shape from the smaller, more angular inclusions in the clay matrix. As in the previous example, this fabric would be described as bimodal. Again, the obviously bimodal nature of Fig. 217, with its similarly sized, larger inclusions, suggests the deliberate addition of the latter, even though the rounding shown by some would often be used as an argument for their being natural inclusions.

In contrast, the pronounced angularity and numerical frequency of the inclusions shown in both plane- and cross-polarized light (Figs. 187 and 186) would, at first, suggest that they are additions. However, they are all monocrystalline, indicating that the crystals have not been derived from crushed rock and their angularity is therefore probably natural. Consequently, it is difficult to determine whether these inclusions occur naturally in a clay which has not been transported far from its site of formation or have been added, from a sand deposit occurring close to the parent rock.

The nature of pot fabrics and their interpretation through the use of thin sections can therefore be seen to be full of complications. The fabrics of most British prehistoric pots usually contain a limited range of inclusions and problems do not frequently arise: this is rather disappointing, for, as has been pointed out earlier, prehistoric pottery, as a result of its coarse and open nature, should provide plentiful opportunities for provenance studies through the identification of the rock fragments present. However, the nature of the most common inclusions (grog (Figs. 128, 129, 130), flint (Figs. 9, 169) and quartz sand (Fig. 10), and the fact that they do not exhibit any optical properties which allow them to be traced to a particular geological source have limited the successful use of basic thin-section studies in Britain.

Textural analysis
Technique applied to the examination of **thin sections**, which involves the recording of shape, size and amount of mineral inclusions present in a **fabric**. Recently, size has been the main feature employed, yielding results that can be further refined via statistical analytical techniques.

Textural analysis has been used with some success for the characterization of sandy fabrics (Peacock 1971, Darvill and Timby 1982, Betts 1982), where the inclusions do not exhibit any optical properties that may allow them to be assigned to a particular geological source. Various methods (point-, line-, ribbon- and area-counting) have all been employed and there is still some debate as to which method is best; all have been succinctly reviewed by Middleton *et al.* (1985). The results from the four basic methods are not strictly comparable, as point-counting measures the area of the thin section occupied by the inclusions, whereas area- and ribbon-counts give a numerical frequency. Of the four methods, area- and ribbon-counts appear to give the most reliable results, but point-counting yields percentage figures which may be more easily appreciated by archaeologists and which may be related to estimations made by the use of the low-power binocular microscope and **visual percentage estimation charts.**

Thermal shock
When vessels are repeatedly heated and cooled, they may become subject to thermal shock. In cooking pots placed directly on the fire, the side of the vessel in contact with the heat will expand more than the inside surface of the vessel, which is considerably colder, as it is in contact with the substance being heated. Small cracks develop and spread from the cooler surface into the body of the vessel, weakening it and eventually causing breakage. (See Lawrence and West 1982 and Rye 1976 for fuller discussions.) Thermal shock is a problem in modern high-fired fine wares which are oven- but not flame-proof: because they contain few non-clay **inclusions** and are fired to temperatures high enough to promote **vitrification**, their bodies are rigid and cannot accommodate rapid heating and cooling. It appears unlikely that British prehistoric pottery was ever affected by thermal shock: **open firing** usually results in very porous wares with little vitrification of the **fabric** and such bodies are able to expand and contract repeatedly without suffering damage. See **thermal shock resistance.**

Thermal shock resistance
Resistance to **thermal shock** can be increased in several ways. Firstly, vessel shape is considered to be important and a round-based, globular pot with no sharp **carinations** should be able to expand and contract more evenly. Secondly, a porous **body**, with large **voids**, will ensure that crack propagation is limited. Thirdly, **inclusions** present in the body which have a low coefficient of thermal expansion, or one similar to that of fired clay, will provide good resistance. For this reason, **grog, calcite** and plagioclase feldspar are supposed to be good inclusion types for cooking vessels, while quartz, which has a high coefficient of thermal expansion, is not. See Rye (1976) and Woods (1986) for more detailed discussions of this problem.

Thin section
A slice of pottery used by ceramic petrologists for examining the mineral content and technology of pottery. The method has been borrowed from geology and is essentially the same as that employed in the examination of rocks. A slab of pottery about 4 mm thick and at least 2 cm long is consolidated and one side is polished to provide a smooth face. This is

mounted on a microscope slide and the pottery is then ground away until it is 30 microns thick: at this thickness, quartz and feldspar **inclusions** will be pale yellow, white or grey when viewed under cross-polarized light (XPL) in the **polarizing microscope**, these colours indicating that the correct thickness has been obtained. The section is then trimmed and covered with a glass cover slip. Slices of pottery taken for thin sections are usually cut vertically down the pot, perpendicular to the rim and base, and this type of section is known as a normal or vertical section. On occasions, horizontal or tangential sections may also be used, the latter being essential for the determination of the method of manufacture (Woods 1985).

At the correct thickness, most of the minerals present in a thin section will be transparent and will exhibit a range of optical properties that allow their identification. Some of the properties frequently used are shape (Figs. 218, 219, 220), **cleavage** (Figs. 73, 75, 220), **pleochroism** (Figs. 193, 194) and twinning (Fig. 221).

Thin-section identification of mineral and rock fragments can provide evidence on the origin of pottery and they can also be used to determine whether opening materials are naturally occurring in or were added to the clay (see **temper**). It is, however, important to remember that the technique only provides information on the inclusions present and not about the clay: most clay minerals are too small to be identified with an optical microscope and, in addition, may be destroyed during the firing process. Provenance studies conducted using thin sections, therefore, are concerned only with inclusions present in the **fabric** and cannot provide concrete evidence of the origin of the clay itself. Similarly, they are usually not appropriate for the study of fine wares which, by virtue of their definition, have few inclusions

Fig. 218   Typical gypsum crystals. Scale in centimetres.

Fig. 219 A gypsum crystal in a thin section of fired clay from Northants. The shape should be compared with those of the crystals in Fig. 218 and the voids in Fig. 233. XPL, × 110.

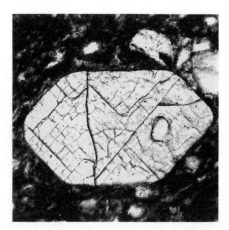

Fig. 220 The clear, octagonal shape of this pyroxene crystal is diagnostic. The cleavage traces, intersecting at angles of roughly 90°, should also be noted, for they are also characteristic. From a Roman amphora of unknown provenance, PPL, × 125.

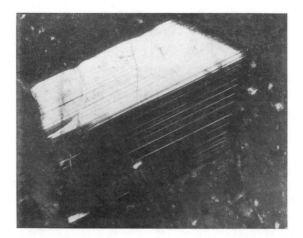

Fig. 221 Twinning in a feldspar in thin section. The crystal shows simple twinning (one half black, the other half white) and multiple twinning (the striped effect). XPL, × 75.

present. Problems are also encountered in the study of sandy fabrics, because quartz has no distinguishing features in thin section, regardless of origin; it is therefore not possible to determine the provenance of sandy wares in this way. Good results have, however, been obtained in such cases through the use of **heavy mineral analysis** (Williams 1977).

Thin sections are also of use in the identification of methods of manufacture (see **particle orientation**) and can also be used to examine surface treatments (for example, Figs. 124, 203, 205, 206) and to obtain information on firing (Hodges 1963, 107-9).

Tooled decoration

A term usually used in conjunction with Iron Age pottery to refer to decoration that has been very lightly executed with a smooth, blunt object. The decoration is executed in a similar fashion to **incised decoration**, except that the tool only lightly scores the outer surface of the pot.

Towthorpe bowl (Fig. 222)

Yorkshire variant of **Grimston–Lyles Hill** pottery of the fourth and third millennia, characterized by simple, hemispherical, bowl forms and heavy, out-turned rims (Piggott 1954, 115; Manby 1975). Occasionally **lugs** may be found on the sides of the pots.

Fig. 222 Towthorpe bowl from Towthorpe, Humberside. After Piggott 1954.
Scale = 10 cm.

Trent Valley A ware (Fig. 61)
Weak-shouldered jars originally identified at Breedon-on-the-Hill, Leicestershire (Kenyon 1950). The surfaces of the vessels are covered with random scratches, suggesting that they have been wiped with a coarse material, such as grass or straw. The style is datable to the fifth to second centuries BC. Also known as **Breedon–Ancaster** and **scored wares**. See also **wiped wares**.

Trevisker (Fig. 223)
A second millennium pottery tradition from south-western England seen as a local version of the southern **Deverel–Rimbury** tradition and named after a double enclosure at St Eval in Cornwall (ApSimon and Greenfield 1972). The pottery from Trevisker was locally made from the **gabbroic clays** of the Lizard Peninsula, and four main styles have been identified:
  Style 1 (Fig. 223:1-3) consists of vessels in a red, well-fired **fabric**, with abundant **inclusions**. Rims are everted and have an internal **bevel**, and the form of the vessels is biconical. Bases are flat and may have strengthening cross-ridges on the inner surface. Handles and pierced **lugs** are common; the former broad and decorated and occurring at the shoulder, the latter small and narrow and found in the neck area. The decoration is made by **twisted, plaited** or double **cord**, taking the form of broad zones of running chevron motif, horizontal lines or diagonal lines.
  Style 2 (Fig. 223:4, 5) vessels are in a finer fabric than Style 1, though pots are not so well fired. Surface colouration is duller and often grey rather than red. Vessel forms are straight-sided or shouldered; rim forms are variable, but simple and bevelled forms are the most common. The decoration is similar to Style 1 in technique and motif and is restricted to the upper third of the pots. Paired **fingertip** impressions or dimples are also found on some vessel walls.
  Style 3 (Fig. 223:6) differs from Style 2 only in the use of boldly **incised** decoration; the motifs used are the same.
  Style 4 (Fig. 223:7-9) is in a dark brown to black, well-fired fabric with large and abundant, angular **inclusions**, which give the fabric a rough feel.

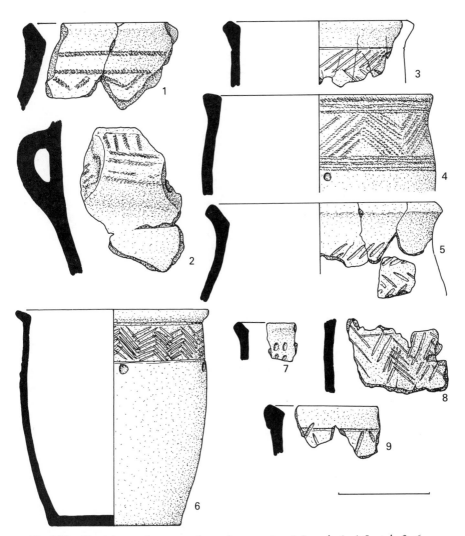

Fig. 223 Trevisker-style pottery from the type site. 1-3, style 1; 4-5, style 2; 6, style 3; 7-9, style 4. After ApSimon and Greenfield 1972. Scale = 10 cm.

Out-turned rims, with or without internal bevels, are common; the bevels are never decorated. Vessel shapes include straight-sided, 'flower-pot'-shaped pots and upright vessels with slightly concave necks. Deep, irregular incision is the main decorative technique used and is normally found below the rim; horizontal lines, running chevrons and herring-bone motifs are used. Occasionally **fingernail impressions** are also found.

At Trevisker itself, it was found that these four styles represented a chronological development from Style 1 through to Style 4.

Tripod vessels (Fig. 224)
These are considered by Thompson (1982) to be in the **Belgic** pottery tradition. They occur in a **grog**-filled or a mica-dusted fabric. They are easily recognized as shallow bowls with three legs or feet, from which their name is derived.

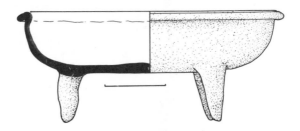

Fig. 224   Belgic tripod bowl from London. After Thompson 1982. Scale = 10 cm.

Triquetra (Fig. 225)
A curvilinear, geometric motif usually occupying a circular space, such as the vessel base, and consisting of three curved and regularly spaced arms radiating from a common centre (like the three-legged symbol of the Isle of Man). The motif is found on **La Tène** decorated pottery, particularly of the **Glastonbury** style (Grimes 1952). It may also be known as a triskele or triskelion.

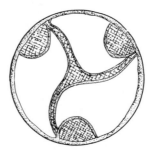

Fig. 225   Triquetra on the base of a bowl from Meare, Somerset. After Grimes 1952. Not to scale.

Trumpet lugs (Fig. 226)
Broad lugs or handles with expanded ends resembling the bell of a brass musical instrument. They are common particularly on the third and second millennia pottery from south-western Britain and are one of the distinctive features of **Hembury ware**.

Fig. 226 Trumpet lug on a bowl in Hembury ware from Hembury, Devon.

Turning

The process used to remove excess clay, tidy up a vessel or create **foot rings** when the clay has reached the **leather-hard** state. It is generally used on **wheel-thrown** vessels but may have been used on some hand-made vessels in later prehistory. The vessel is inverted on the wheel-head and rotated slowly, while a straight-sided turning tool is used to trim away excess clay and remove irregularities. It often leaves facets on the pot surface and may pick up inclusions from near the surface of the pot walls, creating **drag marks** (Fig. 100).

Twisted cord impressions
See **cord**.

Unstan ware (Fig. 227)

Round-based bowls of the third and second millennia from the northern and western isles of Scotland (McInnes 1969) and named after the pottery from the stalled cairn at Unstan on Mainland Orkney (Henshall 1972). The vessels are recognized by their very upright bodies and rounded bases, resulting in a bipartite form. The change in direction between the body and the rounded base is often so severe as to resemble a collar placed on top of a hemispherical bowl (Fig. 227:2). Decoration is by **incision** or **stab and drag** technique and is restricted to the upright portion of the vessel. Motifs employed are simple,

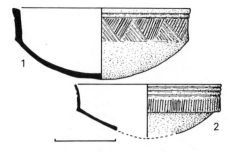

Fig. 227   Unstan bowls. 1, Unstan, Orkney; 2, Midhowe, Orkney. After Henshall 1963. Scale = 10 cm.

consisting of both vertical and horizontal multiple lines or filled chevrons. The origins of the pottery are obscure but may lie in the stab and drag decorated traditions of the Hebrides (Clarke 1983).

Vaul ware (Fig. 228)
Pottery from the western and northern isles of Scotland associated with the builders of brochs (Mackie 1971; 1974). The style is characterized by **barrel** urns with **incised decoration** and filled pendant triangles, often fringed by short incisions (Fig. 228:1). Smaller S-shaped jars with similar decoration are also present (Fig. 228:2).

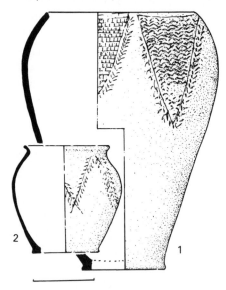

Fig. 228   Vaul ware from Dun Mor Vaul, Tiree. After MacKie 1974. Scale = 10 cm.

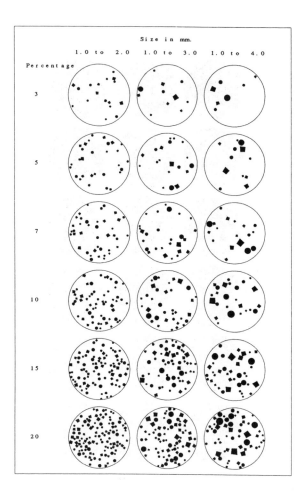

Fig. 229 Visual estimation percentage charts. From Matthew and Woods (in press).

Visual percentage estimation charts (Fig. 229, 230)
Charts used to estimate the proportion of inclusions present in a ceramic body. They may be used in conjunction with a hand lens or low-power binocular microscope and sherd material or with **thin sections** and a **polarizing microscope**. Originally devised for use with sediments, the best-known system was developed in Russia by Shvetsov and published in the West by Terry and Chilingar (1955). Other, newer, more comprehensive charts, involving a greater range of shapes, sizes and materials, and in white-on-black as well as black-on-white format, are now available (for example, the charts of Bacelle and Bosellini, as presented in Flügel 1982, or

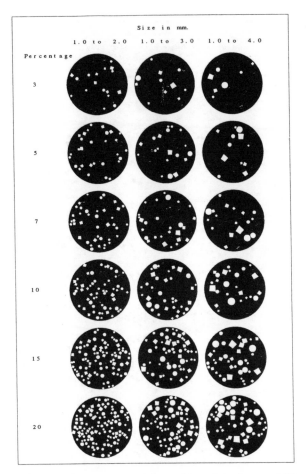

Fig. 230   Visual estimation percentage charts. From Matthew and Woods (in press).

Matthew and Woods, in press), examples of which are shown in Figs. 229 and 230.

Vitrification (Fig. 231)

The formation of a glass and the stage in firing at which the clay particles actually begin to form glassy melts. These flow into the pores between other particles and the fluxing process continues. On cooling, it produces a less porous, harder body. Extreme vitrification results in melting of the clay to such an extent that the pot collapses. Vitrification occurs at relatively high temperatures, which vary according to the types of clay minerals present. However, it rarely occurs below 900°C and consequently is usually not seen in prehistoric pottery.

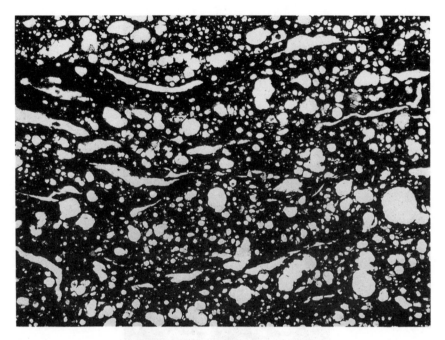

Fig. 231 Vitrification in a thin section of clay fired to 1000°C. The rounded voids are evidence of melting and the elongated voids are the result of firing shrinkage. PPL, × 15.

Void (Figs. 3, 14, 16, 129, 147, 171, 231, 232, 233)
A hole or space in a **fabric**. Voids can be created in several ways. Firstly, they may be the result of **drying shrinkage**; if so, they may be visible in the thin section, surrounding **opening materials** in the clay. Many opening materials are inert and thus are not affected by the water added to make the clay **plastic**; however, the clay itself contracts as it dries, shrinking away from the inclusions and, as a consequence, voids occur around them (Fig. 129). Other voids, also caused by **shrinkage** during drying (for example, some **join voids**), may be evidence of the method of manufacture (Figs. 3, 14, 16, 147). Others may be caused by the burning out of organic material, such as grass, during firing (Figs. 171, 232), or by the dissolution of inorganic material, such as calcite (Fig. 89) or gypsum (Fig. 233) during burial. **Vitrification** also creates voids, because the clay melts, bubbles and shrinks.

Waster (Figs. 5, 59, 101, 111, 112, 234)
A vessel damaged during manufacture, in particular during firing. The most common causes of wasters are **fire spalls**, but others, such as **bloating** (Fig. 59), **dunting** (Fig. 101) and overfiring (Fig. 234:4), are also common.

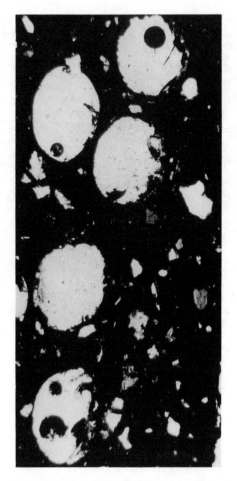

Fig. 232   Highly rounded grass voids in a thin section of a beaker sherd from Northton, Harris. The dune grass originally present has burned out during firing. PPL, × 60.

Wastage did not, however, necessarily render vessels unusable and the large number of spalled vessels excavated from sites of all periods indicates that many were in regular use; some may even have been traded or sold as 'seconds'.

Water of plasticity
The water that is mixed with clay to enable it to become **plastic**. It acts as a lubricant, allowing the clay particles to slide over one another. It is responsible for the greatest problems that occur during firing and accounts for most firing **wasters**: it cannot be completely removed by drying at room

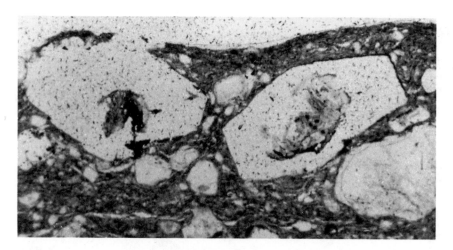

Fig. 233   Two gypsum voids in a thin section of a medieval pot from Brittany. The shapes, and the small 'swallow's tails' in particular, should be compared with the crystals in Fig. 218 and the thin section shown in Fig. 219.

temperature, and a small amount, usually between 3 and 5%, always remains, regardless of how lengthy the drying period has been. It is this that causes **fire spalls**. Water of plasticity is removed during the **water smoking** stage of firing.

Water smoking
The stage in firing around 100°C when remanent **water of plasticity** in the clay boils and turns to steam. This is the most dangerous stage in both **kiln** and **open firings**, when the likelihood of wastage through spalling and explosions is greatest. As the water boils and turns to steam, it increases in volume and, if it cannot escape through the pores in the clay, can exert sufficient pressure to blow flakes of clay (**fire spalls**) out of the walls of the clay vessels. The problem is overcome in kiln firings by raising the temperature of the kiln slowly, thereby gently heating the vessels within. In open firings, where temperature control is not possible, spalling does not occur if the **fabric** of the vessels is sufficiently coarse, i.e. contains relatively large amounts of **opening materials**.

Wessex biconical or handled urns (Figs. 56, 139)
A regional type of **biconical urn**, frequently recognized by the presence of **horseshoe handles** in the neck or immediately below the shoulder of the pot (Calkin 1962; ApSimon 1972). These have been considered either as skeuomorphs of rope carrying-handles or a **plastic** imitation of **cord-**

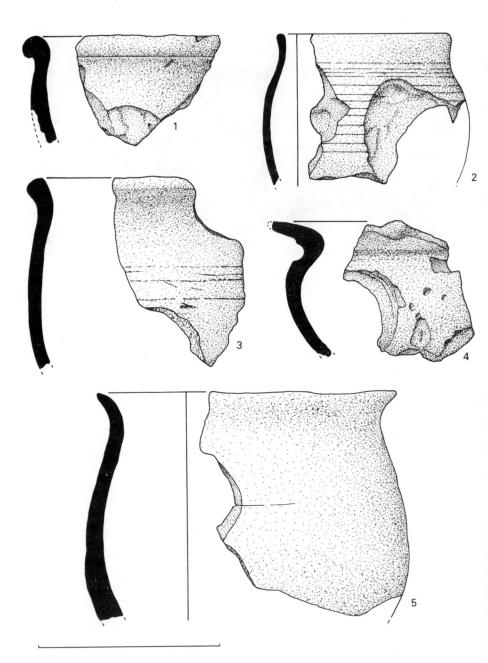

Fig. 234   Waster sherds. Most show characteristic breakage and spalling but 4 is also distorted through over-firing. 1, 3, scored ware sherds from Breedon-on-the-Hill, Leics.; 2, 5, experimental vessels; 4, Romano-British Derbyshire ware, Holbrook, Derbys. Scale = 10 cm.

impressed chevrons. Thought to have developed in the Amesbury region, these urns are generally in a well-fired **fabric** and decorated with cord or other impressions, forming lattice or filled chevron motifs. They may often have a **cordon** decorated with **fingertip impressions** just below the rim or on the shoulder.

West Harling–Staple Howe group (Fig. 235)

Regional group of sixth century BC pottery identified by Cunliffe (1974, 34-5) and distributed between Norfolk and Yorkshire (Brewster 1963). It consists of angular bipartite bowls which are either plain or decorated with simple **incision**. Jars with shoulders, everted necks and neck **cordons** are also found in the assemblage and may be decorated with **fingertip impressions**.

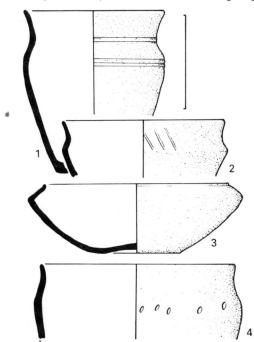

Fig. 235 Pottery of the West Harling–Staple Howe group, as identified by Cunliffe. 1, Creeting St Mary, Suffolk; 2, 4, Staple Howe, Yorks.; 3, West Harling, Norfolk. After Cunliffe 1974. Scale = 10 cm.

Western neolithic pottery

Generic name given to the round-based bowls, with or without **carinations**, of the fourth and third millennia which have close parallels among the Hazendonk, Wijchen and Michelsberg pottery of the Continent. See also **Hembury ware, Windmill Hill ware, Grimston–Lyles Hill ware, Heslerton ware, Boghead bowls.**

Fig. 236 Grooves on the bottom of a wheel-thrown Romano-British pot left by the cheese-wire used to cut the vessel off the wheel-head after throwing. Base diameter = 6.3 cm.

Wheel-thrown (Fig. 174, 192, 236)

The term used to describe vessels that have been made on the potter's wheel. Such vessels are usually, though not always, flat-based. They can be recognized by the presence of **rilling** (Fig. 192), an even wall thickness, diagonal **particle orientation** (Fig. 174) as revealed in **thin section** (Woods 1985) and by **X-radiography** (Rye 1977), and, frequently, by the presence of cheese-wire marks on the base (Figs. 100, 236). The term is not synonymous with wheel-turned, as **turning** (Fig. 100) is a secondary process used to tidy up vessels in the **leather-hard** state; the two processes are therefore quite different and require different terminology.

Writers in Britain frequently refer to slow wheels and fast wheels, the inference being that the former is a simple, one-piece device, sometimes called a *tournette* or turntable, and the latter the more sophisticated wheel with two parts (a flywheel and a wheel-head) with which we, in the twentieth century, are all familiar. To make such a distinction in terminology is clearly nonsensical: any type of wheel can be made to rotate either quickly or slowly and, as long as sufficient speed has been obtained for centrifugal force to be created, vessels can be spoken of as wheel-thrown. It is worth noting that the highly accomplished vessels of the Geometric, Archaic and Classical periods in Greece were all thrown on what many modern writers would describe as a slow wheel (see Noble 1965, Figure 78).

Whipped-cord impressions (Figs. 85, 86)

See **cord impressions** and **barbed wire impressions**.

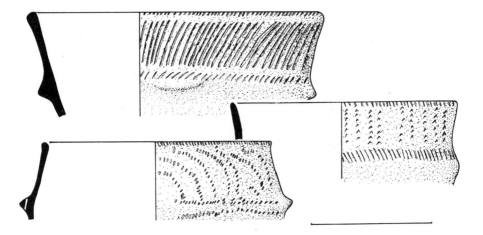

Fig. 237 Whitehawk style, neolithic pottery from Whitehawk in Sussex. After Whittle 1977. Scale = 20 cm.

Whitehawk ware (Fig. 237)

The southernmost style of the early third millennium **southern decorated bowl tradition** (Whittle 1977, 85-97) named after the pottery from the causewayed enclosure at Whitehawk Camp near Brighton (Curwen 1934; Piggott 1954, 74). S-profiled, **closed vessels** and open bowls are both found in the assemblage, as are vessels with everted and thickened rims. Simple **lugs** may be perforated or solid. Ornamentation is rarely elaborate, consisting of **stabs** or **incised decoration** and occasionally **cord** or **fingertip impressions**. It may be arranged in diagonal or vertical lines and is normally restricted to the rim, neck or upper portions of the vessel. **Whipped cord** also makes its first appearance in this style.

Windmill Hill ware (Fig. 238)

This term was first used to describe generically the whole range of undecorated round-based bowls in southern Britain and the name became synonymous with 'early neolithic pottery' (Piggott 1954, 66 ff.). Now, however, Windmill Hill ware has been relegated to the position of a regional style within the **western neolithic pottery** tradition (Smith 1974, 106). The pottery consists of hemispherical and baggy-profiled pots with simple or slightly thickened rims. Some vessels may also have oval **lugs**, which may be perforated or solid. Simple **incised** or **impressed decoration** may be found on the upper portions of vessels, which places some of the pottery of this style in the **southern decorated bowl tradition**. The pottery is named after the neolithic causewayed enclosure of Windmill Hill, near Avebury, from which a substantial assemblage was recovered (Smith 1965).

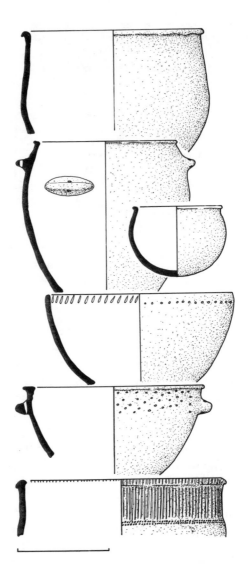

Fig. 238　Windmill Hill ware from the type site. After Smith 1965. Scale = 10 cm.

More recently, vessels from Windmill Hill have been subjected to thin-section analysis and the area around the site itself has been searched for clay deposits that might have been used for pot manufacture in antiquity (Howard 1981). The results indicate that, as is to be expected with hand-made and open-fired pottery, most of the raw materials were available locally. Claims by Howard (1981, 25) for seasonal manufacture by two different groups of potters, however, appear largely unsupported by the evidence.

Wipe marks
See **wiped wares.**

Wiped wares (Fig. 61)
The term given to pottery of the later first millennium which is characterized by the roughening of the surface of the vessel by wiping the wet clay with a coarse material, such as grass, straw or textile. In effect, this is a type of **rustication**, possibly intended as a device to aid handling of the vessel rather than as decoration. This style of pottery is particularly common in eastern England and may also be termed **Trent Valley A ware** (Kenyon 1950) or scored ware and constitutes Cunliffe's **Breedon–Ancaster group** (Cunliffe 1974, 328).

Woodhenge style
Former sub-style of **grooved ware** (Fig. 131).

Woodlands style (Fig. 131:4)
Subs-tyle of **grooved ware.**

X-radiography
X-rays are short wavelength electromagnetic radiation with great penetrating power. They will pass through ceramic objects relatively easily and produce a negative image on film, in which dense, thick areas are white, while less dense, thinner areas are darker. Although they can be used to yield basic information on the texture of pottery, they are primarily used in the examination of ceramic artefacts to ascertain technological data. They can be used to elucidate details of primary methods of manufacture: in all vessels, diagnostic **particle orientation** may be revealed (Rye 1977), and some techniques, such as **ring-building**, may be indicated by the presence of **join voids.** Secondary methods of manufacture, such as the use of a **paddle** and **anvil,** or the addition of parts, such as handles and spouts, may also show on X-ray.

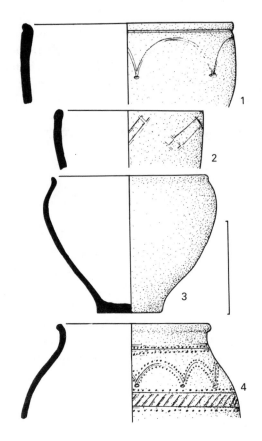

Fig. 239   Pottery in the Yarnbury–Highfield style, as identified by Cunliffe. 1, 3, Fifield Bavant, Wilts.; 2, Yarnbury, Wilts.; 4, Highfield, Wilts. After Cunliffe 1974. Scale = 10 cm.

Yarnbury–Highfield style (Fig. 239)
A local Wiltshire variant, as identified by Cunliffe (1974, 43), of the **saucepan pots** of the third to first centuries BC. Also in the assemblage are jars with simple **tooled** arcs and circular impressions.

Yorkshire vase (Fig. 114:2)
Distinctive type of **food vessel**.

Bibliography

Place of publication not given if London

Abercromby, J., 1902. 'The oldest bronze age ceramic type in Britain; its close analogies on the Rhine; its probable origin in central Europe', *Journal of the Anthropological Institute*, **32**: 373-97.

Abercromby, J., 1904. 'A proposed chronological arrangement of the Drinking cup or Beaker class of Fictilia in Britain', *Proceedings of the Society of Antiquaries of Scotland*, **45**: 323.

Abercromby, J., 1912. *A Study of the Bronze Age Pottery of Great Britain and Ireland*. Oxford University Press.

Allen, C.S.M., Harman, M. and Wheeler, H., 1987. 'Bronze Age cremation cemeteries in the East Midlands', *Proceedings of the Prehistoric Society*, **53**: 187-221.

Annable, F.K. and Simpson, D.D.A., 1964. *Guide Catalogue of the Neolithic and Bronze Age Collections in Devizes Museum*. Wiltshire Archaeological and Natural History Society, Devizes.

ApSimon, A.M., 1957-8. 'Cornish bronze age pottery', *Proceedings of the West Cornwall Field Club*, **2:2**: 36-46.

ApSimon, A.M., 1972. 'Biconical urns outside Wessex', in F. Lynch and C. Burgess (eds.), 1972, pp. 141-60.

ApSimon, A.M. and Greenfield, E., 1972. 'The excavation of the bronze age and iron age settlement at Trevisker Round, St. Eval, Cornwall', *Proceedings of the Prehistoric Society*, **38**: 302-81.

Arnal, G.B., 1988. 'La fabrication des poteries préhistoriques', *Dossiers Histoire et Archéologie*, **126**: 38-45.

Arnold, D.E., 1971. 'Ethnomineralogy of Ticul, Yucatan potters: etics and emics', *American Antiquity*, **36**: 20-40.

Arnold, D.E., 1972. 'Native pottery-making in Quinua, Peru', *Anthropos*, **67**: 858-72.

Arnold, D.E., 1985. *Ceramic Theory and Cultural Process*. Cambridge University Press.

Avery, M., 1973. 'British La Tène decorated pottery: an outline', *Etudes Celtiques 13-2, Actes du Quatrième Congrès International d'Etudes Celtiques*, **2**: 522-51.

Avery, M., 1982. 'The neolithic causewayed enclosure, Abingdon', in H.J. Case and A.W.R. Whittle (eds.), *Settlement Patterns in the Oxford Region: Excavations at the Abingdon Causewayed Enclosure and Other Sites*. Council for British Archaeology Report No. 44, pp. 10-50.

Bakker, J.-A., 1979. *The TRB West Group*. University of Amsterdam.

Bamford, H., 1975. *Briar Hill Excavations 1974-78* Northampton Development Corporation Archaeological Monograph No. 3.

Barfield, L. and Hodder, M., 1987. 'Burnt mounds as saunas, and the prehistory of bathing', *Antiquity*, 61: 370-9.

Baring Gould, S., 1896. 'Third Report of the Dartmoor Exploration Society', *Transactions of the Devonshire Association*, 28: 174-99.

Baring Gould, S., 1897. 'Fourth Report of the Dartmoor Exploration Society', *Transactions of the Devonshire Association*, 29: 145-65.

Barrett, J.C., 1976. 'Deverel-Rimbury: problems of chronology and interpretation', in C.B. Burgess & R. Miket (eds), 1976, pp. 289-307.

Barrett, J.C. and Bradley, R. (eds.), 1980. *Settlement and Society in the British Later Bronze Age*. British Archaeological Reports No.83, Oxford.

Barrett, J.C., Bradley, R., Cleal, R. and Pike, H., 1978. 'Characterisation of Deverel–Rimbury pottery from Cranbourne Chase', *Proceedings of the Prehistoric Society*, 44: 134-42.

Bateman, T., 1861. *Ten Years' Diggings in Celtic and Saxon Grave Hills in the Counties of Derby, Stafford and York, from 1848 -1858*. Allen and Sons.

Betts, I.M., 1982. 'Roman brick and tile: a study in fabric variability', in I. Freestone, C. Johns and T. Potter (eds.), *Current Research in Ceramics: Thin-section Studies*. British Museum Occasional Paper No. 32, pp. 63-71.

Birchall, A., 1965. 'The Aylesford-Swarling culture: the problem of the Belgae reconsidered', *Proceedings of the Prehistoric Society*, 31: 241-367.

Bjørn, A., 1969. *Exploring Fire and Clay*. New York: Van Nostrand Rheinhold.

Blanchet, J.-C., 1984. *Les Premiers Metallurgistes en Picardie et dans le Nord de la France*, Memoirs de la Societe Prehistorique Française, Tome 17.

Bradley, R., 1972. 'Prehistorians and pastoralists in neolithic and bronze age Britain', *World Archaeology*, 4: 192-204.

Bradley, R., 1984. *The Social Foundations of Prehistoric Britain*, Longman.

Bradley, R. and Gardiner, J. (eds.), 1984. *Neolithic Studies. A Review of Some Current Research*. British Archaeological Reports No. 133, Oxford.

Bradford, J.S.P. and Goodchild, R.G., 1939. 'Excavations at Frilford, Berkshire, 1937-8', *Oxoniensia*, 4: 1-80.

Brewster, T.C.M., 1963. *The Excavation of Staple Howe, 1963*. East Riding Archaeological Research Committee, Wintringham.

Brothwell, D., 1972. 'Palaeodemography and earlier British populations', *World Archaeology*, 4: 258-325.

Bryant, G.F., 1970. 'Two experimental Romano-British kiln firings at Barton-on-Humber, Lincs.', *Journal of the Scunthorpe Museum Society*, **3**: 1-16.

Bryant, G.F., 1979. 'Romano-British experimental kiln firings at Barton-on-Humber, England, 1962-1975', *Praehistorica et Archaeologica*, 9/10: 13-22.

BuLock, J.D., 1961. 'The bronze age in the North West', *Transactions of the Lancashire and Cheshire Archaeological Society*, **71**: 1-42.

Burgess, C.B., 1974. 'The Bronze Age'. in C. Renfrew (ed.), 1974, pp. 165-232.

Burgess, C.B., 1976*a*. 'Meldon Bridge: a neolithic defended promontory complex near Peebles', in C. B. Burgess and R. Miket (eds.), 1976, pp. 151-80.

Burgess, C.B., 1976*b*. 'An early bronze age settlement at Kilellan Farm, Islay, Argyll', in C.B. Burgess and R. Miket (eds.), 1976, pp. 181-208.

Burgess, C.B., 1980. *The age of Stonehenge*. Dent.

Burgess, C.B., 1986. '"Urnes of no small variety": collared urns reviewed', *Proceedings of the Prehistoric Society*, **52**: 339-51.

Burgess, C.B., and Miket, R. (eds.), 1976. *Settlement and Economy in the Third and Second Millennia BC*. British Archaeological Reports No.33, Oxford.

Burl, H.A.W., 1984. 'Report on the excavation of a neolithic mound at Boghead, Speymouth Forest, Fochabers, Moray, 1972 & 1974', *Proceedings of the Society of Antiquaries of Scotland*, **114**: 35-74.

Bushe-Fox, J.P., 1915. *Excavations at Hengistbury Head, Hampshire, in 1911-12*. Oxford University Press.

Calder, C.S.T., 1956. 'Stone age house sites in Shetland', *Proceedings of the Society of Antiquaries of Scotland*, **84**: 340-97.

Calkin, J.B., 1962. 'The Bournemouth area in the middle and late bronze age with the Deverel-Rimbury problem reconsidered', *Archaeological Journal*, **119**: 1-65.

Callander, J.G., 1930. 'Two short cists at Kilspindie golf-course, Aberlady, East Lothian', *Proceedings of the Society of Antiquaries of Scotland*, **64**: 191-9.

Callander, J.G., 1937. Report on the pottery, in C.S.T. Calder (ed.), 'A neolithic double-chambered cairn of the stalled type and later structures on the Calf of Eday, Orkney', *Proceedings of the Society of Antiquaries of Scotland*, **71**: 115-54.

Cantrill, T.C. and Jones, O.T., 1911. 'Prehistoric cooking-places in South Wales', *Archaeologia Cambrensis*, **11**: 253-86.

Cardew, M., 1969. *Pioneer Pottery*. Longman.

Case, H.J., 1955. 'Abingdon Ware', *Antiquity*, **29**: 236-7.

Case, H.J., 1956. 'The neolithic causewayed camp at Abingdon, Berkshire', *Antiquaries Journal*, **36**: 11-30.

Case. H.J., 1969. 'Neolithic explanations', *Antiquity*, **43**: 176-86.

Case, H.J., 1977. 'The beaker culture in Britain and Ireland', in R. Mercer (ed.), 1977, pp. 71-101.

Case, H.J. *et al.*, 1964. 'Excavations at City Farm Hanborough, Oxon.', *Oxoniensia*, **29/30**: 1-98.

Case, H.J. and Whittle, A.W.R., 1982. *Settlement Patterns in the Oxford Region: Excavations at the Abingdon Causewayed Enclosure and Other Sites*. Council for British Archaeology Research Report No. 44.

Childe, V.G., 1931. *Skara Brae*, Kegan Paul, Trench, Trubner & Co. Ltd.

Childe, V.G., 1940. *Prehistoric Communities of the British Isles*. Chambers.

Childe, V.G. and Grant, W.G. 1949. 'A stone age settlement at the Braes of Rinyo, Rousay, Orkney (second report)', *Proceedings of the Society of Antiquaries of Scotland*, **81**: 16-42.

Childe, V.G. and Paterson, J.W., 1929. 'Provisional report on the excavations at Skara Brae, and on finds from the 1927 and 1928 campaigns', *Proceedings of the Society of Antiquaries of Scotland*, **63**: 225-80.

Clark, J.G.D., 1931. 'The dual character of the Beaker invasion', *Antiquity*, **5**: 415-26.

Clark, J.G.D. and Fell, C.I., 1953. 'An early iron age site at Micklemoor Hill, West Harling, Norfolk', *Proceedings of the Prehistoric Society*, **19**: 1-40.

Clark, J.G.D. and Godwin, H., 1962. 'The neolithic in the Cambridgeshire Fens', *Antiquity*, **36**: 6-23.

Clark, J.G.D., Higgs, E.S. and Longworth, I.H., 1960. 'Excavations at the neolithic site at Hurst Fen, Mildenhall, Suffolk (1954, 1957, and 1958)', *Proceedings of the Prehistoric Society*, **26**: 202-45.

Clarke, D.L., 1970. *Beaker pottery of Great Britain and Ireland*. Cambridge University Press.

Clarke, D.V., 1976. *The Neolithic Village at Skara Brae, Orkney. Excavations 1972-73: An Interim Report*. H.M.S.O., Edinburgh.

Clarke, D.V., 1983. 'Rinyo and the Orcadian Neolithic', in A. O'Connor and D.V. Clarke (eds.), 1983, pp. 45-56.

Clarke, D.V., Cowie, T.G. and Foxon, A., 1985. *Symbols of Power at the Time of Stonehenge*. H.M.S.O., Edinburgh.

Coleman-Smith, R., 1971. 'Experiments in ancient bonfire-fired pottery', *Ceramic Review*, **12**: 6-7.

Coles, J.M., 1960. 'Scottish late bronze age metalwork: typology, distributions and chronology', *Proceedings of the Society of Antiquaries of Scotland*, **93**: 16-134.

Coles, J.M. and Coles, B., 1986. *Sweet Track to Glastonbury*. Thames and Hudson.

Collis, J., 1977. 'The proper study of mankind is pots', in J. Collis (ed.), 1977, *The Iron Age in Britain – A Review*. University of Sheffield.

Colt Hoare, R., 1812. *Ancient Wiltshire*, 1975 facsimile edition, edited by Simmons and Simpson, Vol. I, Wakefield.

Cooper, N. and Bowman, J., 1986. 'Studying the effect of heat on clay using X-ray diffraction analysis: the role of firing duration in the assessment of ancient firing temperatures', *Bulletin of the Experimental Firing Group*, 4: 37-48.

Corder, P. and Kirk, J.L., 1932. 'A Roman villa at Langton, near Malton, E. Yorks.', *Roman Malton and District*, Report No. 4, Yorkshire Archaeological Society.

Cornwall, I.W. and Hodges, H.W.M., 1964. 'Thin sections of British neolithic pottery: Windmill Hill – A test-site', *Bulletin of the Institute of Archaeology, University of London*, 4: 29-33.

Cowie, T.G., 1978. *Bronze Age Food Vessel Urns*. British Archaeological Reports No. 55, Oxford.

Crichton Mitchell, M.E., 1934. 'A new analysis of the early bronze age Beaker pottery from Scotland', *Proceedings of the Society of Antiquaries of Scotland*, 68: 132-89.

Cunliffe, B., 1974. *Iron Age Communities in Britain. An Account of England, Scotland and Wales from the Seventh Century BC until the Roman Conquest*. Routledge and Kegan Paul.

Cunliffe, B., 1978. *Hengistbury Head*. Elek.

Cunliffe, B., 1983. *Danebury. Anatomy of an Iron Age Hillfort*. Batsford.

Cunliffe, B. *et al.*, 1964. *Winchester Excavations 1949-60, Vol. 1*. Winchester.

Cunnington, M.E., 1926. 'A list of bronze age 'Drinking Cups' found in Wiltshire', *Wiltshire Archaeological and Natural History Magazine*, 43: 267-84.

Curwen, E.C., 1934. 'Excavations at Whitehawk neolithic camp, Brighton, 1932-3', *Antiquaries Journal*, 14: 99-133.

Darvill, T.C., 1979. 'A petrological study of LHS and TPF stamped tiles from the Cotswold region', in A. McWhirr (ed.), *Roman Brick and Tile: Studies in Manufacture, Distribution and Use in the Western Empire*. British Archaeological Reports No. S68, pp. 309-49.

Darvill, T. and Timby, J., 1982. 'Textural analysis: a review of potentials and limitations', in I.C. Freestone, C. Johns and T. Potter (eds.), *Current Research in Ceramics: Thin-section Studies*. British Museum Occasional Paper No. 32, pp. 73-87.

DeBoer, W.R. and Lathrap, D.W., 1979. 'The making and breaking of

Shipibo-Conibo ceramics', in C. Kramer (ed.), *Ethnoarchaeology*. New York: Columbia University Press, pp. 102-38.

Dumont, L., 1952. 'A remarkable feature of South Indian pot-making', *Man*, 52: 81-3.

Elsdon, S.M., 1975. *Stamp and Roulette Decorated Pottery of the La Tène Period in Eastern England: A Study in Geometric Designs*. British Archaeological Reports No.10, Oxford.

Elsdon, S.M., 1989. *Later Prehistoric Pottery in England and Wales*. Shire Publications, Aylesbury.

Erith, F.H. and Longworth, I.H., 1960, 'A bronze age urnfield on Vince's Farm, Ardleigh, Essex', *Proceedings of the Prehistoric Society*, 26: 178-92.

Evans, E.E., 1953. *A Neolithic Site at Lyles Hill, Co. Antrim*. H.M.S.O., Belfast.

Evans, J., 1984. 'Identification of organic residues in ceramics', *Bulletin of the Experimental Firing Group*, 2: 82-5.

Farrar, R.A.H., 1976. 'Interim report on excavations at the Romano-British potteries at Redcliff near Wareham', *Proceedings of the Dorset Natural History and Archaeology Society*, 97 (1975): 49-51.

Feacham, R.W., 1961. 'Unenclosed platform settlements', *Proceedings of the Society of Antiquaries of Scotland*, 94: 79-85.

Fell, C.I., 1937. 'The Hunsbury hillfort, Northants: a new survey of the material', *Archaeological Journal*, 93: 57-100.

Field, N.H., Matthews, C.L. and Smith, I.F., 1964. 'New neolithic sites in Dorset and Bedfordshire with a note on the distribution of neolithic storage pits in Britain', *Proceedings of the Prehistoric Society*, 30: 352-81.

Flügel, E., 1982. *Microfacies Analysis of Limestones*. Translated by K. Christenson. Springer-Verlag.

Foster, I.L. and Alcock, L. (eds.), 1963. *Culture and Environment: Essays in Honour of Sir Cyril Fox*. Routledge and Kegan Paul.

Fox, A., 1954. 'Excavations at Kestor, an early iron age settlement near Chagford, Devon', *Transactions of the Devonshire Association*, 86: 21-62.

Fox, C., 1927. 'An encrusted urn of the bronze age from Wales with notes on the origin and distribution of the type', *Antiquaries Journal*, 7: 115-33.

Fraser, D., 1982. *Land and Society in Neolithic Orkney*. British Archaeological Reports No. 117, Oxford.

Freestone, I.C. and Rigby, V., 1982. 'Class B cordoned and other imported wares from Hengistbury Head, Dorset', in I. C. Freestone, C. Johns and T. Potter (eds.), *Current Research in Ceramics: Thin-section Studies*. British Museum Occasional Paper No. 32, pp. 29-41.

Gabasio, M., 1986. 'Recherches sur l'application de la méthode du carbone 14 à la datation des tessons de poterie', *Archéologie Expérimentale*, 2: 51-67.

Gibson, A.M., 1976. *Bronze Age Pottery in the North East of England*. British Archaeological Reports No. 56, Oxford.

Gibson, A.M., 1980. '"Potbekers" in Britain ?', *Antiquity*, 54: 219-21.

Gibson, A.M., 1982. *Beaker Domestic Sites: A Study in the Domestic Pottery of the Late Third and Early Second Millennia BC in the British Isles*. British Archaeological Reports No. 107, Oxford.

Gibson, A.M., 1984. 'The problems of beaker ceramic assemblages: the north British material', in R. Miket and C.B. Burgess (eds.), 1984, 74-96.

Gibson, A.M., 1986a. *Neolithic and Early Bronze Age Pottery*. Shire, Aylesbury.

Gibson, A.M., 1986b. 'Diatom analysis of clays and late neolithic pottery from the Milfield Basin, Northumberland', *Proceedings of the Prehistoric Society*, 52: 89-103.

Gibson, A.M., 1986c. 'The excavation of an experimental firing area at Stamford Hall, Leicester, 1985', *Bulletin of the Experimental Firing Group*, 4: 5-14.

Gibson, A.M., 'The pottery from Ell's Knowe, Northumberland'. Forthcoming.

Gibson, A.M., 'Excavation and survey on Eastern Dartmoor'. In preparation.

Gillam, J.P., 1951. 'Dales ware, a distinctive Romano-British cooking pot', *Antiquaries Journal*, 31: 429-37.

Gillam, J.P., 1957. 'Types of Roman coarse pottery vessels in northern Britain', *Archaeologia Aeliana*, 35: 180-251.

Gillam, J.P., 1960. 'The coarse pottery', in K.A. Steer (ed.), 'Excavations at Mumrills Roman fort 1958-60', *Proceedings of the Society of Antiquaries of Scotland*, 94: 113-29.

Gingell, C., 1980. 'The Marlborough Downs in the bronze age: the first results of current research', in J.C. Barrett and R. Bradley (eds.), 1980, pp. 209-22.

Glasbergen, W., 1963. 'De Hilversum-pot van Budel/Weert', *Helinium*, 2: 260-65.

Green, H.S., 1976. 'The excavation of a late neolithic settlement at Stacey Bushes, Milton Keynes, and its significance', in C.B. Burgess and R. Miket (eds.), 1976, pp. 11-28.

Greenwell, W., 1877. *British Barrows*. Clarendon Press, Oxford.

Grimes, W.F., 1952. 'The La Tène art style in British early iron age pottery', *Proceedings of the Prehistoric Society*, 18: 160-75.

Grimshaw, R.W., 1971. *The Chemistry and Physics of Clays*. 4th edition. Ernest Benn.

Hamer, F., 1975. *The Potter's Dictionary*. Cambridge: Pitman.

Hamer, F. and Hamer, J., 1977. *Clays*. Pitman.

Hamilton, J.R.C., 1968. *Excavations at Clickhimin, Shetland*. H.M.S.O., Edinburgh.

Harding, D.W., 1972. *The Iron Age of the Upper Thames Basin*. Clarendon Press, Oxford.

Harding, D.W., 1974. *The Iron Age in Lowland Britain*. Routledge & Kegan Paul.

Hastings, F.A., 1965. 'Excavation of an iron age farmstead at Hawke's Hill, Leatherhead', *Sussex Archaeological Collections*, 62: 1-43.

Hawkes, C.F.C., 1935. 'The pottery from the sites on Plumpton Plain', *Proceedings of the Prehistoric Society*, 1: 39-59.

Hawkes, C.F.C., 1968. 'New thoughts on the Belgae', *Antiquity*, 42: 6-16.

Hawkes, C.F.C. and Fell, C.I., 1945. 'The early iron age settlement at Fengate, Peterborough', *Archaeological Journal*, 100: 188-223.

Hawkes, C.F.C. and Hull, M.R., 1947. *Camulodunum*. Society of Antiquaries Research Report No. 14.

Hayes, R.H. and Whitley, E., 1950. *The Roman Pottery at Norton. Roman Malton and District*, Report No. 7, Leeds.

Hencken, T.C., 1938. 'The excavation of the iron age camp at Breedon Hill, Gloucestershire, 1935-7', *Archaeological Journal*, 95: 1-111.

Helbaek, H., 1952. 'Early crops in southern England', *Proceedings of the Prehistoric Society*, 18, 194-233.

Henshall, A.S., 1963. *The Chambered Tombs of Scotland, I*. Edinburgh University Press.

Henshall, A.S., 1972. *The Chambered Tombs of Scotland, II*. Edinburgh University Press.

Henshall, A.S., 1983. 'The neolithic pottery from Easterton of Roseisle, Moray', in A. O'Connor and D.V. Clarke (eds.), 1983, pp. 19-44.

Herne, A., 1988. 'A Time and a Place for the Grimston Bowl', in Barrett, J.C. and Kinnes, I.H. (eds.), *The Archaeology of Context in the Neolithic and Bronze Age: Recent Trends*. Department of Archaeology and Prehistory, University of Sheffield.

Hodges, H.W.M., 1962. 'Thin sections of prehistoric pottery: an empirical study', *Bulletin of the Institute of Archaeology, University of London*, 3: 58-68.

Hodges, H.W.M., 1963. 'The examination of ceramic materials in thin section', in E. Pyddoke (ed.), *The Scientist and Archaeology*. Phoenix, pp. 101-10.

Hodges, H.W.M., 1976. *Artifacts*. 2nd edition. John Baker.

Hodson, F.R., 1962. 'Some pottery from Eastbourne, the "Marnians" and the pre-Roman Iron Age in southern England', *Proceedings of the Prehistoric Society*, 28: 140-55.

Hull, M.R., 1932. 'The pottery from the Roman signal-stations on the Yorkshire coast', *Archaeological Journal*, **89**: 220-51.

Jackson, D.A., 1979. 'A middle iron age site at Geddington', *Northamptonshire Archaeology*, **14**: 10-16.

Jansma, M.J., 1977. 'Diatom analysis of pottery', in B.L. van Beek, R.W. Brandt and W. Groenman-van Waateringe (eds.), *Ex Horreo*. University of Amsterdam.

Jobey, G., 1977. 'Iron age and later farmsteads on Belling Law, Northumberland', *Archaeologia Aeliana*, 5th series, **5**: 1-38.

Jobey, G., 1978. 'Green Knowe unenclosed platform settlement and Harehope cairn, Peeblesshire', *Proceedings of the Society of Antiquaries of Scotland*, **110**: 72-113.

Jobey, G., 1983. 'Excavation of an unenclosed settlement on Standrop Rigg, Northumberland, and some problems related to similar settlements between the Tyne and Forth', *Archaeologia Aeliana*, 5th series, **11**: 1-22.

Jobey, I. and Jobey, G., 1987. 'Prehistoric Romano-British and later remains on Murton High Crags, Northumberland', *Archaeologia Aeliana*, 5th series, **15**: 151-98.

Kenyon, K., 1950. 'Excavations at Breedon on the Hill, 1946', *Transactions of the Leicestershire Archaeological Society*, **26**: 17-82.

Kenyon, K., 1954. 'Excavation at Sutton Walls, Herefordshire, 1948-51', *Archaeological Journal*, **110**: 1-87.

Kinnes, I.A., 1985. 'Circumstance not context: the neolithic of Scotland as seen from outside', *Proceedings of the Society of Antiquaries of Scotland*, **115**, 15-58.

Kinnes, I.A. and Longworth, I.H., 1985. *Catalogue of the Excavated Prehistoric and Romano-British Material in the Greenwell Collection*. British Museum.

Kitson-Clark, M., 1938. 'The Yorkshire vase food vessel', *Archaeological Journal*, **94**: 43-63.

Laird, R.T. and Worcester, M., 1956. 'The inhibiting of lime-blowing', *Transactions of the British Ceramic Society*, **55** (8): 545-63.

Lanting, J.N. and van der Waals, J.D., 1972. 'British beakers as seen from the continent: A review article', *Helinium*, **12**: 20-46.

Lanting, J.N. and van der Waals, J.D., 1976. 'Beaker culture relations in the lower Rhine basin', in J.N. Lanting and J.D. van der Waals (eds.), 1976, *Glockenbeckersymposion Oberried 1974*, Bussum/Haarlem, pp. 1-80.

Lauer, P.K., 1972. 'A neglected aspect of New Guinea pottery technology: firing', *Pottery in Australia*, **11** (1): 7-16.

Lauer, P.K., 1974. *Pottery Traditions in the d'Entrecasteaux Islands of Papua*. Anthropology Museum, University of Queensland, Occasional Papers in Anthropology No. 3.

Lawrence, W.G. and West, R.R., 1982. *Ceramic Science for the Potter.* Radnor: Chilton Book Co.

Lawton, A.C., 1967. 'Bantu pottery of southern Africa', *Annals of the South African Museum,* **49**: 1-440.

Layard, N., 1922. 'Prehistoric cooking places in Norfolk', *Proceedings of the Prehistoric Society of East Anglia,* **3**: 483-98.

Leeds, E.T., 1922. 'Further discoveries of the Neolithic and Bronze Age at Peterborough', *Antiquaries Journal,* **2**: 235-6.

Leeds, E.T., 1928. 'A neolithic site at Abingdon, Berks. (second report)', *Antiquaries Journal,* **8**: 461-77.

Letsch, J.W. and Noll, W., 1983. 'Phase formation in several ceramic subsystems at 600°–1000°C as a function of oxygen fugacity', *Ceramic Forum International/Berichte der DKG,* **60**: 259-67.

Liddell, D.M., 1929. 'New light on an old problem', *Antiquity,* **3**: 283-91.

Litto, G., 1976. *South American Folk Pottery.* New York: Watson-Guptill Publications.

Longacre, W., 1982. 'Kalinga pottery: an ethnoarchaeological study', in I. Hodder, G. Isaac and N. Hammond (eds.), *Patterns of the Past.* Cambridge University Press, pp. 49-66.

Longworth, I.H., 1967. 'Further discoveries at Brackmont Mill, Brackmont Farm, and Tentsmuir, Fife', *Proceedings of the Society of Antiquaries of Scotland,* **99**: 60-92.

Longworth, I.H., 1969. 'Five sherds from Ford, Northumberland, and their relative date', *Yorkshire Archaeological Journal,* **42**: 258-61.

Longworth, I.H., 1983. 'The Whinny Liggate perforated-wall cup and its affinities', in A. O'Connor and D.V. Clarke (eds.), 1983, pp. 65-86.

Longworth, I.H., 1984. *Collared Urns of the Bronze Age in Great Britain and Ireland.* Cambridge University Press.

Longworth, I.H., Wainright, G.J. and Wilson, K.E. 1971. 'A Grooved Ware site at Lion Point, Clacton', *British Museum Quarterly,* **35**: 93-124.

Loughlin, N., 1977. 'Dale ware: a contribution to the study of Roman coarse pottery', in D.P.S. Peacock (ed.), *Pottery and Early Commerce,* Academic Press, pp. 85-162.

Louwe Kooijmans, L.P., 1976. 'The neolithic at the lower Rhine', in S.S. de Laet (ed.), *Acculturation and Continuity in Atlantic Europe.* Dissertationes Archaeologicae Gandensis, Ghent, pp. 150-73.

Lynch, F. and Burgess C.B., (eds.), 1972. *Prehistoric Man in Wales and the West: Essays in Honour of Lily F. Chitty.* Adams & Dart, Bath.

MacKie, E.W., 1963. 'A dwelling site of the earlier iron age at Balevullin, Tiree', *Proceedings of the Society of Antiquaries of Scotland,* **96**: 155-83.

MacKie, E.W., 1971. 'English migrants and Scottish brochs', *Glasgow Archaeological Journal,* **2**: 39-71.

MacKie, E.W., 1974. *Dun Mor Vaul: An Iron Age Broch on Tiree.* Glasgow Archaeology Society.

Maggetti, M., 1982. 'Phase analysis and its significance for technology and origin', in J.S. Olin and A.D. Franklin (eds.), *Archaeological Ceramics.* Washington, D.C.: Smithsonian Institution Press, pp. 121-33.

Manby, T.G., 1957. 'Food Vessels of the Peak District', *Yorkshire Archaeological Journal*, 77: 1-29.

Manby, T.G., 1975. 'Neolithic occupation sites on the Yorkshire Wolds', *Yorkshire Archaeological Journal*, 27: 23-60.

Martin, E., 1988. 'Swales Fen, Suffolk: A Bronze Age cooking pit?', *Antiquity*, 62: 358-9.

Matthew, A.J., and Woods, A.J., 'Spots before the eyes: new comparison charts for visual percentage estimation in archaeological material', in A. Middleton and I. Freestone (eds.), *Recent Developments in Ceramic Petrology.* British Archaeological Reports. In press.

May, J., 1976. *Prehistoric Lincolnshire.* History of Lincolnshire Committee, Lincoln.

Maniatis, Y. and Tite, M.S., 1979. 'Examination of Roman and medieval pottery using the scanning electron microscope', *Acta Praehistorica et Archaeologica*, 9/10: 125-30.

Martlew, R.D., 1983. 'Experimental firings using peat at the Dun Flodigarry excavations, Skye', *Bulletin of the Experimental Firing Group*, 1: 31-6.

Mayes, P., 1961. 'The firing of a pottery kiln of Romano-British type at Boston, Lincs.', *Archaeometry*, 4: 4-30.

Mayes, P., 1962. 'The firing of a second pottery kiln of Romano-British type at Boston, Lincs.', *Archaeometry*, 5: 80-103.

McInnes, I.J., 1964. 'The Neolithic and Bronze Age Pottery from Luce Sands, Wigtownshire', *Proceedings of the Society of Antiquaries of Scotland*, 97: 40-81.

McInnes, I.J., 1969. 'A Scottish neolithic pottery sequence', *Scottish Archaeological Forum*, 1: 19-30.

Mears, J.B., 1937. 'Urn burials of the Bronze Age at Brackmont Mill, Leuchars, Fife', *Proceedings of the Society of Antiquaries of Scotland*, 71: 252-78.

Megaw, J.V.S., 1976. 'Gwithian, Cornwall: some notes on the evidence for neolithic and bronze age settlement', in C. Burgess and R. Miket (eds.), *Settlement and Economy in the Third and Second Millennia B.C.* Oxford: British Archaeological Reports No. 33, pp. 51-79.

Megaw, J.V.S. and Simpson, D.D.A., 1979. *Introduction to British Prehistory.* Leicester University Press.

Mercer, R.J. (ed.), 1977. *Beakers in Britain and Europe: Four Studies.* British Archaeological Reports No. S26, Oxford.

Mercer, R.J., 1981. 'Excavations at Carn Brea, Illogan, Cornwall, 1970-73. A neolithic fortified complex of the third millennium BC', *Cornish Archaeology*, **20**: 1-204.

Middleton, A.P., 1987. 'Technological investigation of the coatings on some "haematite-coated" pottery from southern England', *Archaeometry*, **29**:250-61.

Middleton, A.P., Freestone, I.C. and Leese, M.N., 1985. 'Textural analysis of ceramic thin sections: evaluation of grain-sampling procedures', *Archaeometry*, **27**: 64-74.

Miket, R.M., 1976. 'The evidence for neolithic activity in the Milfield Basin, Northumberland', in C.B. Burgess and R. Miket (eds.), 1976, pp. 113-42.

Miket, R. and Burgess C.B., (eds.), 1984. *Between and Beyond the Walls: Essays on the Prehistory and History of North Britain in Honour of George Jobey*. John Donald, Edinburgh.

Musson, R.C., 1954. 'An illustrated catalogue of Sussex beaker and bronze age pottery', *Sussex Archaeological Collections*, **92**: 106-11.

Musty, J., 1974. 'Medieval pottery kilns', in V. Evison, H. Hodges and J.G. Hurst (eds.), *Medieval Pottery from Excavations*, pp. 41-65.

Needham, S.P. and Sørensen, M.L.S., 1988. 'Runnymede Refuse Tip: A Consideration of Midden Deposits and their Formation', in Barrett, J.C. and Kinnes, I.A. (eds.), *The Archaeology of Context in the Neolithic and Bronze Age: Recent Trends*. Department of Archaeology and Prehistory, University of Sheffield, pp. 113-26.

Newbold, P., 1912. 'The pottery', in W. Hornsby and R. Stanton 'The fort at Huntcliff, near Saltburn', *Journal of Roman Studies*, **2**: 215-32.

Noble, J.V., 1960. 'The technique of Attic vase painting', *American Journal of Archaeology*, **64**: 307-18.

Noble, J.V., 1965. *The Techniques of Painted Attic Pottery*. Faber and Faber, London.

Oakley, K.P., 1943. 'A note on haematite ware', in R.E.M. Wheeler (ed.), *Maiden Castle*. Report of the Research Committee of the Society of Antiquaries No. 12, pp. 379-80.

O'Brien, C., 1980. 'An experiment in pottery firing', *Antiquity*, **54**: 57-9.

O'Connor, A. and Clarke, D.V., (eds.), 1983. *From the Stone Age to the Forty-Five. Studies presented to R.B.K. Stevenson, former Keeper, National Museum of Antiquities of Scotland*. John Donald, Edinburgh.

O'Kelly, M.J., 1954. 'Excavations and experiments in Irish cooking places', *Journal of the Royal Society of Antiquaries of Ireland*, **84**: 105-55.

Patchett, F.M., 1944. 'Cornish bronze age pottery', *Archaeological Journal*, **101**: 17-49.

Patchett, F.M., 1951. 'Cornish bronze age pottery, part 2', *Archaeological Journal*, **108**: 44-65.

Peacock, D.P.S., 1968. 'A petrological study of certain iron age pottery from western England', *Proceedings of the Prehistoric Society*, **34**: 414-27.

Peacock, D.P.S., 1969*a*. 'A contribution to the study of Glastonbury ware from south-western Britain', *Antiquaries Journal*, **49**: 41-61.

Peacock, D.P.S., 1969*b*. 'Neolithic pottery production in Cornwall', *Antiquity*, **43**: 145-9.

Peacock, D.P.S., 1971. 'Petrography of certain coarse pottery' in B. Cunliffe (ed.), *Excavations at Fishbourne, 1961-1969*. Society of Antiquaries of London Research Report No. 27, Volume 2, pp. 255-9.

Peacock, D.P.S., 1977. 'Ceramics in Roman and medieval archaeology', in D.P.S. Peacock (ed.), *Pottery and Early Commerce*. Academic Press, pp. 21-33.

Peacock, D.P.S., 1982. *Pottery in the Roman World*. Longman.

Peacock, D.P.S., 1988. 'The gabbroic pottery of Cornwall', *Antiquity*, **62**: 302-4.

Pearce, S.M., 1981. *The Archaeology of South-West Britain*. Collins.

Piggott, S., 1936. 'A potsherd from the Stonehenge ditch', *Antiquity*, **10**: 221-2.

Piggott, S., 1954. *Neolithic Cultures of the British Isles*. Cambridge University Press.

Piggott, S., 1962. *The West Kennet Long Barrow*. H.M.S.O., London.

Piggott, S., 1963. 'Abercromby and after: the beaker cultures of Britain re-examined', in I.L. Foster and L. Alcock (eds.), 1963, pp. 53-92.

Pitt-Rivers, Lt.-Gen., 1898. *Excavations at Cranborne Chase, near Rushmore, on the Borders of Dorset and Wilts, 1893-1896, IV*. Privately published.

Pollard, S.H.M. and Russell, P.M.G., 1969. 'Excavation of round barrow 248B, Upton Pyne, Exeter', *Proceedings of the Devon Archaeological Society*, **27**: 49-78.

Quinnell, H., 1987. 'Cornish gabbroic pottery: the development of a hypothesis', *Cornish Archaeology*, **26**: 7-12.

Radford, C.A.R., 1951. 'Report on the excavations at Castle Dore', *Journal of the Royal Institution of Cornwall*, N.S. 1: 1-119.

Raven-Hart, R., 1962. 'The beater-and-anvil technique in pottery-making', *Man*, **62**: 81-3.

Rechnitz, W., 1959. 'The earth oven', *Man*, **59**: 21.

Reina, R.A. and Hill, R.M., 1978. *The Traditional Pottery of Guatemala*. Austin, University of Texas Press.

Renfrew, C., (ed.), 1974. *British Prehistory: a New Outline*. Duckworth.

Reynolds, B., 1964. 'Domestic fuel in primitive society', *Man*, **64**: 76-7.

Reynolds, P.J., 1979. *Iron-Age Farm. The Butser Experiment*. British Museum Publications.

Richards, C. and Thomas, J., 1984. 'Ritual activity and structured deposition in later neolithic Wessex', in R. Bradley and J. Gardiner (eds.), 1984, pp. 189-218.

Richardson, K.M. and Young, A., 1951. 'An iron age site in the Chilterns', *Antiquaries Journal*, **31**: 132-48.

Ritchie, J.N.G. and Welfare, H.G., 1983. 'Excavations at Ardnave, Islay', *Proceedings of the Society of Antiquaries of Scotland*, **113**, 302-66.

Robinson, A.M., 1979. 'Three approaches to the problem of pottery fabric descriptions', *Medieval Ceramics*, **3**, 3-35.

Ryder, M.L., 1969. 'Paunch cooking', *Antiquity*, **43**, 218-20.

Rye, O.S., 1976. 'Keeping your temper under control: materials and the manufacture of Papuan pottery', *Archaeology and Physical Anthropology in Oceania*, **11** (2): 106-37.

Rye, O.S., 1977. 'Pottery manufacturing techniques: X-ray studies', *Archaeometry*, **19**: 205-11.

Rye, O.S., 1981. *Pottery Technology: Principles and Reconstruction*. Washington, D.C.: Taraxacum.

Rye, O.S. and Evans, C., 1976. *Traditional Pottery Techniques of Pakistan: Field and Laboratory Studies*. Washington, D.C.: Smithsonian Institution Publications.

Savory, H.N., 1937. 'An early iron age site at Long Wittenham, Berks.', *Oxoniensia*, **2**: 1-11.

Savory, H.N., 1957. 'A corpus of Welsh bronze age pottery, part II: Food vessels and enlarged food vessels', *Bulletin of the Board of Celtic Studies*, **17**: 196-233.

Savory, H.N., 1980. *Guide Catalogue to the Neolithic and Bronze Age Collections*. National Museum of Wales, Cardiff.

Scott, G.J., 1964. 'The chambered cairn at Beacharra, Kintyre, Argyll', *Proceedings of the Prehistoric Society*, **30**: 134-58.

Scott, W.L., 1951. 'Eilean an Tighe: A pottery workshop of the second millennium B.C.', *Proceedings of the Society of Antiquaries of Scotland*, **85**: 1-37.

Shepard, A.O., 1980. *Ceramics for the Archaeologist*. Washington, D.C.: Carnegie Institution Publications No. 609. 5th printing.

Shepherd, I.A.G., 1986. *Powerful Pots: Beakers in North-east Prehistory*. Anthropological Museum, University of Aberdeen.

Simmons, I.G., Dimbleby, G.W. and Grigson, C., 1981. 'The Mesolithic', in I.G. Simmons and M.J. Tooley (eds.), 1981, pp. 82-124.

Simmons, I.G. and Tooley, M.J. (eds.), 1981. *The Environment in British Prehistory*. Duckworth. London.

Simpson, D.D.A., 1965. 'Food vessels in south-west Scotland', *Transactions of the Dumfriess and Galloway Natural History and Archaeological Society*, **42**: 26-50.

Simpson, D.D.A., 1976. 'The later neolithic and beaker settlement at Northton, Isle of Harris', in C.B. Burgess and R. Miket (eds.), 1976, pp. 221-32.

Skinner, B.J., 1966. 'Thermal expansion', in S.P. Clark (ed.), *Handbook of Physical Constants*. Geological Society of America Memoir 97, pp. 76-96.

Smith, A.G., Grigson, C., Hillman, G. and Tooley, M.J., 1981. 'The Neolithic', in I.G. Simmons and M.J. Tooley (eds.), 1981, pp. 210-49.

Smith, I.F., 1956. *The decorative art of neolithic ceramics in south-eastern England, and its relations*. Ph.D. thesis, University of London.

Smith, I.F., 1965. *Windmill Hill and Avebury. Excavations by Alexander Keiller, 1925-1939*. Clarendon Press, Oxford.

Smith, I.F., 1974. 'The Neolithic', in C. Renfrew (ed.), 1974, pp. 100-36.

Smith, I.F., 1981. 'The neolithic pottery', in R.J. Mercer, 'Excavation at Carn Brea, Illogan, Cornwall – A neolithic fortified complex of the third millennium BC', *Cornish Archaeology*, 20: 1-204.

Stead, I., 1979. *The Arras Culture*. York: Yorkshire Philosophical Society.

Stevenson, R.B.K., 1939. 'Two bronze age burials', *Proceedings of the of Antiquaries of Scotland*, 73, 229-40.

Stevenson, R.B.K., 1953. 'Prehistoric pot-building in Europe', *Man*, 53: 65-8.

Stokes, M.A., 1985. 'Experimental trials of die-stamps and Anglo-Saxon pottery firing', *Bulletin of the Experimental Firing Group*, 3: 87-92.

Stone, J.F.S., 1949. 'Some grooved-ware pottery from the Woodhenge area', *Proceedings of the Prehistoric Society*, 15: 122-7.

Swan, V., 1984. *The Pottery Kilns of Roman Britain*. H.M.S.O.

Thompson, I.M., 1982. *Grog-Tempered 'Belgic' Pottery of South-Eastern England*. British Archaeological Reports No. 108, Oxford.

Threipland, L.M., 1957. 'An excavation at St Mawgan-in-Pydar, North Cornwall', *Archaeological Journal*, 113, 33-81.

Thurnham, J., 1871. 'On ancient British barrows, especially those of Wiltshire and the adjoining counties (Part 2, Round barrows)', *Archaeologia*, 43: 285-560.

Tite, M.S., 1969. 'Determination of the firing temperature of ancient ceramics by measurement of thermal expansion: A reassessment', *Archaeometry*, 11: 131-43.

Tite, M.S., 1972. *Methods of Physical Examination in Archaeology*. Seminar Press.

Tite, M.S. and Bimson, M., 1986. 'Faience: an investigation of the microstructures associated with the different methods of glazing', *Archaeometry*, 28: 69-78.

Tite, M.S., Bimson, M. and Freestone, I.C., 1982a. 'An examination of the high gloss surface finishes on Greek Attic and Roman samian wares', *Archaeometry*, **24**: 117-26.

Tite, M.S., Freestone, I.C., Meeks, N.D. and Bimson, M., 1982*b*. 'The use of scanning electron microscopy in the technological examination of ancient ceramics', in J.S. Olin and A.D. Franklin (eds.), *Archaeological Ceramics*. Washington, D.C.: Smithsonian Institution Press, pp. 109-20.

Tite, M.S. and Maniatis, Y., 1975. 'Examination of ancient pottery using the scanning electron microscope', *Nature*, **257**, No. 5522, 122-3.

Todd, M., 1987. *The South West to AD 1000*. Longman.

Topping, P., 1986. 'Neutron activation analysis of later prehistoric pottery from the Western Isles of Scotland', *Proceedings of the Prehistoric Society*, **52**: 105-29.

Topping, P.G. and MacKenzie, A.B., 1988. 'A test of the use of neutron activation analysis for clay source characterization', *Archaeometry*, **30**: 92-101.

Vandiver, P., 1982. 'Technological change in Egyptian faience', in J.S. Olin and A.D. Franklin (eds.), *Archaeological Ceramics*. Smithsonian Institution Press, Washington, D.C., pp. 167-79.

Varley, W.J., 1938. 'The Bleasdale Circle', *Antiquaries Journal*, **18**, 154-71.

Vine, P.M., 1982. *The Neolithic and Bronze Age Cultures of the Middle and Upper Trent Basin*. British Archaeological Reports No. 105, Oxford.

Waals, J.D. van der and Glasbergen, G., 1955. 'Beaker types and their distribution in the Netherlands', *Palaeohistoria*, **4**: 5-46.

Wainwright, G.J., 1980. 'A pit burial at Lower Ashmore Farm, Roseash, Devon', *Proceedings of the Devon Archaeological Society*, **38**: 13-5.

Wainwright, G.J. and Longworth, I.H., 1971. *Durrington Walls: Excavations 1966-1968*, Society of Antiquaries Research Report No.29.

Ward, J., 1902. 'Prehistoric interments near Cardiff', *Archaeologia Cambrensis*, **2**: 25-32.

Warren, S.H., Piggott, S., Clark, J.G.D., Burkitt, M.C., Godwin, H. and M.E., 1936. 'Archaeology of the submerged land surface of the Essex Coast', *Proceedings of the Prehistoric Society*, **2**: 178-210.

Wheeler, H., 1979. Excavation at Willington, Derbyshire, *Derbyshire Archaeological Journal*, **99**: 58-220.

Wheeler, R.E.M., 1936. 'The excavation at Maiden Castle, Dorset: The second interim report', *Antiquaries Journal*, **16**: 265-83.

Wheeler, R.E.M., 1943. *Maiden Castle, Dorset*. Society of Antiquaries Research Report No.12.

Whitbread, I.K., 1986. 'The characterisation of argillaceous inclusions in ceramic thin sections', *Archaeometry*, **28**: 79-88.

Whittle, A.W.R., 1977. *The Earlier Neolithic of Southern England and its Continental Background*. British Archaeological Reports No. S35, Oxford.

Whittle, A.W.R., 1986. *Scord of Brouster: An Early Agricultural Settlement on Shetland*. Oxford University Committee for Archaeology Monograph No. 9.

Williams, D.F., 1977. 'The Romano-British black-burnished industry: An essay on characterisation by heavy mineral analysis', in D.P.S. Peacock (ed.), *Pottery and Early Commerce*. Academic Press, pp. 163-220.

Woods, A.J., 1983. 'Smoke gets in your eyes: Patterns, variables and temperature measurement in open firings', *Bulletin of the Experimental Firing Group*, 1: 11-25.

Woods, A.J., 1984*a*. 'The old pot-boiler', *Bulletin of the Experimental Firing Group*, 2: 25-40.

Woods, A.J., 1984*b*. 'Methods of pottery manufacture in the Kavango region of South West Africa/Namibia: Two case studies', *Colloquies of Art and Archaeology in Asia*, No. 12. Percival David Foundation, 303-25.

Woods, A.J., 1985. 'An introductory note on the use of tangential thin sections for distinguishing between wheel-thrown and coil/ring-built vessels', *Bulletin of the Experimental Firing Group*, 3: 100-14.

Woods, A.J., 1986. 'Form, fabric and function: Some observations on the cooking pot in antiquity', in W.D. Kingery (ed.), *Technology and Style*. Columbus: American Ceramic Society, pp. 157-72.

Woods, A.J., 1989. 'Fired with enthusiasm: experimental open firings at Leicester University', in A.M. Gibson (ed.), *Midlands Prehistory*. British Archaeological Reports 204, pp. 196-226.

Woods, A.J., 'Experiment and ethnography: open firings and opening materials', in A.J. Woods (ed.), *Ceramic Technology: Ethnography and Experiment*. Experimental Firing Group Monograph No. 1. In press.

Woods, P.J. and Hastings, B.C., 1984. *Rushden: The Early Fine Wares*. Northamptonshire County Council.

Wulff, H.E., Wulff, H.S. and Koch, L., 1968. 'Egyptian faience', *Archaeology*, 21: 98-107.

Wyman Abbott, G., 1910. 'The discovery of prehistoric pits at Peterborough', *Archaeologia*, 62: 333-352.